Political Theory and the European Union

The political development of the European Union has now reached the point where governments and citizens of Europe are confronted with constitutional choices that raise issues of fundamental political principle. The EU's continuing democratic deficit, decisions about political organisation within Europe and the associated structures of political representation are all the subject of intense political debate and analysis.

The contributors to *Political Theory and the European Union* examine the issues of constitutional choice that face the government and citizens of today's Europe. They ask central questions such as: what constitutional principles are appropriate for protecting rights in Europe?; should there be a constitutionally entrenched European bill of rights on the model of the USA?; and what rights are due to the citizens of the EU? In order to answer these key questions the chapters are divided into three parts which include: questions of political legitimacy and the meaning of the democratic deficit; the reality of institutional reforms in decision-making processes are possible; and the rights of citizenship and values that should be protected.

These studies highlight the complexities and difficulties in constructing a European constitutional blueprint. It will be essential reading for those studying European politics and society.

Albert Weale is Professor of Government in the Department of Government, University of Essex. **Michael Nentwich** is a senior researcher with the Institute for Technology Assessment of the Austrian Academy of Sciences in Vienna.

ROUTLEDGE/ECPR STUDIES IN EUROPEAN POLITICAL SCIENCE

Edited by Hans Keman, *Vrije University, The Netherlands* and Jan W. van Deth, *University of Mannheim, Germany on behalf of the European Consortium for Political Research*

The Routledge/ECPR Studies in European Political Science Series is published in association with the European Consortium for Political Research – the leading organisation concerned with the growth and development of political science in Europe. The series presents high-quality edited volumes on topics at the leading edge of current interest in political science and related fields, with contributions from European scholars and others who have presented work at ECPR workshops or research groups.

Also available from Routledge in association with the ECPR:

Political Theory and the European Union

Legitimacy, constitutional choice and citizenship

Edited by Albert Weale and Michael Nentwich

London and New York

First published 1998
by Routledge
11 New Fetter Lane, London EC4P 4EE

Simultaneously published in the USA and Canada
by Routledge
29 West 35th Street, New York, NY 10001

© 1998 Edited by Albert Weale and Michael Nentwich

Typeset in Baskerville by Routledge
Printed and bound in Great Britain by TJ International Ltd.,
Padstow, Cornwall

British Library Cataloguing in Publication Data
A catalogue record for this book is available from the British Library

Library of Congress Cataloguing in Publication Data
Political theory and the European Union: legitimacy, constitutional choice
    and citizenship / edited by Albert Weale and Michael Nentwich.
        p.   cm.
      Includes bibliographical references and index.
        1. Political participation – European Union countries.
        2. Citizenship – European Union countries. 3. Legitimacy of
    governments – European Union countries. 4. Democracy – European
    Union countries. 5. European Union. I. Nentwich, Michael. II. Weale,
    Albert.
    JN40.P65   1998
    320.44'09'049–dc21   98–4174
                                             CIP

ISBN 0–415–17313–2

Contents

Contributors

Heidrun Abromeit is Professor of Political Science (Comparative Politics) at the Technical University in Darmstadt, Germany. She has published books and articles on the relations between state and industry, on British public enterprise and privatisation, on federalism, on Swiss politics and (recently) on the future structure of the EU.

David Beetham is Professor of Politics and Director of the Centre for Democratisation Studies, University of Leeds, UK. Recent works include *The Legitimation of Power, Bureaucracy* (second edition) and, with Kevin Boyle, *Introducing Democracy*. A fuller, more developed version of the argument of the chapter in this volume is to appear in a forthcoming book with Christopher Lord entitled *Legitimacy in the European Union*.

Thomas Christiansen is Jean Monnet Lecturer in European Studies in the Department of International Politics at the University of Wales, Aberystwyth, UK. He has published on territorial politics and subnational governments in Europe, German policy on European integration, the European Commission and on conceptual and normative questions of European governance.

Dimitris Chryssochoou is Lecturer in Pan-European Politics in the Department of Politics at the University of Exeter, UK. His research focuses on democracy and European integration, and he has published in various academic journals and edited volumes in English, Greek and Italian. His latest book is *Democracy in the European Union*, 1998.

Carlos Closa is Lecturer in EU Politics and Comparative Politics at the Universidad Complutense, Madrid, Spain. He was formerly Jean Monnet Fellow at the European University Institute, Florence. He has published books and articles on the EU political system, EU citizenship, European political cooperation and the IGC negotiations. He is currently researching the Europeanisation of the Spanish political system.

Andreas Føllesdal is Senior Researcher with the programme of Advanced Research on the Europeanisation of the Nation-State (ARENA) located at the University of Oslo, Norway, where he coordinates the Research Group on

Normative Political Theory. He publishes in the field of political philosophy, with a focus on issues of international political theory, particularly those arising in the wake of changes in Europe. Current research projects include the political theory of federalism, minority rights and European citizenship.

Sverker Gustavsson is Jean Monnet Professor at the Department of Government at Uppsala University, Sweden. His publications are on research policy, welfare state theory and European integration. Currently he is doing research on the future options concerning the democratic deficit, the pillar structure and variable geometry. His research perspective is that of comparative federalism.

Theodora Kostakopoulou is Jean Monnet Lecturer in the Law and Politics of European Integration, and Deputy Director of the Centre for European Law and Practice at the University of East Anglia, UK. Her principal research interests lie in the intersection of the European Union and political theory. She has published articles on EU citizenship and immigration, and is the author of a forthcoming book, *The Politics of Belonging and Exclusion in the European Union: Citizenship and Immigration.*

Richard Kuper was Senior Lecturer in Politics at the University of Hertfordshire, UK, when his chapter was written. He has since taken early retirement to pursue an involvement in an organic farm/eco-village project in France. His work on institutional forms and democratic practices – from the local to the European level – continues, and he is currently writing about the politics of the ECJ and the making of a constitution for Europe.

Christopher Lord is Jean Monnet Senior Lecturer in European Parliamentary Studies in the Department of Politics, University of Leeds, UK. Recent works include, with Simon Hix, *Political Parties in the European Union.* A fuller, more developed version of the argument of this volume is to appear in a forthcoming book with David Beetham entitled *Legitimacy in the European Union.*

Michael Nentwich is a senior researcher at the Austrian Academy of Sciences in Vienna. He has published books and articles on institutional and procedural questions in the context of European integration, European food law, environmental and consumer law, democracy and the EU and technology assessment. He is also the editor of the *European Integration online Papers.*

Michael Tsinisizelis is Associate Professor of Political Science in the Department of Political Science and Public Administration at the University of Athens. He has published on European integration and comparative politics and is the author and editor of various volumes on the EU in Greek. He is currently completing a book (co-authored) on the 1996–7 Inter-Governmental Conference.

Albert Weale is Professor of Government at the University of Essex, UK. He is the author of a number of works in the fields of contemporary political theory, the theory of choice and the analysis of public policy, especially health and environmental policy. He is currently working on the theory of democracy and also on environmental policy in Europe.

Marcel Wissenburg is a research fellow at the Foundation of Law and Policy at the Netherlands Organization for Scientific Research (NWO/REOB) and Lecturer in the Department of Political Science, University of Nijmegen. He has published articles on Kant, Spinoza, Popper, social justice and green political theory. His book, *Green Liberalism*, was published by UCL Press London in 1998.

Series editor's preface

Ever since the European Union has come into existence on paper (i.e. after the Maastricht Treaty in 1992) its institutional shape as a *trans*-national political system has been hotly and intensively debated by politicians, journalists, parties, organised interests and, of course, citizens. This is quite comprehensible because more and more matters of common if not national interest are now slowly, but inevitably, influenced or actually under the aegis of EU decision-making.

Whereas the history of European co-operation was marked by economic interdependence and functional integration based upon the idea that intergovernmental decision-making was still, by and large, based on national sovereignty of the participating states involved. These states are, in turn, adequately controlled by their democratic institutions. However, one may well question whether or not this is also the case with respect to the institutional framework of the EU after its foundation as a *political* union.

Yet, and this is one of the purposes of this new volume of the *Routledge/ECPR Studies in European Political Science* series, the question of political accountability, responsiveness and legitimacy of the EU should not, and can not, be postponed. In other words: the much-used phrase of the 'democratic deficit' has become an urgent issue that must be addressed seriously, if and when all participating nation-states – recognised as 'democratic' systems – wish to develop the new union as a truly democratic system concurrent with their own national systems. This being the case a new situation is emerging: the debate of the EU as a political system implies an inevitable discourse regarding its future shape as a *democratic* union. It involves substantial discussion about the fundamental principles, which are conducive to the *constitutional choices* to be made in this respect.

Constitutional choices always involve the discussion of the leading principles underlying the organisation of decision-making, implementation and the accountability of those in control. This book attempts to structure this debate by discussing the weight and depth of democratic principles as regards crucial topics of organising a democratic EU. In addition, and this is a much-needed point of departure, the contributions share the view that insights generated by means of normative political theory must be combined with elements of institutional analysis. This is important because it compels the analyst to match ideas with practical solutions of organising the democratic polity of the EU. Furthermore it enables him or her to compare other constitutional experiences with the emerging practices within the EU.

Of course, the contributions that make up this volume do not produce a 'blueprint' for the (near) future but they certainly develop 'building blocks' for increasing the 'democratic-ness' of the European Union.

The contributions to this book are organised around three themes:

- Political legitimacy and democracy;
- Decision rules and democratic performance;
- Citizenship and political representation.

Obviously all three themes are interconnected, but represent at the same time a different dimension as regards constitutional choice. Legitimacy implies the acceptance of political authority representing the common interests of all involved. Therefore one must discuss the delegation of powers, the role of the national states and the political influence of the individual. What is the role of the European Parliament (particularly after the Amsterdam Summit in 1997)? How can we institutionalise 'power-sharing' within the EU (in particular after the increase of the member-states)? To what extent are national, regional or functional interests represented in such a way that one can indeed govern by consent rather than by decisions made by veiled bodies or agencies? These questions touch upon both the principles of democratic-ness (accountability and responsiveness) and the feasibility of institutional devices to produce a legitimate political order.

Such a political order, as is often argued, should also be capable of efficient and effective decision-making. Yet, how can this be achieved in a European community that is economically, socially and culturally even more diverse than any other large political community (the US, for example)? Several ideas are elaborated in this part of the book, ranging from consociational decision-making, federal safeguards, and functional diversification in implementation. And yet, it appears difficult to square the circle of efficient and effective policy-making, on the one hand, and democratic performance for all involved on the other. For democratic performance involves not only the inclusion of national or regional interests or elites, but also the full recognition of the role of (organised) citizens.

Citizenship and its right of participation by representation is at the core of democratic theory and one of the central issues of how to institutionalise democratic-ness in any society. Therefore, a discussion on the relationship between individuals/citizens and the working of a democratic polity is essential. In effect, this relation must be seen as a process involving individuals and their representatives. On the one hand, the role of parties (e.g. in the European Parliament) must then be scrutinised, on the other, the role of civic-ness and political culture must be assessed. Both are sources for exerting citizens' rights *per se* and for having access to decision-making at the European level.

The contributions to this book demonstrate that there is still a long way to go before the EU can pass the test of a truly democratic polity. At the same time substantial suggestions are brought forward which are not only useful for debate among academics, but are also serious food for thought for politicians, journalists and citizens. I hope therefore that many of them will find time to read it and will benefit from it in discussing the shaping of the EU as a democratic union *in statu nascendi.*

Hans Keman
Weesp, August 1998

Abbreviations

CAP	Common Agricultural Policy
CDM	Constitutional Decision Making
CFSP	Common Foreign and Security Policy
CoR	Committee of the Regions
COSAC	Conference of European Affairs Committees
DG	Directorate-General
EC	European Community
ECB	European Central Bank
ECJ	European Court of Justice
ECPR	European Consortium of Political Research
EMS	European Monetary System
EMU	Economic and Monetary Union
EP	European Parliament
EU	European Union
IGC	Inter-Governmental Conference
JPC	Justice and Police Cooperation
MEP	Member of the European Parliament
NATO	North Atlantic Treaty Organisation
NGO	Non-Governmental Organization
OSCP	Opportunity Structures for Citizens' Participation
POS	Political Opportunity Structure
RSPCA	Royal Society for the Prevention of Cruelty to Animals
POS	Political Opportunity Structure
TEC	Treaty Establishing the European Community
TEU	Treaty on European Union (Maastricht Treaty)
UN	United Nations
WEU	West European Union
WTO	World Trade Organization

1 Introduction

Michael Nentwich and Albert Weale

The political development of the European Union has now reached the point where the governments and citizens of Europe are confronted with constitutional choices that raise issues of fundamental political principle. At one time commentators on the EU hoped that the Inter-Governmental Conference (IGC) leading to the Treaty of Amsterdam would be the forum within which some of these issues could be addressed. In the event, despite a significant strengthening of the powers of the European Parliament, the EU continues to present important unresolved issues of constitutional choice: the continuing democratic deficit; the lack of agreement about the functions that should be exercised at different levels of political organisation within Europe; controversy over the legitimacy of EU decision rules; and the design of structures of political representation. As we seek to show in this introduction, the Treaty of Amsterdam still leaves unresolved fundamental questions of political principle of the sort discussed in this volume. Enlargement, bringing with it the need to confront issues that were postponed at Amsterdam, will make these issues more, not less, serious.

Two features stand out about these questions of constitutional choice. First, they are irreducibly normative, in the sense that the answers that are given to them rely implicitly or explicitly on political principles or values. We cannot, for example, determine how we should rectify the democratic deficit without first deciding on the importance of the principle of democracy in social and political organisation or without appealing to values like political equality or accountability. Second, these normative issues are intertwined with questions of institutional analysis. Evaluating alternative institutional proposals cannot be done without understanding how the existing decision-making institutions of the EU actually work and what the feasible range of alternatives to current practice might be. In other words, issues of European constitutional choice require the skills both of the normative political theorist and of the student of institutional and comparative politics.

It was because they recognised that the political developments of the EU raised these twin sets of issues that the contributors to this volume met at the ECPR Joint Sessions in Oslo between 30 March and 3 April 1996 to examine and discuss some of the questions in detail. As luck would have it, the group began its meeting on the same day as the IGC started its work. The present volume contains the papers from that session revised and rewritten in the light of the discussion in Oslo and of the outcome of the IGC at Amsterdam in 1997.

One assumption of the group, confirmed in its subsequent work, was that advance in the understanding of some of these questions in part involves conceptual work. That is to say, we need to clarify the meaning of key terms that are used in the debates about the political future of the EU. Examples of such conceptual questions include the following. How should we characterise the democratic deficit of the EU? Is it identical to a deficit that might exist in a nation state, or does it have some distinctive features? Is it primarily a matter of decision rules, decision-making structures, lack of accountability, lack of democratic responsiveness, the absence of a European civic culture or what? But the theoretical debate also goes beyond these conceptual questions to issues of political substance, to do with the principled basis on which different political positions may be held about the future of the EU. What would be a justifiable set of decision rules for reformed EU institutions? Should the popular majority principle be given greater scope in EU decision making, or does the social, political and economic pluralism of Europe require a system of concurrent majorities or super-majoritarian decision rules? What are the appropriate structures of political representation within the EU? How should a European constitutional order seek to balance the representation of member states with the representation of individual citizens?

Moreover, the manner in which these questions of institution building are answered has implications for values like social justice, economic efficiency, political equality and human rights. Procedures do not simply define a way of taking decisions: they also encode certain sorts of outcomes rather than others. Hence the answers that are given to the procedural questions also need to be considered alongside issues of substance. What constitutional principles are appropriate for protecting rights in Europe? How far is democracy a matter of economic control as well as political influence? What rights are due to citizens in the EU and to those outside?

Such issues of European constitutional choice tend to be interrelated. Thus, to take a simple example, one's view on the proper role of the member states in the EU decision process has implications for one's view of the extent to which there should be direct participation in the making of decisions by the citizens of Europe. So it is not easy to look at some of these questions without at the same time touching on many of the others. However, as an aid to understanding, it may be useful to see such issues falling into three groups: those concerned with the question of political legitimacy and the meaning of the democratic deficit in the EU; those concerned with the character of the decision rules that can be justified by appeal to the principles of democratic theory; and those concerned with the rights of citizenship and the values that should be protected in the construction of an EU constitutional order. This is how the individual papers are presented in this volume.

In the next section, we provide an outline of these issues as they are raised in the individual papers, before looking at the decisions that were made in

Amsterdam and the bearing that normative political theory might have on their evaluation. To anticipate our conclusion: we suggest that the unresolved issues arising from Amsterdam will need even more intensive normative, as well as institutional, scrutiny.

Political legitimacy and the democratic deficit

The basic principles of political legitimacy in the modern world are democratic in character; the democratic deficit of the EU thus calls into question its political legitimacy. Political legitimacy is a complex concept, however, as David Beetham and Christopher Lord remind us in Chapter 2. They see a political system as being legitimate to the extent that it can meet criteria of legality (political power is exercised through recognised rules), normative justifiability (the rules are justified in terms of the ends of government), and legitimation (governments are authorised by means of institutions of consent).

To identify these three dimensions of political legitimacy provides no more than a conceptual framework to understand questions of legitimacy, but such a framework can be a powerful way of organising our thoughts. Thus, Beetham and Lord argue that, as the powers of the EU have increased, so it can no longer rely upon the principle that its normative justifiability can be wholly derivative from the authority of the nation states who established it as an international organisation. Instead, it must satisfy the general criteria that apply to the justification of any liberal democratic political system, involving some form of shared identity, adequate procedures for the authorisation and accountability of political power, and a certain level of performance in the delivery of rights, goods and services. Though structurally similar to the legitimation requirements of existing liberal democratic nation states, it is no part of Beetham and Lord's argument to deny that the EU is *sui generis*, such that the exact specification that the normative justification takes will vary from that of the typical nation state.

How much should it vary, however? The three subsequent papers by Føllesdal, Weale and Gustavsson take different views on this question. In the first paper, Andreas Føllesdal seeks to develop a contractualist analysis of the democratic deficit in the EU. He notes that one criticism of the EU is that it lacks the institutions of majority rule that characterise liberal democracies at the national level. However, the relationship between political legitimacy and majority rule is not one that can be taken for granted, but needs to be understood in terms of a broader account of justice, which seeks to specify how political power is to be distributed fairly.

To this end, Føllesdal invokes contractualism as a method of reasoning in political theory. Contractualism seeks to derive an account of political evaluation from a thought-experiment about the principles that could be accepted by persons who had to agree on a social contract with one another. Such a theoretical approach provides a justification of majoritarianism in general, seeing it as the best way to secure, to an acceptable extent, the relevant interests of affected parties from standard harms. However, majoritarianism is not the sole implication of the contractual method. It also legitimises a concern for minority rights. In this way, standard constitutional protections for minorities, which involve taking certain sorts of issues, like civil and political rights, off the majoritarian political agenda, are also justified.

From this perspective, the legitimate form of the EU would be federal in character, with more decisions being brought within the scope of the majority principle and with a constitutional order in which certain rights were guaranteed to European citizens. Føllesdal acknowledges that this will involve a reduction in the powers of the existing nation states, but sees this as essentially a problem of implementation. It means no more than that any transfer of powers should take place slowly to secure existing expectations. It does not betoken any claim to the independent moral standing of the institutions of the nation state.

Albert Weale too sees the legitimation of any future EU constitution as lying between principles of parliamentary representation and constitutionalism, but he is more willing to see the continued influence of the member states in the European system of governance as being legitimate. He detects two strands in democratic theory: one majoritarian implying institutions of parliamentary government; the other super-majoritarian implying a system of concurrent majorities. Although the general justification of democratic institutions is that they promote certain common interests, this is compatible with recognising that established political identities also have a proper place in any legitimate system of government. Moreover, parliamentary government requires certain conditions to be in place before it can function successfully, and these conditions are not met in the case of the EU. In consequence we may well have an inconsistent triad in which any two, but not all three, of the following are possible: the system of concurrent decision making, the *acquis communautaire* and the promotion of common interests.

Sverker Gustavsson takes this logic a stage further by arguing that it is premature to seek to abolish the EU's democratic deficit. He describes his own position as preservationist, wishing to uphold the asymmetry between suprastatism and democratic accountability. To seek to abolish this asymmetry prematurely would threaten the democratic achievements that have been secured in the member states. He defends this position by an analysis of the arguments used by the German Constitutional Court in its judgment on the Maastricht Treaty of 12 October 1993. The source is an important one because, as Gustavsson notes, for reasons of history the German political system had to use legal means to resolve the conflicts over the Maastricht Treaty that in France and Denmark were resolved by the political device of the referendum. The Court recognised that there was a potential conflict between the principles of parliamentary government and the ceding of powers to the EU. It sought to square the circle of this conflict by appealing to certain conditions that should be in place if the yielding of powers was to be regarded as legitimate. In particular, the Court argued that the Bundestag in agreeing to the Maastricht Treaty did not surrender sovereignty but merely delegated its use. Provided delegation of sovereignty met the tests of marginality, predictability and revocability, there could be no constitutional objection.

Gustavsson accepts the logic of this argument but points out the irony that the conditions are not met in respect of the central part of the Maastricht Treaty, namely the arrangements for monetary union. In Gustavsson's view the acceptance by the Court of the arrangements for European Monetary Union are inconsistent with those provisions of the German constitution that establish the principles of democratic government irrevocably as the basis of the German political system. By extension, the argument runs, other countries are ceding important powers to the European Central Bank that ought to be retained as matters of democratic choice by duly elected representative assemblies.

Taken together then these papers respond in different ways to the challenge to produce arguments of normative justifiability contained in the opening paper of Beetham and Lord. All see a problem in reconciling our understanding of the nation state with a vision of the democratisation of the EU. The tension is felt least sharply in Føllesdal's paper, where the conflict is seen essentially as one of not upsetting existing legitimate expectations in the democratising of the EU. By contrast, though in different ways, Weale and Gustavsson see some connection between the principles of democratic theory and the continued existence of the nation state. One way around the controversy implicit in these different views is to ask whether it is possible to reform the system of political authority in the EU to give sufficient scope to the political pluralism of which the nation state is but one expression. This is the task faced in the second set of papers.

Decision rules and the constitutional construction of the EU

Tsinisizelis and Chryssochoou open the debate by discussing the dynamics of the evolution of the EU using the concept of confederal consocation. The essence of their argument is that the EU continues to act as a means for strengthening the domestic power base of national leaders, in part because the European system of governance rests upon the separate constitutional orders of the member states, and in part because collective decisions within the EU are made by closed processes of bargaining among political elites that resemble the classic forms of consociationalism. Thus, in place of a politically organised demos at the European level, the EU can be seen as the institution of distinct demoi involved in a process of mutual governance. Tsinisizelis and Chryssochoou argue that the dynamics of reform will be governed by the continuing desire of European political elites to manage the processes of institutional reform, so that in consequence it will be difficult for a transnational European demos to emerge. Rather than form following function, function is more likely to follow existing form.

Thomas Christiansen focuses his attention upon the Commission. He argues that the demand for increased political accountability has to be set against the equally legitimate demands for improved system effectiveness and the maintenance of national diversity. Drawing upon empirical evidence, he argues that there are inherent weaknesses in the Commission's mode of working arising from national influences through secondments and comitology. One way to over-come these difficulties, he suggests, might be to take seriously the idea that the regulatory tasks of the Commission could be undertaken through more indepen-dent agencies who would have to render a public account of their decisions.

Questions about the constraints on the reform process do not, however, entirely determine the character and limits of possible reforms. In her paper Heidrun Abromeit proposes one possible way in which transnational democratic rights might be enhanced. She starts from the assumption that democracy is not the same as parliamentary government, but she is also critical of the existing system of EU governance for its ability to impose external costs upon those actors not involved in the decision process. Using a contractarian form of argu-ment (borrowed from James Buchanan, not, like Føllesdal, from John Rawls), she argues for the establishment of veto rights on policy formation. Regions and transnationally organised groups would be able, through the device of a refer-endum, to veto policy initiatives decided upon by normal EU processes of decision making. One advantage of such an arrangement, Abromeit argues, is that the ability to impose external costs would be reduced, since those who were most likely to bear the costs would be able to protect themselves through the exercise of the veto. Abromeit acknowledges that the use of the veto might involve increasing the transaction costs associated with decision making, but she points out that the use of a blocking referendum would prevent the EU inter-vening in too many areas and would also prevent the inefficiencies associated with the creation of package deals under existing arrangements.

If the idea of countervailing democratic rights is to be developed, then it will require the creation of opportunity structures for citizen participation, and the range and form of such opportunity structures is the theme of the paper by Michael Nentwich. His account of such structures reveals a wide possible range, involving the referendum but also including an interactive network of communi-cation, changing the rules of standing in the European Court of Justice, deliberative opinion polling and various experiments with teledemocracy. He argues that there is a powerful case for extending the use of such devices at the European level in order to counterbalance the loss of participatory opportunities for citizens of the member states as functions and competences move upwards.

Citizenship and constitutional choice

Issues of citizen participation raise questions about the substantive values that may be promoted or hindered by various institutional arrangements. And this brings us to the topics of the last set of papers, all of which are concerned with citizens' rights in the new Europe.

Richard Kuper argues that one must move beyond a conception of democ-racy as a set of institutional arrangements to the conception of democracy as a process. Political legitimacy is not created by institutional reforms but by engage-ment with the political concerns of citizens, as expressed, for example, through social movements. There is thus a need to ensure the capacity of members of society to participate actively as democratic citizens. Since the outcomes of democratic decisions can affect the capacity of people to participate in future decisions, issues of substance and process cannot easily be separated, and there is a need for Europe both to incorporate social rights in its political order and to allow the flourishing of economic organisation at the regional level.

Dora Kostakopoulou takes up the theme of exclusion that is touched upon in Kuper's analysis. She argues that the EU provides a context in which it should be possible to fashion a post-national view of citizenship around new concepts of community thereby encouraging the possibilities of multiple membership. In this view, there are various measures that are necessary to overcome the democratic deficit of the EU including both institutional reforms to strengthen the powers of the European Parliament and an ending to the unjust exclusions from citizenship that apply, for example, to resident aliens.

Carlos Closa takes up a similar set of themes, arguing that it is possible to establish a coherent and strong notion of EU citizenship. Although individuals are embedded in particular communities, the qualities that are needed for active citizenship, in particular agency and responsibility, are universal in character. Hence, we should think of these qualities as deriving from different sources but feeding the creation of a European political culture orientated to democratic constitutional arrangements.

How inclusive should constitutional reform be, however? Marcel Wissenburg is concerned with the extent to which there should be a concern for the protection of nature included in a European constitution. He argues that there are various logical possibilities in this respect, including an anthropocentric perspective, in which only human beings are assigned moral value, and ecocentrism, in which value is assigned to the whole of nature. Wissenburg argues that only an anthropocentric ethic based on the principle of equality of moral worth is compatible with the assumptions of a liberal democratic constitutional order for the EU.

Constitutional choice after Amsterdam

It should be clear from the above summary of the papers that once the questions of constitutional design and evaluation are opened up, the range of possibilities becomes very radical indeed. How far have current processes of institutional reform responded to the challenges posed by such questions of value and principle?

The Amsterdam European Council in June 1997 agreed on the so-called 'Draft Treaty of Amsterdam', which was signed at a special summit on 2 October 1997, again in Amsterdam. In what follows, we base our assessment on the version of the Treaty of Amsterdam that was circulated in August 1997 (CONF/4004/97). The Amsterdam Treaty is not a 'constitutional charter' in the sense that it lays down the foundations of the EU in a systematic way. Rather, it marks another step on the path of incremental changes that were already characteristic in the development of the EU hitherto.

Its most important result is the reform of the codecision procedure, which was shortened and simplified. More importantly, the changes eliminated to a large extent the procedural imbalances between the two major institutional players, the Council and the European Parliament (EP). Remaining differences can be assimilated to a useful distribution of roles, while the overall political weight of the two institutions within the codecision procedure may now be considered equal. Amsterdam thus finally puts the EP on an essentially equal footing with the Council.

Codecision was not made the sole uniform decision procedure of the EU, but the EP's involvement in the decision-making processes was broadened. There were numerous specific changes, but the following are the most important. The cooperation procedure has been replaced by codecision in most cases, with the exception of EMU. In future, the EP will thus be a co-legislator in thirty-seven different types of issue. By contrast, in some central issues where the Amsterdam Treaty introduces new provisions or amends existing ones, there is still only consultation of the EP (e.g. most decisions on asylum/immigration; agricultural policy; the harmonisation of legislation concerning indirect taxes; and the so-called 'subsidiary competence' provision Article 235 TEC). There are even some new instances of non-involvement of the EP, for example when decisions are taken on recommendations on employment policy, and on adaptation or supplementation of RD programmes. No changes were agreed on the EP participation in the budgetary procedure, and there is still either no involvement, or only consultation, in the second and third pillars of the EU (i.e. in the Common Foreign and Security Policy (CFSP) and Justice and Police Affairs Cooperation (JPC)). To sum up, the IGC did not result in a 'landslide' increase in parliamentary competence in EU decision making. However, codecision will henceforth be perceived as the standard procedure in legislative matters, while consultation or cooperation will increasingly be considered as exceptions to the rule.

There was much debate about how to make the European Commission more efficient, more coherent, and capable of meeting the challenges of a further enlarged EU. The issue of the reduction of the size of the college of Commissioners was 'settled' by postponement. At the date of entry into force of the first enlargement of the EU, the Commission will comprise only one national per member state, *provided* that the issue of the weighting of votes in the Council of Ministers is settled by the same date. With respect to the internal organisation of the Commission, the Commission President was strengthened by giving him/her organisational prerogatives, and it is envisaged that there will be a reorganisation of the Commission's structure with the possibility of centralising specific policy areas in the hands of a few higher-order Commissioners (vice-presidents). According to the Amsterdam Treaty, the assent of the EP will be needed for the designation of the Commission President, in addition to the approval of the new team of Commissioners. Furthermore, the nominee for President will be given a greater say in the choice of the members of the college.

The Amsterdam Treaty fixes a maximum number of 700 Members of the European Parliament and envisages that, when adjusting the present numbers in the course of future enlargement negotiations, 'appropriate representation of the peoples' of the member states has to be ensured.

Giving the national parliaments a greater say in European politics is not just an additional way to improve the status of democracy in the EU, but for some is better than strengthening the EP. The Amsterdam Treaty will include a Protocol 'on the role of national parliaments in the European Union' which states in its preamble that the Conference desires the encouragement of greater involvement of national parliaments in the activities of the EU. However, 'greater involvement' does not, as the Protocol shows, refer to formal participation, but only to an exchange of views. The Protocol has two parts. The first aims at improving and fastening the transfer of information between the two layers of decision making. The second deals with the future role of COSAC, the Conference of European Affairs Committees. This will be given the right to give its opinion on EU matters, though its view will not be binding either at national or at European levels.

The new Treaty consolidates the status and institutional position of the Committee of the Regions by separating its structure from the Economic and Social Committee; by giving it the power to adopt its own rules of procedure without approval of the Council; and by involving it on a consultative basis in more cases of EU decision making.

With respect to the Council of Ministers, the Amsterdam Treaty tackles the issue of more efficient policy making by the extension of the scope of qualified majority voting to a series of competences, for example the implementation of decisions in the second (CFSP) and third pillars (JPC). By contrast, unanimity will still be required for a series of new competences (e.g. the implementation of the Schengen *acquis*) as well as for some existing competences such as industrial policy. In order to facilitate the shift from unanimity to majority voting, the new Treaty introduces three innovative formulae. First, for basic decisions in CFSP, unanimity is kept as a general rule, but where a member state is against the decision which is about to be taken it may abstain from the vote without preventing the decision being taken; the state is, however, not bound by the decision, and does not have to participate in its financing (so-called 'constructive abstention'). Second, in a series of decisions taken under the third pillar (JPC), the new Treaty replaces unanimity by the 'extra-qualified' majority already known from those cases where the Council has hitherto acted without a proposal from the Commission (at least ten member states have to be in favour of a measure). Finally, in three cases (e.g. for implementing measures in CFSP) the new Treaty provides for a formula which might be nicknamed the 'Amsterdam Compromise'. A member of the Council may declare that, for important and stated reasons of national policy, it intends to oppose the granting of an authorisation by qualified majority. In this case (and as with the 1966 'Luxembourg Compromise'), a vote shall not be taken, but the Council may, acting by a qualified majority, request that the matter be referred to the European Council for decision by unanimity.

The new Treaty also puts an end to the secrecy in the Council, with new rules on transparency. In particular, the rules previously contained in mere interinstitutional agreements and rules of procedure are now part of the primary law of the EU. The latter has to be respected by the institutions, which will be checked by the ECJ. In material terms, a general right of access to EP, Council, and Commission documents is established. This right of access is, however, subject to the principles and the conditions to be defined by codecision of the Council and the EP within two years of the coming into force of the new Treaty. Based on this basic decision, the three institutions shall elaborate in their rules of procedure specific provisions regarding the access to their documents. The Amsterdam Treaty includes some qualifications which restrict the Council's room for manoeuvre when adapting its rules of procedure: in contrast to the present situation, the results of the votes, the explanations of votes, and the statements in the minutes will be made public automatically in cases where the Council acts in its legislative capacity.

How do these reforms look in the light of the principles of democratic legitimacy discussed in this volume? A first assessment (Nentwich and Falkner 1997) of this new *de facto* constitutional framework reveals that the Amsterdam Treaty brought to an end what the Single European Act began and the Maastricht Treaty continued: the process of making the EP a co-legislator, as powerful as the Council in the codecision procedure. Hitherto, this decision mode has been biased in favour of the Council and was the exception rather than the rule in EU policy making. In both respects, the Amsterdam Treaty marks a sea change. To be sure, there are still instances where the Community legislates without the EP being involved on an equal footing with the Council. Such cases will be the exception, however, and codecision the rule. The EP involvement in the investiture of the Commission, too, was reformed. The genuine political role of the Commission (notably its President) will in the future be accentuated, especially at the time of its investiture, when the envisaged activities of an incoming Commission will be a matter of parliamentary, and thus public, debate.

Looking at the institutional balance emerging from the Amsterdam Treaty in a perspective that measures it against basic democratic principles of governance instead of comparing it with the traditional national models, our assessment is mixed. On the one hand, it seems obvious that the balance was altered in favour of the EP which is the directly legitimated body of the EU; the Commission's new investiture procedure is finally drawn out of the mists of secret intergovernmental bargain into the light of public hearings; the principle of openness and transparency has at least been introduced in the primary law. This suggests that the EU will be somewhat more democratic after the Treaty of Amsterdam comes into force. On the other hand, a set of agencies now fulfil tasks that were previously under the direct control of national democratic institutions. Much of the implementation of EU policies is done without any control by the EP, and most of political decisions tend nowadays to be taken 'in the shade' of the representative institutions only. Whilst these trends exist at the national level, the EU nevertheless represents an extreme case with some 85 per cent of all decisions *de facto* decided in working groups. Making transinstitutional and transnational policy networks the subject of democratic accountability is a question to be confronted at all layers of the European multi-level system.

Thus, in terms of the principles discussed in this volume, the results of Amsterdam only highlight the relevance of the discussion of political principles. Although in some respects the new Treaty has added democratic legitimacy to the EU's decision-making structure, the observations and discussions on legitimacy and the democratic deficit by Beetham and Lord, Føllesdal, Weale as well as Tsinisizelis and Chryssochoou highlight continuing issues for the future. It seems that the German Constitutional Court's Rubicon has not yet been crossed by the Amsterdam agreements (Gustavsson). Nor was the role of citizenship in a united Europe (on this see Kuper, Kostakopoulou, and Closa) altered by the new Treaty. Moreover, the need to bring European politics back to the people, as Abromeit and Nentwich argue, still remains open. The role of the Commission in the political framework of the Union (Christiansen) remains a topical issue as does the future of EU environmental policy (Wissenburg).

Conclusion

These then are the themes pursued in the present volume. What conclusion do they indicate about the political theory of European constitutional choice?

There is no sense in which the workshop emerged with a European constitutional blueprint. Indeed, a number of papers explicitly reject the idea that it is possible to derive such a blueprint from normative considerations. Normative political theory does not typically generate consensually agreed solutions to problems, and in any case the purpose is to identify the points of principle, rather than focus upon points of institutional detail. But we hope that the papers show that, if our understanding of principles needs to be informed by an appreciation of institutional process, the analysis of institutions needs to be supplemented by evaluation in the light of political principles in the important task of constructing a democratic, just and inclusive European political order.

Reference

Nentwich, M. and Falkner, G. (1997) 'The Treaty of Amsterdam: Towards a New Institutional Balance', *European Integration online Papers* (EIoP) 1 (15); http://eiop.or.at/eiop/texte/1997-015a.htm.

Part I

Political legitimacy and the democratic deficit

2 Legitimacy and the European Union

David Beetham and Christopher Lord

Introduction: legitimacy and the European Union

The concept of legitimacy

The question of the legitimacy or rightfulness of political authority is of central concern to both normative political philosophy and explanatory political science, yet a satisfactory definition of the concept remains elusive, and the connection between the respective concerns of political philosophy and political science is obscure. To avoid lengthy preliminaries, we propose to follow Beetham's (1991) analysis of political legitimacy as a multi-dimensional concept, comprising the different elements of legality, normative justifiability and legitimation. Political power is legitimate, we can say, to the extent that:

- it is acquired and exercised according to established rules (legality); and
- the rules are justifiable according to socially accepted beliefs about (1) the rightful source of authority and (2) the proper ends and standards of government (normative justifiability); and
- positions of authority are confirmed by the express consent or affirmation on the part of appropriate subordinates, and by recognition from other legitimate authorities (legitimation).

Each of these elements or components has its distinctive negative: illegitimacy (breach of the rules); legitimacy deficit (weak justifiability, contested beliefs); delegitimation (withdrawal of consent or recognition).

Much follows from this conceptual framework, not only for the critique of other conceptions of legitimacy as uni-dimensional, but also for understanding the history of philosophical disagreements about legitimacy (Beetham 1998). For our present purposes, however, it will be sufficient to emphasise two points. First, from the standpoint of comparative political science, the above framework offers no more than a heuristic device for identifying the elements which have to be 'filled in', so to say, for each distinctive type of political order, whether past or present. It is the differences under each dimension (the form of legality, normative justifiability, legitimation), and the characteristic institutional arrangements appropriate to each, that help define the specificity of different political systems. Second, of the three dimensions, it is the criteria of normative justifiability (authorisation and performance standards) that provide the key site for the analysis of legitimacy, since it is problems in this domain that typically find expression in breaches of legality or acts of delegitimation.

The legitimacy of liberal democracy

Leaving aside for the present the form of legality characteristic of liberal democracy (constitutional rule of law) in order to concentrate on the key dimension of normative justifiability, we can identify its distinctive source of authority in the principle of popular sovereignty, and its acknowledged ends of government to be the protection of basic rights (freedom, security, welfare, albeit in variable or contestable order). Each of these legitimating criteria is complex, though in different ways. From the principle of popular sovereignty derives, most obviously, the electoral authorisation of government, and the criteria of representation, accountability, and so forth, that comprise the manifestly democratic aspects of legitimacy. At the same time, however, the legitimating belief that the people constitute the ultimate source of political authority raises acutely the question 'Who constitutes the people?' and makes issues of political identity, of territoriality, of inclusion and exclusion, equally crucial for political legitimacy.

The complexity of performance criteria, on the other hand, is of a different kind. Although Lockean rights protection, complemented by welfare rights and economic growth, best summarises the core purpose of liberal democratic government, there is obviously considerable variation of popular expectation within and around this core over time. We must also distinguish here between the legitimacy of individual governments and of the political order itself. Less important than the success or failure of individual governments for political legitimacy is that the system of rule should be seen to facilitate rather than hinder the attainment of its performance criteria, and above all should effect the prompt removal of those who have 'failed'.

What, finally, of the other dimension, that of legitimation through consent? 'Consent' is a notoriously problematic concept, including as it does states of mind and 'tacit consent' or inaction, as well as actions that may be interpreted in ways unintended by the agents themselves (Horton 1992, Pateman 1985). What is important for legitimation is the public recognition or affirmation of authority by those qualified to give it, through actions conventionally acknowledged to have this significance. Legitimation in this sense is a feature of all political orders. What is distinctive about liberal democracy in contrast to others is that the act of appointing the political authority and the act of publicly affirming it is one and the same – an election – since, uniquely, those subordinate to authority are also its appointing agents. 'Consent' therefore disappears as a separate moment in liberal democratic legitimation, since it is subsumed under the act of authorisation.

In this central domain of normative justifiability, then, the legitimacy of a liberal democratic system depends on three criteria: an agreed definition of the people or 'political nation' as defining the rightful bounds of the polity; the appointment of public officials according to accepted criteria of popular authorisation, representativeness and accountability; and the maintenance by government of defensible standards of rights protection, or its routine removal in the event of 'failure'. Of course the particular form these criteria take in any given country will depend upon its distinctive tradition and historical evolution, including the survival of pre-democratic modes of legitimation.

Legitimacy in the European Union

Having established the conceptual framework for our analysis, we can usefully approach the subject of legitimacy and the European Union by considering the sceptical question as to whether this framework is at all appropriate to the EU. It is at first sight a plausible contention that such legitimacy as the EU enjoys must be quite different from that of the states which compose it, and more akin to that of other international authorities, whose membership comprises states rather than individual citizens. This is a legitimacy constructed on the one hand at the level of legality – a superior jurisdiction to which national legal systems are subordinate – and on the other at the level of legitimation – the public recognition and affirmation by established legitimate authorities – rather than at the level of *normative justifiability*. That is to say, the legitimacy of the EU is a wholly derivative one, following the principle: that system of authority is legitimate whose authority is recognised and confirmed by the acts of other legitimate authorities. It is not a matter of its own normative justifiability directly, and therefore the standard liberal democratic criteria are not relevant to its analysis. This is because the EU does not need them for its effective operation. Its addressees are primarily member states and their own legal authorities; and it no more requires obedience and cooperation from ordinary citizens than do NATO, the WTO or the UN itself.

To rebut such scepticism, it is not necessary to take a view about precisely what kind of political animal the EU is, or is on the way to becoming, whether more or less state-like, whether federal or confederal, whether decentred, postmodern, or whatever (Caporaso 1996). Nor is it necessary to commit oneself to one particular model of analysis of EU institutions and processes from among the many available (Hix 1994, Risse-Kappen 1996). It is sufficient to acknowledge that the EU is simply not like other intergovernmental bodies, and that the authority of its institutions requires, and is in the process of acquiring, a measure of normative validity in its own right, alongside the indirect legitimacy deriving from recognition by its member states and their political elites. This is so for a number of reasons.

First, viewed as a regulatory regime, EU law impacts directly on citizens, as producers, employees, consumers, etc., and requires their acknowledgement of it as binding on them, and therefore their recognition of the EU as a rightful source of valid law. This is evident, for example, across the range of quota policy

– the preservation of fish stocks, the reduction of agricultural surpluses, the rundown of rust-belt industries – where decisions jeopardise the livelihood of individuals directly, and have significant distributional consequences. The tendency of national governments to offload the odium for such decisions very publicly onto the EU only makes the issue of its legitimacy more, not less, salient.

Second, from a dynamic point of view, the development of the EU historically has exposed the inadequacy of a legitimacy confined to elite consensus. The debates over Maastricht demonstrated the vulnerability of the EU to popular countermobilisation, and the necessity to secure not only public support for the expansion of its powers, but also a more direct legitimacy for the institutions that were to exercise them. Whatever disadvantages greater transparency and accountability may bring for the distinctive modes of EU decision making, it is now commonly accepted that the further extension of jurisdiction needs to be balanced by a larger electoral and parliamentary role. Those who are opposed to the former will also oppose the latter. The issues of the EU's legitimacy and the extension of its powers are thus intimately connected (Taylor 1983: 1–26).

A final, and arguably the most important, reason for treating the legitimacy of EU institutions seriously is the impact it has on the legitimacy of the member states themselves. The latter can no longer be regarded as independent of the former. Just as it was the acknowledged deficiency of individual nation states in market regulation and economic performance that led to the surrender of powers to the European level, so the latter's performance affects the standing of national governments for good or ill. So too the inadequacy of parliamentary scrutiny of national legislation is compounded by the expansion of European law, and intensifies in turn the democratic deficit at the supranational level. At the same time the existence of a European authority provides a focus for regions and peoples which dilutes the monopolistic claims for allegiance of the nation state, even though a common European identity lies in the future. The legitimacy of political authority in Europe is now a 'two-level process' (see Dyson 1993), which cannot be analysed at one level alone, but only as a process of interaction between the EU and its member states.

Such an analysis will necessarily bring the EU level within the frame of the liberal democratic criteria of normative justifiability already outlined: agreement on political identity, or who counts as the 'people'; popular authorisation and accountability of public officials; effective performance or removal from office in the event of 'failure' (see Graeger 1994). Although we call them liberal democratic it should be evident that these criteria cannot be reduced to the question of 'democratic deficit' alone. If expanded powers require a greater measure of authorisation and accountability, democratisation in turn may prove unsustainable without some development of a European political identity alongside a national one (Habermas 1992, Weiler 1992, Laffan 1996). At the same time, however, we should not expect these criteria to be fulfilled by exactly the same political or institutional forms as at the level of the national state, not least because they coexist with an indirect mode of legitimation, rather than being completely self-sufficient (so-called 'double legitimacy', Dehousse 1995: 22–6).

The assumptions of our analysis, then, can be summarised in the following propositions:

- EU institutions require an increasing degree of direct or substantive legitimacy alongside the procedural legitimacy derived from the respective treaties, and the indirect legitimation provided by the member states.
- Such legitimacy can only be found in the three criteria of normative validity characteristic of liberal democratic polities, though the institutional forms through which they are realised may differ, and are still in the process of evolution.
- In respect of all three criteria, legitimacy is an increasingly interactive process between the EU and national levels, which cannot be analysed exclusively at either one.
- The EU impacts *differentially* on the legitimacy of its member states, according to their respective size, character and distinctive legitimation problems.

The three criteria and two levels provide us with a ready-made plan for the rest of the chapter. Figure 2.1 shows how they can be used to generate six questions of critical importance to the politics of legitimation in the EU. In the sections that follow we will consider each of the questions in turn, developing indices and case studies that illustrate the various ways in which they may be answered. The further we delve, the more apparent it will become that our two levels, three criteria and six questions are interactive; that different 'solution sets' can be established across the criteria and levels; and that there is a time dimension involved, with various possibilities for the incremental legitimation (or delegitimation) of the EU that aim to satisfy the criteria in different ways and at varying speeds. By breaking things down in this way, we seek to clarify process dynamics and not to deny their existence. Our six questions, in other words, provide us with an effective analytical tool for identifying points of legitimacy strength and weakness in the developing relationship between political authority at the EU and national levels, without this committing us either to a particular view about how the relationship should develop, or to the idea that a perfect solution exists to the legitimation problems so identified.

Identity: who are the people?

The central issue to be discussed here is whether the inhabitants of the EU consider themselves to be 'a people'. There are three reasons why this is not as simple a question as it first appears. First, feelings of a common European political identity vary across countries, regions and social groups. Second, there is no neat separation between what people expect to get out of a political system and the extent to which they identify with it. The distinc-

| | | Criteria of political legitimation | | |
		Identity	Authorisation & Accountability	Performance
Levels of Political Legitimation	EU Political System	1. Is there a European Political Identity?	2. Can EU institutions be directly authorised and accountable to the public?	3. How might European integration be justified in terms of superior economic and political performance?
	Member states of the EU	4. How do different concepts of national identity interact with the process of European integration and with what consequences for legitimacy at the two levels?	5. What is the relationship between national representative institutions and EU decision-making?	6. How do the performance of the EU and its member states affect one another and with what consequences for the legitimacy of each?

Figure 2.1 Levels and dimensions of legitimation in the European Union

tion between the instrumental/utilitarian (*Gesellschaft*) and identitive (*Gemeinschaft*) dimensions to politics is clearer in logic than it is in fact, so it may not be possible to keep the analysis in this chapter rigidly distinguishable from what we have chosen to call performance-related factors of legitimation. Third, feelings of shared identity can be constructed from within a political system (endogenously) and do not necessarily need to exist *toute entière* before it can begin to function (exogenously). Our challenge is, accordingly, to develop indices that do justice to the complexity with which feelings of European identity can be constructed across space, time, types of political relationship, and to the various ways with which they may be cultivated from within existing power relations.

EU-level indices

One way to measure concepts of political identity is simply to go out and ask the public. Opinion polls – such as those organised by Eurobarometer – ask just the questions that would help us discover whether the inhabitants of the EU feel themselves to be a 'people' and with enough strength and consistency to underpin the acceptability of EU decisions. Table 2.1 shows that although very few people across the EU consider themselves to be entirely European, a clear majority feel that they are at least partly so and that they, accordingly, have a dual national and European identity. But what we really need to know is how they would trade off the two identities in the event of conflict. Although Table 2.1 shows that those with mixed feelings of identity consistently prioritise the 'national' across all the member states of the EU, Table 2.2 is even more helpful. It explicitly tests the dilemma at the heart of any transnational political system that is in need of some measure of democratic legitimation: if a majority established at the supranational level clashes with a national one, which should be considered the more legitimate (Dahl 1989)? On this question, it would seem that opinion across the EU is evenly split. This would, in turn, explain several patterns of contemporary integration from the continued need to mix and match intergovernmental and supranational methods to the increasing use of variable geometry.

But opinion polls are not real choices, or what economists call revealed preferences. Unfortunately, there are very few case studies that unambiguously probe the acceptability of a European popular sovereignty through actual political behaviour. This is because the EU rarely tests the direct compliance of the public, preferring, instead, to tax and regulate through the indirect medium of national revenue-raising powers and EU directives that have also to be legislated into national law. However, a possible indicator of the relative acceptability of democratic majorities based on a single European people, rather than several national peoples, is provided by participation in elections to the European Parliament. Average participation across the EU is, indeed, around 10–15 per cent lower than for national elections, suggesting a lower perceived legitimacy of a European-level popular sovereignty. However, before we get carried away with this point we need to notice that participation in

Table 2.1 Concepts of European and national identity, EU (12). Question: In the near future do you see yourself as . . . ?

	Nationality only	*Nationality and European*	*European and nationality*	*European only*
Bel	29	42	14	10
DK	48	44	4	3
D	29	43	15	9
Gr	46	48	4	2
E	34	51	5	5
F	22	52	12	11
Irl	38	50	6	3
It	25	55	12	4
L	17	51	13	12
NL	33	50	9	6
P	41	49	4	3
UK	49	34	7	7
EU	33	46	10	7

Source: Eurobarometer 42 (1995): B42.

Table 2.2 Public attitudes in EU (12) towards majority decision making

	Countries should not have to submit to majority decisions	Majority of countries should decide on some matters
Bel	32	35
DK	49	34·
D	33	42
Gr	31	39
E	37	30
F	38	37
Irl	47	28
It	35	38
L	22	56
NL	34	49
P	45	23
UK	46	29
EU	38	36

Source: Eurobarometer 42 (1995): B50.

Euro-elections remains higher than for US Presidential elections and that in so far as it is lower than in national general elections this may be because the EP continues to be perceived as insufficiently empowered, rather than lacking in all right to further powers.

None of this, however, addresses more philosophical questions about the future prospects for identity formation at the European level. Now there are those who are sceptical on this count, either because the EU lacks the 'essentialist' qualities that make the nation appear natural and uncontested as a focus for identity (Obradovic 1996) or because the nation state may have been constructed as a kind of 'final equilibrium' in identity formation (Cederman 1996). Without being able to settle such a speculative question conclusively, we are more sanguine for three reasons. First, the EU may not need an identity rooted in the past if it can construct a forward-looking identity based on shared commitments to termination of conflict and continued democratisation of the European continent. Second, and closely related to this, we are attracted by Jo Weiler's argument that constitutional patriotism offers an alternative to ethnic homogeneity and that a stable relationship can develop between European and national identities precisely because they can take up very different – and complementary – positions on either side of this distinction (Weiler 1997). Third, we have to question whether the 'thick' identities of communitarian politics really are appropriate to a construction like the EU, or, indeed, to contemporary conditions. There may be much to be said for the 'thin' – and lightly held – identities that consist of little more than shared norms and idioms of communication (which may not even require people to speak the same language). These allow people to interact flexibly in the spirit of Ernest Gellner's joke that the contemporary citizen needs to be 'modular man' (Gellner 1994); they leave room for critical and reflexive attitudes to loyalties (Giddens 1996, Weiler 1997), and they can be developed endogenously within institutional structures: joining in the game can create the identity (Scharpf 1997).

Interaction with the national level

Concepts of national identity can be constructed in ways that are of varying helpfulness to European political integration. There are a number of possible variables that may account for these differences.

Large and small states

It is possible that people who live in small states are more aware of the limited capacity of their governments to ensure physical protection, economic performance and welfare entitlements. For these essentially performance-related reasons, they may be readier to identify with an EU that is capable of providing valuable state-supplementing roles and to accept the legitimacy of an EU-level popular sovereignty. Smaller states may also prefer a supranational approach to European integration in which decisions are made by impartial institutions to an intergovernmental one in which large states are likely to dominate.

Considerations such as these explain high levels of support for an ambitiously defined EU in Belgium, Ireland, Luxembourg and the Netherlands. However, the Scandinavian countries, which are all small in terms of population, provide instances of small states where European integration is viewed with some suspicion. One reason for this is that the limited capacity of small states has to be set against their intimacy as political arenas. Perceptions of whether a country is part of the core or the periphery of the EU's political system also have to be taken into account. These will be governed by geography (distance from Brussels) and history (length of membership), on both of which scores the Benelux countries are central and the Scandinavians peripheral. Nor do the large member states show any uniformity in the extent to which their publics have developed feelings of European identity. The UK and Germany would seem to be at the opposite ends of the spectrum in this regard. We clearly need to turn to factors other than state size to explain different levels of identification with a European whole.

Divided national communities and European integration

Another possibility is that feelings of European identity will be stronger where the state has not succeeded in capturing all sentiments of political loyalty for the nation. This would suggest that support for European integration will be greater amongst the more internally divided of the member states, amongst minority communities, in peripheral regions and in countries where state formation has in some sense been imperfect. Belgium with a 40:60 divide between two different ethno-linguistic communities – Flanders and Wallonia – is the most internally divided of the EU countries and also one of the most Euro-enthusiastic. Likewise, high levels of support for the EU in Italy are often related to marked divisions between the North and the South and the failure of the Italian state to secure universal acceptance of its legitimacy across all regions and social segments. It is also significant that support for European integration is higher than the national average in Scotland and Wales in the UK and in the Basque and Catalan regions of Spain. However, perhaps the most telling example of the hypothesis that support for the EU may be linked to problematic patterns of national identity formation is provided by the case of West Germany between 1949 and 1989. It was not only for historical reasons that postwar Germans found a more attractive sense of collective identity in commitment to European unification. The latter also offered a substitute identity for a nation that was divided by the Cold War and uncertain as to the exact status and permanence of the West German state.

European integration and histories of state failure

Another possibility is that identification with the EU is linked to different histories of state success and failure. The most obvious way in which a state can fail to protect its citizens is in war and there would seem to be some link between different experiences of international conflict in the twentieth century and attitudes towards European integration. The original six – France, Germany, Italy and Benelux – were all countries that had at some point been defeated, occupied or implicated in the crimes of the Second World War. By contrast, the UK, which had in many ways been a socially divided country before 1939, emerged from the conflict with renewed confidence in its internal social solidarity and international survival skills. However, perceptions of state success and failure can also be linked to more prosaic considerations of economic performance. This would, for example, explain the renewed interest that France showed in European integration after the failure of the so-called Mitterrand experiment in 1981–4, or the role of poor economic growth in persuading British governments of the need to apply for EC membership in the 1960s.

National elite support

All the foregoing hypotheses provide useful partial answers. They fit some case studies but not others. One reason for this is that structural–historical factors often have to be mediated through national elite interpretations of European integration. Political scientists have long argued about the extent to which communities are natural or imagined into existence by their elites, but few would take an extreme position towards one pole or the other and, when it comes to the EU, there are, indeed, good reasons to expect mass perceptions of the EU to be unusually dependent on elite guidance. Much may, therefore, depend on the willingness of local elites to adapt previously constructed concepts of collective identity to include feelings of identification with a European political system.

Perhaps the three principal possibilities here are provided by the contrasting examples of the UK, France and Germany. German elites have often supported the development of the EU as an alternative to national identity. French elites have often managed to convince their public that both identities can grow and develop at the same time. Senior British government figures have, on the other hand, either been convinced that the identities are competitive or been defensive on this point.

Authorisation, representativeness and accountability

We said earlier that a further dimension to legitimation in liberal democratic systems is that political power should be authorised, representative and account-able. The obvious solution is to have a political leadership elected by all adult members of the political system. But, in the case of the EU, uncertainty as to whether the European electorate is capable of feeling itself to be a 'people' whose popular sovereignty is acceptable to all led, at first, to the development of an institutional structure that piggy-backed on the democratic authority of the state (Wallace and Smith 1995). An ingenious dual political leadership was constructed in which an unelected Commission would lead in the proposal of initiatives, but all final decisions would be taken by Councils of Ministers, whose members were accountable to national parliaments and electorates. Only more recently have there been even hesitant and incremental attempts to develop more direct modes of democratisation at the European level. In this section our European-level case study will look at the relationship of the Commission to the EP, and our national-level case study will consider the relationship between members of the Council of Ministers and domestic parliaments. This will provide a neat way of comparing supranational and intergovernmental paths to the democratic legitimation of EU power. What will emerge is that both suffer from structural defects from a point of view of authorisation, representativeness and accountability. This suggests that there are no easy solutions to the demo-cratic deficit.

EU level: the Commission and problems of authorisation, accountability and representation

The Maastricht Treaty attempted a limited movement towards a more direct form of representation in the EU by requiring new Commissions to be confirmed in office by newly elected European Parliaments. When it came to use this power for the first time in 1994, the EP deftly maximised its potential by unbundling it into a three-stage obstacle course stretched over six months: first, a vote would be taken on the new Commission President; then, there would be hearings of individual Commissioners before the committees of the EP; and, finally, a vote would be taken on the Commission as a whole and its programme. There are, however, three structural defects to this procedure (Hix and Lord 1996):

- Because they are still 'second order' in character, European elections are not really about the institution that is in fact being elected – the EP (Reif and Schmitt 1980). It is hard to see the EP as having a strong popular authorisation that it passes on in turn to the new Commission, when it is the chance agglomeration of fifteen contests that usually centre on issues and power in the national arena.

- The member states are reluctant to give the EP more than a drastic 'take it or leave it' choice over the authorisation of the Commission. The right to appoint remains firmly with the member governments, with the European Council collectively selecting the Commission President and the individual states each nominating one or two Commissioners. At the end of the day, the EP can only exercise influence by rejecting the whole Commission, at the risk of an institutional crisis and without guaranteed influence over any proposed alternative.

- The Commission does not have to rest on a continuing majority of the EP. Once it has been confirmed in office it is 'safe' for four and half years, except in the unlikely event of a two-thirds vote of the EP, and even then it is unclear what would happen, as the member states possess the vital right of reappointment. This limits the ultimate accountability of Commission to Parliament, in spite of the detailed arrangements for the Commission to answer MEPs' questions and so on.

All of these difficulties – the second-order elections, continued insistence that the appointment of the Commission should be distributed between states, and a Commission that does not rest on a continuing majority in the EP – are all ultimately linked to a common limiting factor in supranational democratisation of the EU: the reluctance of many – at both elite and mass levels – to be governed by simple majoritarian politics at the EU level (Dehousse 1995).

National level: the Council of Ministers/European Council and domestic political arenas

The Council of Ministers and the European Council – and the relationship of individual ministers to national parliaments – were the means by which the EU originally sought to solve problems of authorisation, accountability and representation. Such indirect democratisation was most popular in those countries with a low sense of the EU constituting a single democratic people and a high sense of national parliamentary sovereignty. However, there are, once again, structural defects to this model:

- It presupposes the retention of national vetoes. If governments are not in a position to veto proposals, they cannot be held accountable to their national parliaments for the decisions of the Councils. On the other hand, national vetoes may be incompatible with another criterion for the legitimation of the EU: its effective performance. This problem has grown increasingly acute with the expansion of the EU's membership. Thus, even when the formal rules retain the veto, the EU frequently resorts to an informal kind of majority voting, where the minority drops its objections and allows the President to sum up the mood of the meeting in a manner that is not in its favour (Hayes-Renshawe and Wallace 1995). Such informalities – not to mention the practice of not publishing voting behaviour in order to lessen the frictions of majoritarian politics – would scarcely be compatible with a real accountability of ministers to national parliaments.

- Attempts to democratise one political arena (the EU) through the apparatus of another (the state) are bound to be suboptimal. Ministers may be individually authorised in their member states, but at no point in time are the Council of Ministers or the European Council authorised as collective entities, although the decisions they make clearly reflect more than the sum of their parts. Likewise, the idea that national parliaments can bring the EU to account falls down, first, because of lack of information or continued presence at the heart of the EU's complex institutional structure and, second, because national representatives can only go in hot pursuit of national ministers and not the many others who may be responsible for decisions.

- The notion that it does not matter that the policy-initiating body – the Commission – is unelected because all final decisions have to be approved by the indirectly elected Council is deeply unsatisfactory. It ignores the point that agenda setting may be an independent source of political power, because it determines whether questions are to be discussed at all and it problematises them in a restrictive manner (Lukes 1974, Peters 1994).

- By a paradox, the principle of subsidiarity – that the EU should only concern itself with those things that cannot be done more effectively by the state – has the potential further to erode any claim that the public can be adequately represented by the Council and national parliaments alone. For, it suggests that the EU ought to concern itself with just those problems that spill across political boundaries and cross-cut the national–cultural segmentation of the EU. Differences in political preferences in relation to such an agenda would tend to be poorly correlated with national divisions. They would justify present tendencies towards a dual mode of representation in the EU, in which a directly elected Parliament, organised for transnational alignments, can also assume some powers of accountability and review (Hix and Lord 1996).

In sum, the legitimacy of EU institutions is weak, whether we adopt an intergovernmental or supranational conception of authorisation and accountability. In falling between the two, the EU satisfies the criteria for neither. At the same time it also serves to erode the legitimacy of national parliaments, in a number of ways. The inability of representatives at the national level to scrutinise EU legislation effectively weakens the authority of their assemblies. The ability of regions and localities to lobby the EU directly for funds strengthens their own representative status *vis-à-vis* national centres. And the right of individuals to challenge national legislation directly at the European Court emphasises the subordinate status of supposedly sovereign parliaments. The effects of such erosion could be expected to be most corrosive in those states, such as the UK, where the central parliament claims a monopoly of decisional authority and representative legitimacy.

Performance

The EU is developing policies that entail substantial costs and intrusions into the lives of citizens. The single market programme has affected the employment prospects of whole industrial sectors, changed the location of where production is likely to take place and altered the human skills that have to be embedded in local populations if they are to remain competitive. It has also radically altered relationships between the individual and the state in the national arena by greatly constraining the manner in which the latter can shelter various forms of economic activity. A single currency would further erode the role of the state as a manager of economic prospects by taking away its ability to change exchange rates, interest rates and the supply of money. In so doing it would constitute a very different system for deciding on the incidence and location of inflationary and recessionary pressures in West Europe. Such developments inevitably raise the question: what right does the EU have to make such momentous decisions about individual life-chances and the distribution of key values, imposing sacrifices on some and opening opportunities to others? This question usually elicits a utilitarian answer that justifies EU action on the grounds that it is likely to enhance the overall performance of West Europe's political and economic systems. Table 2.3 shows that the public has some clear views on those policy areas in which it would prefer to be governed in part by the EU or in whole by the nation state. It is reasonable to assume that these figures are linked to popular perceptions of the relative capacity of the state and the EU to deliver various kinds of policy performance. However, in the case studies that follow we will also want to isolate the structural factors that are likely to affect the relative performance claims of the two levels.

Economic and social/welfare rights protection

One element within the literature argues that in an interdependent and globalised market economy the EU will always be able to do two things better than the state: mop up harmful cross-border flows (externalities) and correct the underprovision of public goods (Moravcsik 1993). The need to match the lowering of economic frontiers with common environmental standards and action against crime are conspicuous examples of both the public goods and externalities arguments, while more contested instances are provided by social and monetary policy. Although such factors clearly do justify substantial elements within the EU's policy portfolio, they should not be used to suggest that form will ineluctably follow function and that the EU will always develop to fill

Table 2.3 Public preferences for 'national action only' or 'some role for the EU' in particular policy areas. Average of EU (12) as a whole

Policy area	National action only	EU
Defence	43	51
Industrial policy	43	49
Environment	33	63
Cultural policy	58	35
Currency	43	50
Immigration	39	54
Third World cooperation	16	77
Asylum rules	37	56
Health and social welfare	66	30
Health and safety at work	56	39
Broadcasting rules	51	41
Unemployment	49	47
VAT rates	42	47
Drugs	25	71
Foreign policy	21	70
Education	67	29
Workers' participation rights	54	33

Source: Eurobarometer No. 42.

the gaps left by the state in the management of externalities and international public goods. Such functionalist logic understates the importance of historically embedded notions of political appropriateness. Those things that are considered to be the rightful ends of governance may both go beyond – and fall short of – the efficiency considerations associated with the correction of market failure. Indeed, from the point of view of a legitimacy-winning political performance the EU may even find it easier to introduce measures that go with the grain of marketisation (negative integration), and increase the incidence of externalities and public goods failure, rather than set up the common policy regimes and institutions that are needed to mop up these problems (positive integration). This corresponds to Habermas's observation that a seemingly 'natural' order – such as a frontier-free market – will usually find it easier to command public consent than a policy regime with its more concentrated and visible power relations (Habermas 1976).

Citizen rights protection

The EU has developed a role in the protection of citizen rights, in part, as a deliberate attempt to cultivate a sense of European political identity. However, there are also important performance-related considerations that could be used to legitimise the extension of its activities in this area. First, political systems are not justifiable on performance grounds if they are partial and leave just a few better off. They are, therefore, compelled to address questions of basic citizen entitlements. As Elizabeth Meehan has suggested, the notion of a European Community that is just about economics is fundamentally incoherent: it is impossible to define economic relationships without begging questions of social and legal rights (Meehan 1993: 146). Second, one enormous advantage from the citizens' point of view of a two-level – European and national – political system is that there is now a degree of competition in rights delivery that breaks the previous monopoly of the state. The citizen has a double guarantee in the event of a failure of state performance in this area.

Security rights protection

Apart from the all-important point that the EU creates dependable expectations that member states will not use force against one another to bring about political change within the EU area, security is the area of rights protection in which the EU is probably least developed. Although external security policy can be discussed in the 'second pillar', the EU is not itself a security provider. Provision has been made for collaboration in internal security – immigration, drugs trafficking and terrorism – in the 'third pillar'. But the results are so far unimpressive and the methods strictly intergovernmental (Bieber and Monar 1996). The example of security rights protection is instructive of two further limits of purely performance-related criteria as bases for legitimating European integration. First, the EU is not the only international grouping that is available to compensate for the state's lack of scale or capacity. Any belief that form should follow function might presuppose a world of overlapping international and supranational groupings, each of varying size, membership and constitution, according to the task in question. In the area of security, it is not the EU, but a North Atlantic grouping, with the USA as dominant partner, that has been considered by most governments to be the optimum policy-making area. Second, the extension of the EU into the security domain creates highly problematic interactions with our other dimensions of legitimation. Some consider responsibility for the physical security of citizens to be the core activity of the state, without which it would be greatly diminished as an organisational focus for feelings of social–psychological community, possibly without any guarantee that the EU would, in the meantime, develop the very considerable reserves of political identity needed to undertake shared risks of life and limb in security policy.

Interaction with the national level

Although there would seem to be some relationship between the diminishing capacity of the state to respond to societal needs and the development of thè EU, this would not seem to be the whole story. By improving the ability of the nation state to make choices, the EU can even be seen as rescuing rather than replacing the state (Milward 1992). Innis Claude's useful distinction between the 'state-substituting' and the 'state-supplementing' roles of international organisation alerts us to the possibility that the relationship between European integration and the state may be one of relegitimisation and not just delegitimisation (Claude 1964). Indeed, the precise arrangements by which European integration has been institutionalised makes it impossible to assess the political performance of state and Union as separate phenomena. One author evocatively describes the two as existing in a joint-decision trap: neither can really deliver economic, social and security rights protection without relying to a degree on the efforts of the other (Scharpf 1988). Yet, individual member states clearly differ in the steepness of the trade-offs they face between national ineffectiveness and European effectiveness; in the manner in which their own performance and that of the EU interact; in the extent to which EU actions complicate – as well as relieve – performance difficulties at the national level; and in the way in which national elites conceptualise interdependencies of performance between the levels and the prescriptions they are, accordingly, prepared to accept.

EU/national-level performance: examples of a positive relationship

Where the EU improves rights delivery – and political performance in general – public satisfaction with domestic political systems may also increase. Thus rapid economic growth, facilitated by the formation of the EC, helped marginalise the opponents of the new liberal democratic regimes in postwar Western Europe. Democratisation and Europeanisation are also thought to have gone hand in hand in Southern Europe in the 1970s and 1980s, with new government elites taking credit for the entry of their country to the EU, and the EU, in turn, consolidating the domestic position of democratic politicians with generous payments from the structural funds. Membership of the EU has frequently been used to facilitate state adjustment strategies that would otherwise be blocked in the domestic arena. The practice of legitimating a difficult decision by presenting it as an unavoidable EU obligation has been described as the 'alibi function' of EU membership (Hill 1983).

EU/national-level performance: examples of a negative relationship

In spite of the foregoing, the EU may intensify, as well as solve, many of the performance problems of the contemporary West European state. One of the problems of belonging to the EU is that the state ceases to be the 'one institution that is sovereign and self-validating' (Beetham 1991). At one level, this may mean that it is compelled by majority voting to accept certain policies and rules that are inappropriate to its own circumstances. At another, it diminishes the capacity of the state to set its own criteria of good performance: to head off public discontent by reducing expectations of what is possible rather than improving delivery itself. Membership of the EU makes the comparative performance of each state much more transparent to the citizens of the others.

Conclusion

In this chapter, we have argued that one reason why the EU is more than a conventional international organisation is that it requires, and is in the process of acquiring, a measure of political legitimation in its own right. It is no longer sufficient to argue that its legitimacy can be a wholly derivative one that follows the principle that an international body is legitimate if recognised by states whose domestic political systems are themselves legitimate. Because the EU requires its own normative justification, it must satisfy the general criteria that apply to the legitimation of any liberal democratic political system. These we have identified as the existence of some form of shared political identity, authorisation and accountability of political power and performance in the delivery of rights, goods and values. None of this, however, is to suggest that the politics of legitimation are going to be the same for the EU as for the nation state. On the contrary, we have identified two essential differences. First, the EU is not a self-contained political system, but a two-level one of transnational institutions and member states. Legitimation opportunities and problems, accordingly, spill across different levels of political authority to a greater extent that in single-state politics. Second, our three criteria for the legitimation of a liberal democratic political system are general in nature. Specific solutions that are available to the state are not always available to the EU, and vice versa. Indeed, an unthinking transposition of arrangements for identity formation, accountability or political performance from the state to the EU may cause – rather than solve – legitimation problems. At a level of both political theory and political science, it is essential to recognise that (unlike most states) the EU is transnational; that it is developing at a different historical conjuncture to the state; and that, in the case of the EU, it is often a process of integration, and not just a state of affairs, that requires normative justification.

References

Beetham, D. (1991) *The Legitimation of Power*, London: Macmillan.

Beetham, D. (1998) 'Legitimacy', in *Routledge Encyclopaedia of Philosophy*, London: Routledge.

Bieber, R. and Monar, J. (eds) (1996) *Justice and Home Affairs in the European Union: The Development of the Third Pillar*, Brussels: European Interuniversity.

Caporaso, J. (1996) 'The European Union and Forms of State: Westphalian, Regulatory or Post-Modern?', *Journal of Common Market Studies* 34(1): 29–52.

Cederman, L.-E. (1996) 'Nationalism and Integration: Merging Two Literatures in One Framework', ECPR Joint Sessions, Oslo, 29 March–3 April 1996.

Claude, I. (1964) *Swords into Ploughshares: the Problems and Progress of International Organization*, New York: Random House.

Dahl, R. (1989) *Democracy and its Critics*, New Haven, CT: Yale University Press.

Dehousse, R. (1995) *Institutional Reform in the European Community: Are there Alternatives to the Majoritarian Avenue?*, EUI Working Paper RSC No. 95/4, pp. 33.

Dyson, K. (1993) *Elusive Union*, London: Longman.

Gellner, E. (1994) *Civic Society and its Enemies*, Harmondsworth: Penguin.

Giddens, A. (1996) *Beyond Left and Right*, Cambridge: Polity.

Graeger, N. (1994) *European Integration and the Legitimation of Supranational Power*, Oslo: Oslo University Department of Political Science.

Habermas, J. (1976) *Legitimation Crisis*, London: Heinemann.

Habermas, J. (1992) 'Citizenship and National Identity: Some Reflections on the Future of Europe', *Praxis International* 12(1): 1–19.

Hayes-Renshawe, F. and Wallace, H. (1995) 'Executive Power in the European Union: The Functions and Limits of the Council of Ministers', *Journal of European Public Policy* 2(4): 559–82.

Hill, C. (ed.) (1983) *National Foreign Policies and European Political Co-operation*, London: Allen & Unwin.

Hix, S. (1994) 'The Study of the European Community: The Challenge of Comparative Politics', *West European Politics* 17(1): 1–30.

Hix, S. and Lord, C. (1996) 'The Making of a President: The European Parliament and the Confirmation of Jacques Santer as President of the Commission', *Government and Opposition* 31(6): 62–76.

Horton, J. (1992) *Political Obligation*, London: Macmillan.

Laffan, B. (1996) 'The Politics of Identity and Political Order in Europe', *Journal of Common Market Studies* 34(1): 81–103.

Lukes, S. (1974) *Power, a Radical View*, London: Macmillan.

Meehan, E. (1993) *Citizenship and the European Community*, London: Sage.

Milward, A. (1992) *The European Rescue of the Nation State*, Berkeley, CA: University of California Press.

Moravcsik, A. (1993) 'Power and Preferences in the European Community', *Journal of Common Market Studies* 31(4): 473–524.

Obradovic, D. (1996) 'Policy Legitimacy and the European Union', *Journal of Common Market Studies* 34(2): 191–221.

Pateman, C. (1985) *The Problem of Political Obligation*, Cambridge: Polity.

Peters, B. G. (1994) 'Agenda-setting in the European Community', *Journal of European Public Policy* 1(1): 9–26.

Reif, K. and Schmitt, H. (1980) 'Nine Second-Order National Elections: A Conceptual Framework for the Analysis of European Election Results', *European Journal of Political Research* 8(1): 3–44.

Risse-Kappen, T. (1996) 'Exploring the Nature of the Beast: International Relations Theory and Comparative Policy Analysis Meet the European Union', *Journal of Common Market Studies* 34(1): 53–80.

Scharpf, F. (1988) 'The Joint Decision Trap: Lessons from German Federalism and European Integration', *Public Administration* 66(3): 239–78.

Scharpf, F. (1997) 'Economic Integration, Democracy and the Welfare State', *Journal of European Public Policy* 4(1): 18–36.

Taylor, P. (1983) *The Limits of European Integration*, London: Croom Helm.

Wallace, W. and Smith, J. (1995) 'Democracy or Technocracy? European Integration and the Problem of Popular Consent', *West European Politics* 18(3): 137–57.

Weiler, J. H. H. (1992) 'After Maastricht: Community Legitimacy in Post-1992 Europe', in William James Adams (ed.), *Singular Europe: Economy and Polity of the European Community after 1992*, Ann Arbor, MI: University of Michigan Press, pp. 11–41.

Weiler, J. H. H. (1997) 'Legitimacy and Democracy of Union Governance', in G. Edwards and A. Pijpers (eds), *The Politics of European Treaty Reform: The 1996 Intergovernmental Conference and Beyond*, London: Pinter, pp. 249–88.

3 Democracy, legitimacy and majority rule in the European Union

Andreas Føllesdal

Introduction: the double duty of 'democracy'

When it is said that the European Union has suffered from a democratic deficit, the term 'democracy' is used to lament several separate lacunas. The aim of the present chapter is to explore the relations between two of the senses in which 'democracy' is said to have been missing in the EU.

Democracy as legitimacy

Institutions, as all other rules that regulate behaviour, should be legitimate in several senses. We are only morally obligated to obey normatively legitimate institutions. That is, they must be justifiable to the 'demos', to all affected parties. Normative legitimacy requires a presentation and justification of such principles of legitimacy for the EU, as well as transparency of its institutions. Only then can the public assess whether principles of legitimacy are satisfied. At present, we have neither such a theory of justice, nor the requisite transparency. These flaws are in part due to the lack of a constitutional dimension to the institutions of the EU. There is no explicit presentation and systematic defence of the *de facto* constitutive rules, rules of mechanisms, and purposes of the EU (Castiglione 1995: 62–3). In so far as these institutions are deficient in this respect, they lack the requisite moral authority and might not deserve the support of the populations. As a first step towards increased legitimacy, many (including the European Council and the IGC 1996 Reflection Group) recommended that there should be more transparency regarding the work of EU bodies. The Amsterdam Treaty takes steps in this direction by requiring timely information to national parliaments, and allowing them six weeks for debates before legislative proposals are placed on the Council agenda. More drastic suggestions, not adopted, included a European Constitution explicitly established and recognised as such, and procedures for holding Council members accountable for their votes.

Democracy as majority rule

'Democracy' is also used to describe the decision procedures of institutions whereby the preference of the majority of the electorate determines the result (Dahl 1989: chs 10 and 11). The democratic deficit of the EU sometimes refers to this notion of democracy. There is a

> gap between the powers transferred to the Community level and the control of the elected Parliament over them, a gap filled by national civil servants operating as European experts or as members of regulation and management committees, and to some extent by organised lobbies, mainly representing business.
>
> (Williams 1991: 162)

Suggestions abound that the institutions should be changed to increase the role of majority rule as a central structure for citizen participation (Christiansen, this volume, provides helpful overviews of the problems and suggestions, and see Nentwich, this volume, for alternative opportunity structures for participation). The Amsterdam Treaty introduces some changes which reduce the democratic deficit. It increases the power of directly elected representatives in the European Parliament, moving towards a system of bicameral parliamentary democracy, possibly leading to codecision with the Council as the standard procedure (Nentwich and Falkner 1997). Furthermore, the Treaty increases the use of qualified majority voting among the government representatives in the Council of Ministers. These changes highlight some of the central topics of a normative political theory for the EU: the legitimate significance of states; the proper scope and application of the principle of subsidiarity; and the content of 'vital national interests' or 'important and stated reasons of national policy' which protect a domain of domestic sovereignty from outside intervention, originating with the 1966 Luxembourg Compromise and re-emerging in the Amsterdam Treaty.

These two senses of democracy are related in several interesting ways. The lack of specific majoritarian decision procedures can be lamented only from the perspective of a sound political theory of legitimacy. Only then can we understand why such majority rule is appropriate for certain kinds of decision in the first place. Second, contractualist theories of normative legitimacy appeal to consent by all affected parties, and are thus reminiscent of democratic elections. Considerations of possible consent bring out whether the interests of each are secured well enough by the institutions. Thus 'the notion that government must rest on the consent of the governed has become an article of political faith, a conviction that much contemporary political philosophy labours to secure' (Flathman 1993: 528).

However, the precise relations and implications between these two senses of democracy – of normative legitimacy and of majority rule – are contested and obscure. A better account of legitimacy must draw on a broader theory of justice for Europe. Such a theory may allow us to understand and judge the case for particular majoritarian mechanisms within the EU. We need such an account in order to assess the suggestions for institutional changes mentioned above.

The aim of this chapter is to explore these relations from a particular contractualist perspective, addressing some specific issues regarding the relevance of consent, and indicating how this approach frames the practical arguments about institutional reform witnessed in the Amsterdam Treaty and beyond. The next section provides a sketch of a liberal contractualist theory of normative legitimacy. The second section brings this perspective to bear on claims to majoritarian mechanisms, and the third section considers some contractualist constraints on majority rule. In conclusion I note how the contested ends of the EU are central to a satisfactory resolution of these issues.

A contractualist account of legitimacy

General structure

The term 'legitimacy' is used in several different, yet interrelated, ways (Beetham 1991, Flathman 1993, Beetham and Lord, this volume). Laws and authorities are legally legitimate in so far as they are enacted and exercised in accordance with constitutional rules and appropriate procedures. Laws and authorities are socially legitimate if the subjects actually abide by them. Finally, they are normatively legitimate in so far as they can be justified to the people living under them, and impose a moral duty on them to comply. Normative legitimacy is often taken to be fundamental, but the three senses of legitimacy are related: legal legitimacy and the rule of law is often regarded as a necessary, though not sufficient, condition of normative legitimacy. Sociological legitimacy often requires that the population believe that the institutions are normatively legitimate. Moreover, some normative theories in the discourse ethics tradition hold that the actual acceptance of a normative justification is required for normative legitimacy (Habermas 1979: 200, McCarthy 1994: 46). Other normative theories, including the contractualist account presented here, recognise that actual acceptance of arguments is important, but insist that the role of acceptance is not to define legitimacy, but rather to aid in discovery.

The contractualist account of normative legitimacy which we bring to bear takes as its main subject the rules of practices and social institutions. It addresses the conditions under which citizens of Europe have reason to accept European-level institutions as normatively legitimate. On this view, institutions are legitimate only if they can be justified by arguments in the form of a social contract of a particular kind. The principles of legitimacy to which we should hold institutions are those that the persons affected would unanimously consent to, under conditions which secure and recognise their status as appropriately free and equal. The set of social institutions as a whole should secure the interests of all affected parties to an acceptable degree. These interests include peace, stability, satisfaction of basic needs, and fair shares of goods and powers.

Hypothetical consent plays a particular role in expressing these moral requirements on the legitimate use of power. Our moral obligation to obey the law of the land is justified in part by the claim that this social order could have been the subject of consent among all affected parties. But this does not entail that such hypothetical consent creates the moral obligation or duty in the same way as free and adequately informed consent binds those who so consent. The existing, legitimate institutions are binding on us not because we actually consent, or participate in a daily tacit plebiscite (Renan, in Miller 1993: 11). Thus actual, tacit or hypothetical consent is not the source of moral obligation to comply. Rather, any actual obedience on the part of individuals can at the very most be taken as evidence of their belief about the legitimacy of institutions, rather than as a justification of these institutions themselves (Raz 1994: 338, *pace* Walzer 1977).

Thus, the idea of possible consent in the contractualist tradition does not provide the source of moral duty, but is an expression of one important condition for such duties. Obedience is required only when power is distributed fairly. The requirement of equal respect entails that all individuals must be served by the social institutions: every individual's interests must be secured and furthered by the social institutions as a whole. This commitment is honed by the notion of possible consent, allowing us to bring the vague ideals of equal dignity to bear on pressing questions of legitimacy and institutional design. Appeals to consent thus serve to recognise legitimate authority, but consent is not held to generate the moral authority of institutions (Murphy 1994).

Different theories in the contractualist tradition have different subject matter: some are concerned with principles that are to regulate behaviour generally (Kant 1785, Scanlon 1982), others focus on principles for the fundamental domestic institutions of a state (Locke 1690, Rawls 1971, 1993), or for global regimes (Beitz 1979, Pogge 1989, Føllesdal 1995). In so far as the EU is and should remain *sui generis*, or form the first of a new breed of multi-state polity with federalist features, a new contractualist theory is required. Two subtasks may be suggested.

One important component is to determine which interests are at stake, and how impact on these interests should be weighed. Individuals in Europe have broadly divergent conceptions of value and views about the good life. Acceptance of such pluralism (Rawls 1993) would seem desirable for a theory of justice for Europe. This leads us to focus on how institutions in Europe distribute goods which affect those interests all have reason to recognise as grounds for claims. Survival, protection of basic vital needs, and civil rights must be secured for all. But under reasonably favourable conditions, as in Europe, more can be obtained. When arguing about how institutions should affect the distribution of the further benefits and burdens needed to pursue our diverging life plans, we may do better by focusing on strategic resources: political rights, income and wealth, opportunities for social positions. Social primary goods (Rawls 1971), or subsets of resources (Dworkin 1981) or capabilities (Sen 1993) may be the best available index for arguments of this kind.

Another important task is to determine the effects of the EU on individuals, both within the EU and outside. Much empirical research on these issues is required. In several ways, the EU seems to be moving towards the role which nation states enjoyed previously. With the four freedoms and a European monetary union, the EU has pervasive effects on individuals' lives. The impact increases with the decreasing power of government instruments over legislation and exchange rate policies, which hitherto served as shock absorbers between citizens and the surrounding world. The increased importance of the EU underscores that political control over its institutions is an important good, and explains why the democratic deficit, in both senses, is a most pressing issue.

What contractualism is not

Before turning to the substantive issues, it may be illuminating to distinguish this sort of contractualist theory from some alternatives.

This contractualist theory does not aim to generate principles of legitimacy from a choice situation. Nor is the role to *uncover* pre-existing principles of legitimacy (*pace* Castiglione 1995). The role of arguments about alternative principles of legitimacy is rather to rank such principles by appeal to how well they secure the relevant interests of all affected parties.

Contractualist theories of this kind do not say that what makes principles normatively valid is that they are the outcome of actual dialogue among all affected parties. The standard for moral truth is not held to be dependent on, or constituted by, the result of actual deliberation by particular parties within particular institutions. Contractualism rather suggests how the binding nature of institutions depends on how actual lives are affected within institutions (Weithman 1995). By contrast, the tradition associated with Habermas (1992) is more demanding with regard to the need for actual dialogue, since '[v]alidity construed as rational acceptability is . . . tied to communication processes in which claims are tested argumentatively by weighing reasons pro and con' (McCarthy 1994: 46).

This point has some practical and political implications. If principles of legitimacy require actual participation in order to be appropriate, or for the laws to be experienced as the citizens' own creation (Brown 1994: 181), the EU would appear to require a constitutional convention, as in the American case (Jefferson 1789). Contractualism, on the other hand, insists that political participation, including democratic mechanisms, and constitutional conventions must be justified on the merits of such procedures.

The focus on principles of legitimacy as conditions which particular institutions must satisfy also sets this approach apart from accounts which hold that the role of political theory is to generate blueprints for institutions. The aim of political theory is narrower: to resolve conflicts among considered judgements and clarify our views on areas where more determinate answers are needed.

Finally, contractualism is not committed to holding that a unique set of rules or institutions needs to be identified. The justification offered by contractualism is not one of deduction, but rather of acceptability. Often this is all that is needed for the purpose of identifying some social worlds as out of bounds, as unjust or immoral. On this view, political theory aspires to put some constraints on what kinds of world individuals should acquiesce in, without necessarily pointing to one ideal world (O'Neill 1986: 48). Justification of this kind underdetermines the set of just institutions. Several different institutional arrangements can be equally unobjectionable, and hence permissible from the point of view of justice.

Justifying majority rule

We now turn to consider the case for majority mechanisms within the institutions of the EU. The following sketch is brief: the purpose is to indicate, but not exhaust, contractualist arguments on this issue.

The general case for majoritarian mechanisms

The contractualist case for majoritarian mechanisms in general is that such mechanisms secure the relevant interests of affected parties from standard harms to an acceptable extent. Majoritarian democratic mechanisms are designed to allow all affected parties equal shares of political control in some sense. The argument for such allocations of political power is comparative: it must be argued that majoritarian mechanisms are better suited than alternative allocations of political controls, in that they ensure the relevant interests for all parties. Such arguments rely on substantive empirical information about how democratic measures and alternative procedures are likely to work, including the likely abuses of power they and the alternatives give rise to. Troubling cases include those where there are permanent minorities (cf. Føllesdal 1996), and those where the set of affected parties is contested, such as when the plight of animals or the environment is at stake (Wissenburg, this volume, Føllesdal 1998a).

Two examples of troubling issues can illustrate contractualist arguments regarding institutional reforms aimed at increased majority mechanisms.

Stability

The contractualist approach is concerned to assess stable institutions by their effects, both intended and unintended, on affected parties. We must be attuned to the incentives created by institutions over time, and how they affect individuals' values and perception of themselves and of the community they live in. Long-term unintended effects of social institutions are notoriously difficult to predict and hence assess. Nevertheless, institutional theory may throw some light on these issues. For instance, the case against voting on representative legislators cannot rest with Rousseau's scornful dismissal of voters being free only on the day they vote (Rousseau 1762: bk 3, ch. 15). Rather, the issue must be whether such a method is better than the alternatives in terms of securing the interests at stake, where we consider the incentive effects on voters and representatives. Another relevant example concerns the centralising effects of European institutions.

Some authors note that the current institutional arrangements of the EU are likely to foster the unintended centralisation of powers (Vibert 1995: ch. 7). If a legitimate European order requires more centralised power, we should welcome this tendency, but otherwise not.

Against mixed models

In mixed models of government one body enjoys legislative, executive and judicial powers. To be sure, even in states which split powers the executive and legislative functions are not always clearly aligned with different bodies. Often the executive not only executes laws, but initiates legislation and makes policy, while the legislature often reviews and influences the execution of policy (Vibert 1995: 162). However, the concern for transparency and avoidance of standard threats caution against mixed models of government.

In contrast, those approaches which stress the pervasive need for democratic participation and majority rule might regard all attempt at separating powers as anti-democratic and hence illegitimate. The separation of powers puts some aspects of government out of reach of representatives, and hence of the public.

It is exceedingly difficult, even for intellectually Herculean and virtuous elites, to stick to overriding goals during bargaining and deliberation about laws and policies, and the application of regulations (Mill 1861). And systemic effects are unpredictable at the level of day-to-day decision making. Second, citizens may reasonably want guarantees against likely threats of abuse. Institutions and the allocation of power must be tailored with these sources of instability in mind. To be sure, the representatives and executives must be virtuous, but citizens may reasonably insist on protections against likely threats – including the possibility that some will bend the rules inappropriately. We cannot expect that 'enlightened statesmen will . . . always be at the helm' (Madison 1787: 80). Thus, there is something to be said for a system of checks and balances and a distribution of powers, both from the point of view of efficiency and to protect against standard threats.

The case for majority mechanisms in the EU

What role should majoritarian mechanisms play at the level of the EU? When decisions are moved to the European level, we would suspect that majority rule as a means of accountability and control at the same level secures a better match between the decisions and those affected. Thus majority procedures are often regarded as an improvement over the current situation in the EU. Such arguments favour the increased powers of the directly elected EP. However, there are reasons to be wary about transposing domestic political arrangements to the European level and there are several competing additional suggestions for how to increase majoritarianism in the European institutions. In the following I indicate how contractualism approaches these issues.

The *Commission* has multiple functions: promotion of the common interest, monopoly of legislative initiative and guardianship of Community law. The Commission includes at least one Commissioner from every member state, in fact selected by each Prime Minister. Even though the Commissioners are regarded as civil servants with loyalty only to the EU and the 'European interest' (Ludlow 1991: 122), they frequently defend national positions in the Commission. There is, then, representation in a weak and indirect sense, and the Commission decides by majority vote. However, there is little accountability: the Commissioners are not directly elected, the work of the Commission is notoriously opaque, and selective censure of Commissioners is impossible.

A variety of measures are slowly improving on this situation (Christiansen, this volume). What further should be done? In light of the current powers of the Commission, it would seem unwise to insist that the Commission should be subject to direct election. This might lend it undue authority in interaction with the other institutions (Vibert 1995: 188). This is not to say that parliamentary approval provides sufficient legitimacy. The Amsterdam Treaty has agreed with the IGC reflection group that the multiple powers should remain. I suggest to the contrary that from the contractualist perspective we should be extremely wary of accepting the broad powers of the Commission. This is particularly so when the effectiveness of the Commission depends on the intermingling of executive and legislative, federal and state roles (Ludlow 1991: 87).

The appropriate focus for increased democratic rule should not therefore be the Commission. When the Treaty of Rome was established, member states were regarded as the most likely sources of inappropriate threats to the regime. However, the EU is developing from being institutions created for the effective pursuit of private interests, towards a union with political aspirations guided by a conception of the common good suitable for states. At this later stage, and with these declared aspirations, the central institutions emerge as the salient threat to an appropriate distribution of powers. This may be true of both the Commission and the EP (Vibert 1995), just as has been claimed about the US Congress. These risks increase if the Commission is directly elected, and hence can claim increased legitimacy. Majority procedures may therefore be better established and strengthened elsewhere. The need for a check on centralising tendencies lends support for an increased role for representative bodies based on states, such as the Council of Ministers, or a body representing national parliaments, rather than enhancing the power of the EP.

The *Council of Ministers* has the final word on legal matters, and is the 'ultimate locus of . . . decisionmaking on all major issues' (Wessels 1991: 133). While the number of votes is distributed among states on the basis of size, the Council of Ministers is composed of representatives of the governments of all member states. Members are not under direct majoritarian control: with the exception of Denmark, no national parliament can bind the ministers attending.

Neither the Commission nor the Council of Ministers is directly elected, while both have a large impact on policy. Their respective powers are ill defined, and the secrecy which shrouds their debates and votes allows the Council and the Commission to use each other as scapegoats. There is neither much opportunity nor impact of public scrutiny. This vagueness may give rise to not unreasonable suspicions of abuse of power. In general, the powers of the Council must be delineated more clearly. In addition, I submit that there are good grounds for increasing the power of the Council of Ministers *vis-à-vis* the Commission. The reason is not only worries about the mixed mode of government exercised by the Commission, but also a consideration that the Council of Ministers may check centralising tendencies.

Against majority rule?

We now turn to consider some constraints on the role of majority rule. Contractualism is not of itself sceptical of 'anti-majoritarian' institutions in the EU. I here sketch arguments concerning two issues: the legitimacy of constitutional constraints on the scope of majority rule; and the legitimate role of states' powers, possibly overruling a majority of the citizens in Europe.

A constitution with rights?

Should there be a European constitution with a bill of rights? Few deny the need for clear 'constitutive rules' which specify the various government bodies and their legal powers. The lack of a European Constitution in this sense prevents transparency, which all agree is a minimum condition for legitimacy. However, some writers argue against entrenching some individual rights in a constitution, since a constitution is anti-majoritarian and non-representational. Thus a constitution appears to fly in the face of the principle of rule by the people. More specifically, constitutions are said to be unalterable, and distanced from political debate (Bickel 1962, Bellamy 1995, Harrison 1993).

What does contractualism make of this tension between majority rule and constitutionalism? I shall argue that the objections mentioned against constitutional protections of rights are ill founded. However, other objections may be raised, particularly since the precise content of a such a constitution and set of rights remains to be determined.

Bellamy, accepting the fact of pluralism, holds that

> Within complex and plural societies, containing a variety of cultural traditions and diverse ends and interests, we require a form of on-going constitutional politics to generate a sense of allegiance to common legal norms and political institutions. This argument places democracy, and hence the removal of the democratic deficit within the Community, before rights.
>
> (Bellamy 1995: 153)

Bellamy argues instead for unentrenched rights, claiming that individuals are more likely to accept the legitimacy of decisions they disagree with if they feel they have been involved in making them and there are opportunities for reopening the debate in the future. Democratic politics offers the possibility of a fair compromise for the resolution of issues which allow for reasonable disagreement. Moreover, democracy protects rights, by institutionalising procedures and dispersing power allowing individuals to fight for their rights themselves (Bellamy 1995: 167).

In response, we first note a point of agreement. Clearly, the constitution is anti-majoritarian. One function of constitutional protections through rights is precisely to secure certain interests of every citizen – even those of minorities – against day-to-day majoritarian politics. Some issues are placed off the political agenda. From the point of view of contractualism, this is justifiable in so far as some such arrangement is needed to secure the vital interests of each citizen against standard threats. The important issue is which rights should be entrenched in this way, and how to provide for adjustment and revision of the constitutional protections. For a constitution must also provide channels for changing the constitution by qualified majority, in light of changing circumstances and risks.

From the point of view of justice, this removal of some issues from ongoing political debate is not to be regretted. It is surely not conducive to allegiance, neither of the majority nor of minorities, if the elected representatives are regularly able to redefine the basic rights of some. Furthermore, constitutional protections do not remove all issues from public debate, even though the issues are taken off the political agenda. Constitutional constraints on political debate, for instance by a constitutional court, instead serve to give notice to the public that the political powers now take an extraordinary course, that or the unintended systemic effects of political decisions now cross certain important boundaries. Such warnings do not stifle political debate, since the legislature can revise the constitution if the requisite safeguards are satisfied (Ackerman 1988: 192).

Federalism and state powers

A central political and philosophical issue regarding the future of Europe is the legitimate role of the member states. The reason why small states enjoy disproportionate influence is of course historical. Unlike the USA, the EU developed and develops from pre-existing independent, legally equal, *de jure* sovereign nation states (cf. Weale 1995: 86, citing Mancini 1991: 177). From this starting point, somewhat free and equal parties with a real (though often quite unattractive) no-agreement alternative consented on certain terms. The prior formal sovereignty of each state translated into formal representation which gives citizens of small states disproportionate influence, so that, for example, there are many more members of the EP per thousand citizens for the small states than for the larger ones and small states are overrepresented for their population size in the allocation of votes in the Council of Ministers.

The historical explanation of overrepresentation for citizens of small states does not, however, address the issue of whether such an outcome is normatively legitimate. Indeed, contractualism might seem troubled by this role for states. States do not enjoy an independent moral standing within contractualism of the sort we explore here, which insists on normative individualism. That is, this view insists that only interests of individuals are significant, where the similar interest of each counts equally (cf. Weale, this volume). The interests of states or cultures, therefore, must be expressed as interests of individuals in states or cultures.

The preferred principles of legitimacy are those which would be ranked highest by all affected parties committed to interact on an equal footing, regardless of world view, social standing or natural endowments. Existing states are of value in so far as they maintain individuals' expectations, but this case for states would allow their slow disappearance. A states system would seem difficult to justify in so far as it entails that individuals in different states enjoy different life-chances. So while states may be acceptable as a second-best solution in times of transition, contractualism would seem to insist that, eventually, all social institutions should have a regional and eventually global reach. The current status of states in the EU would appear to be inappropriate, since the interests of small states – or rather the interests of their citizens – are unduly favoured.

Member states will continue to enjoy a variety of powers. From the Amsterdam Treaty it would seem that the trend is towards a bicameral system of governance where the Council continues to be one important source of control. Even though the distribution of votes in the Council varies with population size, it fails to reflect the actual great disparity of population sizes among European states. And in the Commission every state has one Commissioner, with the largest five states having two each until future expansion of the EU. In order to reduce the 'democratic deficit', by ways of equalising citizens' formal influence, the power of states and national parliaments should be reduced by reducing the powers of the Council and possibly of the Commission. Moreover, their votes should reflect population size more exactly (cf. Nentwich and Falkner (1997) for further exploration of some options).

What can be said in defence of the role of states? Some 'communitarian' traditions can accommodate the equal status of states without serious problems, in so far as communities and states are accorded a moral standing in addition to the standing of their constituent individual citizens. However, in contractualism of the sort laid out here only individuals' interests ground normative arguments, and the similar interests of everyone must be accorded equal weight. Political communities have no claims beyond those based on the interests of their citizens. A justification of states with significant powers might be provided within contractualist theory if coalitions of citizens are allowed in the choice situation, parallel to Locke's contractualist argument allowing a property owners' state (Cohen 1986). This strategy may yield communitarian conclusions, but is fraught with great theoretical difficulties.

To be sure, there are reasons to move slowly in reducing the powers of existing states, so as to not upset expectations. As part of a political theory of transition from unjust situations, we could plausibly regard states within the EU as a permissible deviation from institutions which would be acceptable to all. However, this perspective will insist that steps should be taken to reduce the role of states, moving towards regional and global institutions. Thus it might appear that contractualism welcomes slow moves towards the abolition of sovereign states, such as might happen in the EU. However, let me briefly sketch another defence of the significance of states compatible with this contractualist approach (cf. Føllesdal (1991) for other arguments). The primary normative role of states may be to serve as a locus of checks and balances within a federation, confederation or other order with federal features (cf. Tsinisizelis and Chryssochoou, this volume, for further conceptions of integration). The most just stable system of regional institutions may involve a distribution of checks and balances where states play an important role as a check on centralist tendencies. Thus one might argue that member states should retain roles regarding constitutional change to prevent hasty or unwarranted centralisation. This defence is based on the interest of individuals in controlling institutional and cultural change, allowing their expectations to be met. This mode of reasoning may also support giving regions an institutionalised role within the governing bodies of Europe.

Conclusion: the ends of Europe

The objectives of the EU are essential for the development of a normative political theory of Europe. The principle of subsidiarity brings this out:

> The Community shall take action, in accordance with the principle of subsidiarity, only if and in so far as the objectives of the proposed action cannot be sufficiently achieved by the Member States and can therefore, by reason of the scale of effects of the proposed action, be better achieved by the Community.
>
> (Treaty on European Union Article 3b)

Three issues must be clarified. First, an acceptable justification of the principle of subsidiarity itself has of course not yet been offered (cf. Føllesdal 1998b).

Second, who should be authorised to apply this principle? It must be applied by some institution, such as a European Court, when parties disagree about the scope of their powers. This in turn, however, involves considering the general centralising tendency of EU institutions, including the European Court of Justice (Mancini 1991: 179). It might therefore be wise to consider whether other bodies are better equipped and placed as guardian of the separation of powers.

The third, and perhaps most fundamental, issue is that a proper application of the principle of subsidiarity requires us to be clear on the legitimate ends of the EU and those of the member states, respectively. The present uncertainty about the legitimate significance of states and of the powers of the European Commission is due in part to disagreement on this issue. The objectives of the EU are hotly contested, and this has an impact on what powers it should enjoy.

Deliberation about institutional changes is needed to ensure the efficiency of the European institutions after enlargement. However, since, in the absence of objectives, talk of efficiency becomes meaningless, deliberation about institutional change cannot be separated from the question of objectives. To illustrate: the Reflection Group has no qualms about maintaining the powers of the Commission. The Commission is said to work most effectively when it can mix legislation, enforcement and bargaining in furtherance of the goals of the EU. Yet, the mix of bargaining both about and within legal frameworks clearly constitutes an avoidable threat of abuse of power.

The risk is even more pronounced with uncertainty and disagreement about the aims of the EU. This disagreement makes claims of efficiency controversial if not obfuscating. If EU institutions focus exclusively on market efficiency, leaving the distributive tasks solely to member states, the transfer of powers to European institutions might then leave states unable to fulfil the legitimate claims of citizens. Alternatively, the EU may have to assist states, by providing regional transfers aimed at distributive justice among citizens of different states. The extent of any such distributive commitment is contested, and normative theory is urgently needed (Føllesdal 1997, 1998b). EU documents talk of 'convergence' of living standards and 'solidarity', but these terms must be specified: is the aim only to eradicate dire poverty, or also to go beyond that baseline, towards equal living conditions for all Europeans? Any such moves transfer formerly internal issues of domestic policies of states towards centralised institutions, leaving national governments with less leeway in the field of social policy. Some will argue that these obligations cannot be adequately secured by emasculated nation states.

A better understanding of the legitimate aims of the EU is thus crucial for making headway on the issues of legitimacy and democratic mechanisms, both practical and philosophical. As long as the explicit aim of the EU was economic, increased efficiency was easily interpreted as Pareto-improvements within a utilitarian setting. The task of the EU was previously predominantly to secure peace and stability through free markets, leaving matters of distribution and authority aside, in accordance with standard (though by no means uncontroversial, cf. Sen 1982) economic theory. The EU now has much broader political aspirations. Its objectives, criteria of efficiency, and the role of majoritarian mechanisms must be reconsidered accordingly. The choice of means becomes more important as economic benefit is supplemented by other political goals. Transparency and the rule of law, majority rule, distributive justice, and human rights all become central issues. They cannot be regarded merely as ideals to be pursued on a par with economic efficiency, but are conditions of justice if the EU indeed is to become and appear legitimate.

References

Ackerman, B. (1988) 'Neo-federalism?', in Jon Elster and Rune Slagstad (eds), *Constitutionalism and Democracy*, Cambridge: Cambridge University Press and Norwegian University Press, pp. 153–94.

Beetham, D. (1991) *The Legitimation of Power*, London: Macmillan.

Beitz, C. R. (1979) *Political Theory and International Relations*, Princeton, NJ: Princeton University Press.

Bellamy, R. (1995) 'The Constitution of Europe: Rights or Democracy?', in Richard Bellamy, Vittorio Bufacchi and Dario Castiglione (eds), *Democracy and Constitutional Culture in the Union of Europe*, London: Lothian Foundation Press, pp. 153–75.

Bickel, J. (1962) *The Least Dangerous Branch*, New Haven, CT: Yale University Press.

Brown, C. (1994) 'The Ethics of Political Restructuring in Europe – The Perspective of Constitutive Theory', in Chris Brown (ed.), *Political Restructuring in Europe: Ethical Perspectives*, London: Routledge, pp. 163–84.

Castiglione, D. (1995) 'Contracts and Constitutions', in Richard Bellamy, Vittorio Bufacchi and Dario Castiglione (eds), *Democracy and Constitutional Culture in the Union of Europe*, London: Lothian Foundation Press, pp. 59–80.

Cohen, J. (1986) 'Structure, Choice, and Legitimacy: Locke's Theory of the State', *Philosophy and Public Affairs* 15(4): 301–24.

Dahl, R. (1989) *Democracy and Its Critics*, New Haven, CT: Yale University Press.

Dworkin, R. (1981) 'What is Equality? Part 2: Equality of Resources', *Philosophy and Public Affairs* 10(4): 283–345.

Flathman, R. E. (1993) 'Legitimacy', in Robert E. Goodin and Philip Pettit (eds), *A Companion to Contemporary Political Philosophy*, Oxford: Blackwell, pp. 527–33.

Føllesdal, A. (1991) 'The Significance of State Borders for International Distributive Justice' Ph.D. Dissertation, Harvard University. University Microfilms No. 9211679.

Føllesdal, A. (1995) 'Justifying Human Rights: The Challenge of Cross-Cultural Toleration', *European Journal of Law, Philosophy and Computer Science* 2(4): 38–49.

Føllesdal, A. (1996) 'Minority Rights: A Liberal Contractualist Case', in Juha Raikka (ed.), *Do we need Minority Rights? Conceptual Issues*, The Hague: Kluwer Academic/Kluwer Law International, pp. 59–83.

Føllesdal, A. (1997) 'Do Welfare Obligations End at the Borders of the Nation State?', in Peter Koslowski and Andreas Føllesdal (eds), *Restructuring the Welfare State. Studies in Economic Ethics and Philosophy*, Berlin: Springer Verlag, pp. 145–63.

Føllesdal, A. (1998a) 'Sustainable Development, State Sovereignty and International Justice', in William M. Lafferty and Oluf Langhelle (eds), *Sustainable Development: On the Aims of Development and Conditions of Sustainability*, London: Macmillan, pp. 145–63.

Føllesdal, A. (1998b) 'Subsidiarity', *Journal of Political Philosophy* 6(2): 190–218.

Habermas, J. (1979) 'Legitimation Problems in the Modern State', in *Communication and the Evolution of Society*, trans. Thomas McCarthy, Boston: Beacon Press.

Habermas, J. (1992) *Faktizität und Geltung*, Frankfurt: Suhrkamp Verlag. English edition (1995) *Between Facts and Norms*, trans. William Rehg, Cambridge, MA: MIT Press.

Harrison, R. (1993) *Democracy*, London: Routledge.

Jefferson, T. (1789) 'Letter to Madison on the Rights of Each Generation', in John Somerville and Ronald E. Santoni (eds) (1963) *Social and Political Philosophy*, New York: Anchor Doubleday, pp. 261–6.

Kant, I. (1785) *Grundlegung Zur Metaphysik der Sitten*, (1980) *Grounding for the Metaphysics of Morals*, James E. Ellington (ed.), Indianapolis: Hackett.

Locke, J. (1690) *Two Treatises of Government*, (1963) Peter Laslett (ed.), New York: New American Library, Mentor.

Ludlow, Peter. (1991) 'The European Commission', in Robert O. Keohane and Stanley Hoffmann (eds), *The New European Community*, Boulder, CO: Westview Press, pp. 85–132.

McCarthy, T. (1994) 'Kantian Constructivism and Reconstructivism: Rawls and Habermas in Dialogue', *Ethics* 105(1): 44–63.

Madison, James (1787) 'Federalist Paper No. 10', Clinton Rossiter (ed.) (1961) *The Federalist Papers*, New York and Scarborough, Ontario: New American Library.

Mancini, G. Frederico (1991) 'The Making of the Constitution of Europe', in Robert O. Keohane and Stanley Hoffmann (eds), *The New European Community*, Boulder, CO: Westview Press, pp. 177–94.

Mill, J. S. (1861) *Considerations on Representative Government*, reprinted in J. Gray (ed.) (1991) *John Stuart Mill On Liberty and Other Essays*, Oxford: Oxford University Press.

Miller, D. (1993) 'In Defense of Nationality', *Journal of Applied Philosophy* 10(1): 3–16.

Murphy, Mark C. (1994) 'Acceptance of authority and the duty to comply with just institutions', *Philosophy and Public Affairs* 23(3): 271–7.

Nentwich, Michael and Falkner, Gerda (1997) 'The Treaty of Amsterdam: Towards a New Institutional Balance', in *European Integration online Papers* (EIoP) Vol. 1, No. 1; http://eiop.or.at/eiop/texte/1997-015a.htm.

O'Neill, O. (1986) *Faces of Hunger: An Essay on Poverty, Justice and Development*, London: Allen & Unwin.

Pogge, T. W. (1989) *Realizing Rawls*, Ithaca, NY: Cornell University Press.

Rawls, J. (1971) *A Theory of Justice*, Cambridge, MA: Harvard University Press.

Rawls, J. (1993) *Political Liberalism*, New York: Columbia University Press.

Raz, J. (1994) 'The Obligation to Obey: Revision and Tradition', in Jospeh Raz (ed.), *Ethics in the Public Domain*, Oxford: Clarendon Press, pp. 325–38.

Rousseau, J.-J. (1762) *On the Social Contract*, Roger D. Masters (ed.) (1978), trans. Judith R. Masters, New York: St Martin's Press.

Scanlon, T. M. (1982) 'Contractualism and Utilitarianism', in Amartya K. Sen and Bernard Williams (eds), *Utilitarianism and Beyond*, Cambridge: Cambridge University Press, pp. 103–28.

Sen, A. K. (1982) 'Rational Fools: A Critique of the Behavioural Foundations of Economic Theory', in A. K. Sen (ed.), *Choice, Welfare and Measurement*, Cambridge, MA: MIT Press, pp. 84–106.

Sen, A. K. (1993) 'Capability and Well-being', in Martha Nussbaum and Amartya Sen (eds), *The Quality of Life*, Oxford: Clarendon Press, pp. 30–53.

Vibert, F. (1995) *Europe: A Constitution for the Millenium*, Aldershot: Dartmouth.

Walzer, M. (1977) *Just and Unjust Wars: A Moral Argument with Historical Illustrations*, New York: Basic Books.

Weale, A. (1995) 'Democratic Legitimacy and the Constitution of Europe', in Richard Bellamy, Vittorio Bufacchi and Dario Castiglione (eds), *Democracy and Constitutional Culture in the Union of Europe*, London: Lothian Foundation Press, pp. 81–94.

Weithman, P. (1995) 'Contractualist Liberalism and Deliberative Democracy', *Philosophy and Public Affairs* 24(4): 314–43.

Wessels, W. (1991) 'The EC Council: The Community's Decisionmaking Center', in Robert O. Keohane and Stanley Hoffmann (eds), *The New European Community*, Boulder, CO: Westview Press, pp. 133–54.

Williams, Shirley (1991) 'Sovereignty and Accountability in the European Community', in Robert O. Keohane and Stanley Hoffmann (eds), *The New European Community*, Boulder, CO: Westview Press, pp. 155–76.

4 Between representation and constitutionalism in the European Union

Albert Weale

Introduction

Imagine the year is 2007, the fiftieth anniversary of the Treaty of Rome. With the continuing concerns about the democratic deficit in the wake of the Treaty of Amsterdam, a new Inter-Governmental Conference (IGC) is established. Contrary to expectations it proves to be a more radical body than observers and decision makers expect. Indeed, its report issued within one month of its first meeting consists solely of the following short statement:

> We unanimously recommend the abolition of the democratic deficit in accordance with the fundamental principles of parliamentary government. We thus recommend that the sole legislative body of the European Union shall be the European Parliament. No other body shall legislate in matters constitutionally reserved to the European Union. The European Council and the Council of Ministers should be abolished, and the sole right of initiative in matters of European Legislation should pass from the Commission to the European Parliament. The Commission should hence-forth work as the civil service of the government that enjoys the confidence of the Parliament.
>
> Outside its assigned scope the European Parliament shall have no powers. The Parliament shall consist of as many members as necessary to ensure one representative for each one million population of citizens of the EU. The system of election shall be based on the principles of proportional representation. Legislation and policy within the assigned scope of the European Parliament shall be decided by a simple majority of members voting on any issue.
>
> The new constitution should come into effect in 2008 in celebration of the fiftieth anniversary of the founding of the European Economic Community.

The above of course is just a piece of political science fiction. But many people (myself included, but also see the next chapter by Gustavsson) might feel that the prospect is not only unlikely in practice but also undesirable in principle. Why should this be so?

The problem arises because, whatever may be the implausibility of this imagined constitutional proposal, its implementation would at least abolish the
democratic deficit. Parliamentary government is surely one of the options that
would emerge from the sort of contractarian arguments that Føllesdal discusses
in this volume for example. Hence, if it prompts principled objections, either
there must be some non-democratic reason why someone should object, or there
must be some elements in the theory of democracy that would lead us to qualify
the application of principles of parliamentary government to the EU.

One non-democratic reason for finding the proposal for unicameral parliamentary government in the EU objectionable is that the EU lacks the political
identity that is required for such government (compare Closa, this volume). The
peoples of Europe do not constitute a people, which is what is needed for parliamentary government to be successful, even if we imagine the scope of that
government's decisions to be bound by constitutional limitations. This is an
example of what Dahl (1979: 108, 1989: 119–31) has termed the inclusion
problem. Simply stated, this problem is that there is no democratic way of
deciding who is to be a member of the demos. Political democracy already
presupposes that membership of the demos has been decided, otherwise even
elementary procedures, such as counting the ballots of those eligible to vote,
cannot be operated. Yet, this inclusion problem cannot be the basis of the
concern about the prospect of unicameral government in the EU, otherwise
there would be no reasons for insisting that *any* element of the EU's decision
making should have a democratic character.

The alternative possibility is that the principles of simple or unmixed parliamentary government taken without qualification are simply inappropriate for a
political entity like that of the EU. As Abromeit points out in her chapter in this
volume, there are fears about the tyranny of the majority and the protection of
minorities in a majoritarian system of government, and it may be that alternative conceptions of democracy, for example the consociational one suggested by
Tsinisizelis and Chryssochoou in their chapter, are based on more plausible
democratic principles.

It is the theoretical grounds of this possibility that I shall explore in this
chapter. My strategy will be as follows. I shall consider the theory of democratic
institutions in general, and then go on to consider two conceptions of democracy
consistent with that theory, the tradition of representative government and the
tradition of liberal constitutionalism. Neither conception on its own, I shall
argue, provides a set of principles in terms of which one would reasonably base
the reform of existing EU decision-making procedures. Instead, we need to
balance the principles of representative government and liberal constitutionalism
to provide a sound basis for reform.

A theory of democratic institutions

I shall define a democracy as a system of political decision making in which
major decisions of public policy depend in some systematic way upon the opin-

ions of the bulk of the members of the relevant political community. This definition is intended to be broadly encompassing, covering a range of democratic
practices including both direct democracy and indirect or representative democracy. Thus, it is clear that direct democracies of the sort envisaged by Rousseau
(1762) make public policy depend upon the opinions of the majority about the
content of the general will. But even in elitist or protective forms of democracy
associated most notably with the work of Schumpeter (1954), public opinion
plays a negative role by ascribing to the people the power to 'throw the rascals
out' should the decisions of political leaders become too outrageous.

If we ask for the justification of democratic procedures in this broad sense,
then the most persuasive answer, I hold (Weale 1999), is that democratic practices are the most suitable for advancing those common interests of the members
of the political community that need to be determined collectively. In the
absence of a capacity for collective decision making, certain interests – most
notably those associated with the cumulative unintended consequences of individual action within the sphere of civil society – could not be attended to.

Democracy also presupposes an assumption of political equality, however. In
the absence of such an assumption, one might conclude that it would be possible
for a set of Platonic guardians or a technocratic elite to attend to a society's
common interests. Democracy also implies, therefore, that each citizen is as
capable as any other of making a public decision, or, more weakly, that there is
no one class of citizens that can be guaranteed to be superior at making public
decisions (cf. Dahl 1989: 98).

Public decisions also are made in the circumstances of human fallibility so
that collective decision making takes places under circumstances in which there
are differences of judgement over the suitability of alternative policy measures.
It may be that these differences could be reconciled in an open-ended dialogue
in which all participants were honestly and earnestly seeking for the truth, as
Habermas (1985: 344) suggests. Since political decision making is a practical
affair, however, such choices have to be made in a limited period of time and
under imperfect information, so that some procedure has to be found for coming
to a decision in the absence of unanimous agreement.

The essential notion behind this way of looking at things, then, is that democracy is a system of political institutions that enables the members of a political
community to secure their common interests, where those members are
prepared to treat one another as political equals and where there is recognition
of human fallibility. In this sense, we may speak of democracy as a fair scheme
of political cooperation to common advantage among persons who are located
in circumstances of imperfect information. Let me note some points that arise
from this conception of democratic politics.

In the first place, the common interests of the members of a political community will typically operate at a high level of generality and take a somewhat
abstract form. They include such things as defence from external attack, the
maintenance of internal order, a functioning system of property, protection of
the natural resources on which all productive human activity depends, provision

for coping with the familiar occasions of human vulnerability, including dependence in childhood, economic insecurity and declining productivity in old age,
and the maintenance of the cultural capital of a society, including both its
formal educational institutions and the norms of cooperation and reciprocity in
social life. Among the members of any society, we might expect rival conceptions
of these goods, but I cite this list as a way of indexing the main components of
collective human welfare.

The second point is simply to note that established and well-functioning political association is itself an institution to be maintained and developed when it
serves the interests of the members of a community. But this does *not* imply that
political association is, or should necessarily be, based on any 'deep' social characteristic like that of a shared language, religion or ethnicity. In effect I am
denying one-half of the nationalist proposition that there should be an equiva-
lence between state and nation by denying that every state should be a nation,
where a 'nation' is understood as a group of people sharing some pre-political
bond of identity. This is not, of course, the same as denying the right of any
nation to become a state, under appropriate circumstances, but it is simply to
draw attention to the fact that the territorial intermingling of nations means that
not every state can be a nation, and that typically few states are nations within
the boundaries of Europe (Weale 1997: 131–9).

Third, although we need not presuppose any deep structure of social identity
within a political community, an important aid to political citizenship is to be
found in shared habits, customs and conventions that enable a group of people
to work together. A shared language is, for example, an important lubricant of
shared political activity (compare Closa in this volume). Other forms of social
cement (including a common education, shared cultural reference points or
certain common experiences, most notably fighting in a war) need not reflect a
deep underlying identity to be significant nonetheless (compare Barry 1989:
168–70).

Fourth, there is no reason to think that shared interests apply uniformly across
any existing political community. Although politics is about the provision of
public goods in the broad sense of that term, some public goods within a political community may in effect be local public goods, sensibly confined to a subset
of the whole. Since the solution to any problems associated with public goods
will typically take time or effort from a population, it may be that the provision
of public goods is best achieved by calling on the sense of history and identity of
those who have shared political practices over time. In normal cases, for
example, saving historic buildings is a matter of more concern to local populations than to the political community at large. (Exceptions will include buildings
of considerable cultural significance to a large number of people. Thus, I take it
that the fate of the Acropolis is something of interest to more than the resident
population of Athens.) There are, of course, many issues here that gather under
the name of 'subsidiarity', but I shall take it as a general presumption that not all
issues of common interest are of relevance to the widest set of citizens within a
political community.

Fifth, the concept of collectively determined ends through political means itself helps to define when a political community should be established. Not all forms of human interaction will necessarily call for the need to establish mechanisms of political control. For example, if a small proportion of the members of two nations trade with one another, there is unlikely to be the need for common political control over and above the control that is exercised by the individual political units. However, when interaction becomes sufficiently dense and extensive, its cumulative and unintended consequences may require a unit that encompasses the existing political units in order to establish the degree of common political control that is required. It is indeed just such a process that has led to the political structures of the EU.

Two traditions of democratic theory

If we take these various elements in the theory of democracy together, we can see one major tension that is likely to emerge. This is the tension between that element of democratic theory that leads us to focus on the promotion of *common interests* within a political community at any level of organisation and that element of democratic theory that leads us to recognise the importance of *established political identities*. If we recognise the importance of established political practices and the identities that attach to them, then we are forced to find a place within our system of decision making for the representation of established political bodies or units, whereas if we stress the importance of democracy as a method for the promotion of common interests, then we should seek to reduce the influence of established interests and promote institutional arrangements that promote impartial decision making.

The tension between these two elements of democratic theory is represented within the history of political thought by the contrast between James Madison and John Stuart Mill. Madison (1787) argued for a large, diverse and complex republic on the grounds that the best way to prevent the tyranny of the majority was to create a political system in which it would be difficult to assemble a coherent majority. I shall call this the ideal of democracy as liberal constitutionalism, to help focus on the notion that what is essential to a well-functioning democracy is a set of rules that constrain the pursuit of particular purposes among members of the population. Since for the liberal constitutionalist no sectional purpose should become a common purpose, the best way to ensure protection for the political community as a whole is to make it difficult for any purpose to become a common purpose. By contrast, John Stuart Mill (1861) was, on my reading, a majoritarian democrat, though one with misgivings and a desire to protect minorities from the tyranny of the majority. He argued for a legislature based on a national system of proportional representation to foster the independence and impartiality of judgement that was essential in creating a deliberative body that could act in the common interest.

Taken to its logical limits the Madisonian liberal constitutionalism resembles Calhoun's (1953) principle of 'concurrent majorities', in which established political subunits have power of veto over decisions at the highest level of political community. By contrast, the Millian system is majoritarian, with institutional devices in place to ensure that the majority is electoral rather than simply legislative and with a presumption (which Mill never deals with satisfactorily in institutional terms) that there are some matters on which the majority should not legislate because to do so would be oppressive to minorities.

These two traditions of democratic theory map well onto the two elements of democratic theory – identity and common interests – that I have drawn out of the general argument justifying democracy. The reason for this is that one way of ensuring that established political identities are not overridden is to create a system of territorial political representation, which in a federal system gives considerable legislative power to the constituent units. This can be done in various ways including the mode typical of US federalism in which various subjects of legislation are reserved to the states or in the German mode in which the *Länder* governments are themselves represented in the system of national legislation. Either way the principal idea is to use super-majoritarian devices to protect established interests. A concern for established political identity therefore suggests a Madisonian approach.

A concern with common interests, by contrast, maps more naturally onto a Millian conception. This is because John Stuart Mill is Benthamite in his theory of legislation. That is, he inherits the philosophical radicals' opposition to established interests (the church, landed interests, rent-seeking professions and the like), and so wishes to establish a principle of legislation which is in essence strongly majoritarian. This makes representative parliaments the basis for collective decision making. Aside from some rather silly mid-Victorian views about the mental superiority of university graduates over the rest of the population, he has, as I have noted, no institutional mechanisms for dealing with the tyranny of the majority, even though his other writings show that he is extremely concerned about this problem. But in his legislative theory at least he inclines towards simple government, as distinct from complex government, and against the protection of already established interests, including political interests. (It is also highly significant in the present context that in chapter 16 of *On Representative Government* Mill presupposed a sentiment of national identity holding the members of a society together.)

In any highly complex political community, and particularly in a community that emerges as the result of a pact among its constituent political units, there is a need to balance these conflicting elements of identity and common interests. In the next section I seek to characterise how the balance has been struck in the evolution of the EU to date, and what consequences this might have had.

Institutional features of the European Union

What are the principal institutional features of the EU that we should pick out as being relevant to the above traditions of democratic theory?

The first is that decision making is super-majoritarian. Indeed, it resembles, as much as any political institution, the system of 'concurrent majorities' advocated by Calhoun. Even with the system of qualified majority voting in the Council of Ministers, it is clear that there are strong pressures towards unanimity and consequent log-rolling towards package deals that seek to reconcile otherwise conflicting demands. Thus, the policies surrounding the creation of the Single European Market can be seen as a log-roll in which the northern countries, who wanted the single market but not the structural funds, concede on the dimension of lesser importance to them, whilst the southern countries, who wanted the structural funds but not the single market, concede on the dimension less important to them, so that the result is the single market plus the structural funds. Moreover, in routine decision making, even where nations are outvoted in the Council of Ministers, it is not always clear that the national governments are opposed to the measure, as distinct from wanting their populations to believe that they are opposed. Hence, it is difficult to move at the European level without carrying the support of all member states, at least over the medium term.

Second, it would seem that although formally it is the Commission that has the sole right to initiate measures, in practice measures often originate with the member states (indeed, I have heard it claimed that the overwhelming bulk of directives and regulations had their origins in one or other of the national systems). The reasons for this are not difficult to find. The Commission is far from being an overstaffed bureaucracy – indeed it is typically rather short of staff, and given the need for national quota systems, even shorter of effective staff. Hence, when it is under political pressure to develop a measure, the Commission comes to depend on existing approaches already adopted within member states. This is certainly true in the environmental field where the phenomenon has been well studied (Héritier *et al.* 1994), and I suspect is true in other policy sectors. Add to this the incentive that member states have, particularly in, say, a field like that of environmental policy, to generalise the costs of measures across Europe to avoid putting their own industries at a competitive disadvantage, and it is easy to see why the formal and the actual position on the origin of measures diverge so much.

Third, there is a lack of parliamentary accountability in the process of decision making. This applies both at the level of the European Parliament and at the level of the national parliaments. It is certainly true that the EP has come to challenge more forcefully the Commission and the Council of Ministers over certain matters in recent years, and of course the strengthening of the co-decision procedure in the Treaty of Amsterdam means that it will be able to exercise more control than before in the making of decisions, if only in the form of a veto. The procedure also means that the EP negotiates directly with the Council rather than through the Commission as intermediary. But there are still a number of important policy areas outside the scope of the co-decision procedure. These include, for example, anti-discrimination measures and measures on immigration and asylum, which as Kostakopoulou shows in her chapter touch the essence of citizenship. Moreover, many of the other formal powers of the EP are either weak or so apocalyptic in their consequences that rational actors are precluded from using them. At the national level the Danish system of accountability to a specific parliamentary committee obviously provides the strongest mechanism of accountability and the UK once again exhibits the perversities of its constitutional arrangements by making committees of an unelected chamber the most effective instruments of democratic accountability. But it is clear, even in the Danish case, that there is only a certain volume of business that can be dealt with, and that there are tacit conventions between the government and the committee about how to set their collective agendas.

What are the consequences of this structure of decision making? Super-majoritarian systems are likely to create their own decision-making pathologies, in particular a tendency towards pork barrel public finance. There is some dispute, of course, over this assumption in the literature. The original discussion of the problem in Buchanan and Tullock (1962) proposed the view that the pork barrel is a phenomenon of majoritarian politics. Yet, on general theoretical grounds, this seems unlikely, as Brian Barry (1965) pointed out many years ago. Since the core of the majority voting game with a fixed sum to distribute is empty, we ought to expect any majorities attempting the pork barrel to be vulnerable to collapse from inducements offered by those who look as though they might end up in the minority that pays for the majority's benefits. Alternatively, even if the pork barrel operates in majoritarian politics, its effects over a series of decisions would be variable, since the prevailing majority at a particular time a vote was called would be net beneficiaries, but this majority coalition could be expected to be of variable composition over time.

Super-majority coalitions may also have an empty core, but being larger, and therefore more difficult to establish, the last added members are in a strong bargaining position. The consequence of this fact is, as Barry (1965: 317) put it, that the 'nearer a system comes to requiring unanimity for decisions, the more prevalent we may expect to find the "pork barrel" phenomenon'. The reason is that with perfect information and low transaction costs, rational egoists have an incentive to misrepresent their preferences to get the bribe of being induced to join the proto-winning coalition, and under imperfect information, log-rolling will produce specific and visible benefits. Scharpf's (1988) analysis of the 'joint decision trap' in federal systems in which constituent governments are represented supports this conclusion with inductive evidence.

Competing conceptions of democracy

If the institutions of democracy have their rationale in the promotion of a common interest and existing EU institutions are not well structured to pursue a common interest, why do we not simply say that they should be reformed in a more majoritarian direction? In other words, why not simply accept the logic of parliamentary government contained in my opening piece of political science fiction?

Of course, one would not have to go as far as unicameral parliamentary government. There are many suggestions on the table that reflect a desire for less influence of member states in the system of decision making. For example, there are the proposals to strengthen those institutions, like the Parliament and the Court, that are responsive to the widespread, non-territorially based interests of European citizens. One obvious institutional reform here, widely supported by a number of commentators and institutions, is to move towards a fully two-chamber system of decision making, in which the EP was given equal say with the Council of Ministers (for proponents, see Falkner and Nentwich 1995: 112–14). But is the general direction of these proposals right?

In the first place, the promotion of a conception of democracy in which political deliberation is orientated towards the promotion of the common interest is likely to take place only under rather special conditions. As Scharpf (1988: 261–3) has pointed out, it requires a 'problem-solving' frame of mind, which in turn is likely to be based upon a perception of common identity which in turn may require a certain ethnic or cultural homogeneity, or perhaps awareness of a common fate induced by common vulnerabilities. Europe, by contrast, is characterised by its diversity. The histories of its component countries are quite different, involving quite distinct priorities and often competing orientations to the same problem.

Moreover, the problem-solving attitude is more likely to be fostered in small-scale, rather than large-scale, democracies. Such an attitude is, I think, typical of the Nordic democracies, for a variety of reasons connected to their size and political culture. Where a democracy is small, political actors are enmeshed in ongoing relationships, thus tempering their willingness to use public power for their own narrow advantage. Moreover, they are also countries in which small size has historically been accompanied by similarity of socio-economic circumstances for the bulk of the populations, thus lowering preference diversity. It is also possible, I conjecture, that a secularised Protestantism has also been responsible for encouraging a rationalistic problem-solving attitude, and this of course is not a common cultural heritage across Europe. Certainly, the statistical association between Protestantism and democracy is suggestive (Bollen 1979).

It may also be a reasonable hypothesis that an orientation towards common interests is fostered in political systems in which boundaries are relatively closed and fixed. This reinforces that ongoing set of relationships within which political actors are enmeshed, and means that agreements that have taken time and trouble to work out will not be disrupted by new agents coming in with quite different sets of demands. This condition is obviously not met in the case of the EU, where the prospect of enlargement is constantly on the agenda.

One respect in which democratic practice has developed has been in the role of political parties. One can argue that although many people in both the Millian and the Madisonian liberal constitutionalist traditions have been hostile to political parties, the party system plays an important role in structuring public debate and clarifying alternatives. Political democracy requires party government. However, in the European context it is clear that we are a long way from having a European party system, despite the formal creation of parties in the EP (cf. Anderweg 1995). European elections are such in name only; in practice they are a series of national contests fought by the political parties on their own local agendas. The same was even true of the referendums on the Maastricht Treaty, which were in effect voter evaluations of the performance of their own national governments (Franklin *et al.* 1995).

The other obvious problem with the majoritarian conception of democracy at the European level arises from the position of the smaller countries. If we say that the numerical majority should take preference over the concurrent majority, then the smaller countries will correctly fear that their distinct interests will be ignored. One way to make this issue more vivid is to see what would happen were seats in the EP to be allocated strictly on a one-person one-vote basis throughout the EU. The representation from countries like Luxembourg and Portugal would fall significantly.

Supposing we were to accept these points as being valid, what would be implied about the construction of political institutions at the European level?

One obvious response to these problems is the liberal constitutionalist one. This says that, given these decision-making pathologies, it is highly undesirable to increase the spending powers of the EU relative to national governments. The logic here is that, in order to avoid the oversupply of public goods at the European level implicit in its super-majoritarian arrangements, there would need to be strict limits on the extent to which European institutions could engage in public finance activities. Probably the best way of doing this would be to continue the present practice of depriving the EU of its own independent tax base. On this view, expenditure on public goods is best carried on at the national or the subnational level where there is greater homogeneity of preference.

Almost by default, on this view, the chief policy instrument of the EU would be what it now is, namely regulation (in the non-technical sense of that term). The EU would be left to deal with the regulation of the single market and possibly the development of regulation in the field of what is known as the new 'social' regulation, environment, consumer protection and occupational health and safety. These might be regarded as policy sectors in which there was a liberal rationale for market intervention to correct for market failure (Majone 1996: ch. 13). In some cases there is also a clear cross-boundary element (e.g. certain forms of pollution), whilst others acquire significance in the single market because of the dangers of regulatory competition leading to a decline in standards of control. However, it is also worth noting that the liberal constitutionalist proposals for institutional reform from the European Constitutional Group suggest making it impossible to legislate on any other basis than a high super-majority (80 per cent) for regulatory proposals though single-market measures would only require a simple majority (Falkner and Nentwich 1995: 24–5).

If we were to assume that the single market will not realise its full benefits without a single currency, then a further liberal constitutionalist implication is that the political institutions of the EU should not control the currency. In this respect, the present plans for economic and monetary union seem to be running close to liberal constitutionalist form. Placing responsibility for monetary policy with an independent central bank is what we should expect from countries that do not trust themselves to be ruled by a majority sentiment that they do not share.

Liberal constitutionalist proposals of this sort have a number of problems, however. In essence, the main point of the liberal constitutionalist is that, in a political community with the history and complexity of the EU, it is extremely difficult, if not impossible, to move far from the system of concurrent majorities to a more majoritarian system of decision making. But no one who cares about the democratic credentials of political institutions ought to rest content with this conclusion for a number of reasons.

If you create not just a common market but also a single market, and then you impose very tight limits on the tax-raising powers of the EU, you are in effect depriving policy makers at the European level of the ability to develop the flanking policies – particularly in the form of regional transfers – that offset the cumulative, unintended consequence of the single market, in the form of concentrated unemployment or lack of capital investment. Moreover, one of the proposals from the European Constitution Group is to make it easier, in majoritarian terms, to legislate for liberalising the single market than to legislate for regulating the single market. This reinforces the bias in favour of negative integration (the removal of barriers to trade) and against positive integration (the determination of the conditions under which markets operate) which observers have already noted is implicit in the present system of decision making (Scharpf 1996).

However, the justification for this bias is difficult to see. It cannot rest on the need to defend the political identity of member states, since many liberalisation proposals in the single market (e.g. reducing subsidies to national carrier airlines) will undermine politically determined choices to support so-called 'national champions'. Simply to privilege the single market over the potential corrective policies as a matter of policy, however, risks repeating the mistake that Justice Wendell Holmes ascribed to those interpretations of the US Constitution that saw it as prohibiting labour protection laws: 'the Fourteenth Amendment does not enact Mr Herbert Spencer's *Social Statics*' (cited in Atiyah 1979: 323). If the US Constitution does not take this path, why should a European one do so?

The European Constitution Group also proposes a three-chamber system of decision making, with a chamber of parliamentarians alongside a smaller European Parliament (Falkner and Nentwich 1995: 113). The obvious difficulty with this proposal is that it compounds the problem of getting definite agreement, and of overcoming the pork barrel tendencies that are built into all super-majoritarian requirements. It is certainly true, as Riker (1992) argued, that multi-chamber decision making reduces the probability of out-of-equilibrium majorities imposing decisions that could be defeated in a majority rule cycle. But the opposite risk is to impose so many veto points that it is impossible to take corrective political action at the European level.

Moreover, if the pork barrel is a consequence of the super-majority decision making embedded in the existing structure, then a move towards a more majoritarian system of decision making is called for in order to counteract pork barrel effects. This has been the argument of those like David Martin, who have called for more powers to be transferred to the EP, in order to be in a better position to reform the Common Agricultural Policy (CAP). But typically, of course, groups who have been the beneficiaries of public expenditure programmes need to be compensated in some way in the short and medium term if they are not to put up strong resistance to reform. So the price of eliminating wasteful expenditure in the medium to long term is a short-term *increase* in the public budget.

The most important question to deal with, however, is the problem of system capacity. If a political system is to perform the task of coping with the cumulative, unintended consequences of interaction in civil society, it will need a certain level of system capacity in order to be able to cope with the problems that it confronts. After all, it was the realisation by the French government in the 1980s that it was impossible to have Keynesianism in one country that shifted French politics towards the Single European Act. One can argue, of course, that the shocks to the EMS in 1992 and 1993 show that even a unit the size of Europe cannot escape from the power of international capital and currency markets, but it should be apparent that if this is true, it will be true in spades at the level of the nation state.

As Dahl (1982) has pointed out, the criterion of system capacity is often at odds with the criterion of citizen effectiveness and control. The criterion of capacity pushes us towards larger units in our theory of institutional design, whereas the criterion of citizen effectiveness and control – and I would add the criterion of established political identity – pushes us towards smaller units. The implication is that some effective collective capacity is needed at the European level, but we cannot reasonably expect it to take a simple majoritarian form.

Instead of a blueprint

One way of balancing these conflicting considerations that is in principle appealing is to be found in the suggestions of the Monitoring European Integration project at the Centre for Economic Policy Research in London (*Flexible Integration* 1995). The essence of these proposals is to distinguish a *common base* of responsibilities in which all members of the EU would participate from *open partnerships* that allow groups of countries to participate at will. If decision making were moved in a more majoritarian direction in respect of the common base, the goals implicit in the single market and the associated flanking policies would be achieved more fully, whilst the open partnerships would in effect give each nation a veto on participation in matters like currency integration or foreign policy.

The attraction of these principles is that by narrowing the areas on which countries have to cede decision-making competence the dangers of simple majoritarianism are reduced for those countries that are cautious about the scope of European integration. The obvious problem, however, is that the *acquis communautaire* would prevent reducing the common base even to the limited extent that is envisaged in the proposals.

Here there may be an inconsistent triad: three propositions that are incompatible when taken all together, though any two of them are consistent. Thus, one can keep the doctrine of the *acquis communautaire* and the present system of decision making, but lose the capacity to pursue common interests via a strengthening of majoritarian institutions. One can keep the *acquis communautaire* and introduce more majoritarianism, but thereby lose the protection of established political identities. Or one can gain the advantage of majoritarianism and the protection of existing identities, but only at the cost of restructuring the assignment of political competences in ways that are inconsistent with the *acquis communautaire*.

To raise this last possibility is to suggest that there may be a potential conflict between the demands of European integration and the requirements of democracy. The principle of maintaining the *acquis communautaire* has been the device by which the momentum of European integration has been maintained since it has prevented nation states seeking to recover powers in areas they had previously ceded to the EU. The process of constitutional contracting that would be required to renegotiate the balance of powers might therefore risk slowing, or perhaps even reversing, the momentum of European integration, a particularly striking example of the potential conflict between system capacity and size. But the risk of failing to seek to renegotiate the European political order in order to achieve greater democratic legitimacy is perhaps even greater.

References

Anderweg, R. (1995) 'The Reshaping of National Party Systems', in J. Hayward (ed.), *The Crisis of Representation in Europe*, London: Frank Cass, pp. 58–78.

Atiyah, P. S. (1979) *The Rise and Fall of Freedom of Contract*, Oxford: Clarendon Press.

Barry, B. (1965) *Political Argument*, London: Routledge and Kegan Paul.

Barry, B. M. (1989) *Democracy, Power and Justice*, Oxford: Clarendon Press.

Bollen, K. A. (1979) 'Political Democracy and the Timing of Development', *American Sociological Review* 44: 572–87.

Buchanan, J.-M. and Tullock, G. (1962) *The Calculus of Consent*, Ann Arbor, MI: University of Michigan Press.

Calhoun, J. C. (1953) *A Disquisition on Government*, ed. C. Gordon Past, Indianapolis: Bobbs-Merill.

Dahl, R. A. (1979) 'Procedural Democracy', in P. Laslett and J. Fishkin (eds), *Philosophy, Politics and Society*, Oxford: Basil Blackwell, pp. 97–133.

Dahl, R. A. (1982) *Dilemmas of Pluralist Democracy*, New Haven, CT, and London: Yale University Press.

Dahl, R. A. (1989) *Democracy and Its Critics*, New Haven, CT, and London: Yale University Press.

Falkner, G. and Nentwich, M. (1995) *European Union: Democratic Perspectives After 1996*, Vienna: Service Fachverlag.

Flexible Integration: Towards a More Effective and Democratic Europe (1995) London: Centre for Economic Policy Research.

Franklin, M., van der Eijk, C. and Marsh, M. (1995) 'Referendum Outcomes and Trust in Government: Public Support for Europe in the Wake of Maastricht', in J. Hayward (ed.), *The Crisis of Representation in Europe*, London: Frank Cass, pp. 101–17.

Habermas, J. (1985) *The Philosophical Discourse of Modernity*, trans. Frederick Lawrence, Cambridge: Polity.

Héritier, A. *et al.* (1994) *Die Veränderung von Staatlichkeit in Europa*, Opladen: Leske+Buelrich.

Madison, James (1787) 'Federalist Paper No. 10', in Clinton Rossiter (ed.) (1961) *The Federalist Papers*, New York and Scarborough, Ontario: New American Library.

Majone, G. (1996) *Regulating Europe*, London and New York: Routledge.

Mill, J. S. (1861) *Considerations on Representative Government*, reprinted in J. Gray (ed.) (1991) *John Stuart Mill On Liberty and Other Essays*, Oxford: Oxford University Press.

Riker, W. H. (1992) 'The Justification of Bicameralism', *International Political Science Review* 13(1): 101–16.

Rousseau, J.-J. (1762) *The Social Contract*, in G. D. H. Cole (ed.) (1973) *The Social Contract and Discourses*, London: Dent.

Scharpf, F. W. (1988) 'The Joint Decision Trap: Lessons from German Federalism and European Integration' *Public Administration* 66(3): 239–78.

Scharpf, F. W. (1996) 'Negative and Positive Integration in the Political Economy of European Welfare States', in G. Marks *et al.* (eds), *Governance in the European Union*, London: Sage, pp. 15–39.

Schumpeter, J. (1954) *Capitalism, Socialism and Democracy*, London: Unwin University Books.

Weale, A. (1997) 'Majority Rule, Political Identity and European Union', in P. B. Lehning and A. Weale (eds), *Citizenship, Democracy and Justice in the New Europe*, London: Routledge, pp. 125–41.

Weale, A. (1999) *Democracy*, London: Macmillan.

5 Defending the democratic deficit

Sverker Gustavsson

Two main positions may be taken, broadly speaking, in the debate on the democratic deficit. One is to *abolish* the prevailing imbalance between suprastatism and democratic accountability. Thus the European Union would be turned into a democracy in its own right, with the European Parliament serving as the basis for a United States of Europe. The other main option is to *preserve* the established asymmetry, which is done in the Amsterdam Treaty. This means the member states will content themselves with pooling rather than surrendering their sovereignty. Europe should not adopt a constitution of its own, and the several national parliaments should retain the ultimate responsibility for the Treaty between their governments (S. Gustavsson 1996: 102ff.).

The present chapter focuses on the latter of these two options. What is the best conceivable argument for the preservationist position? As far as I can see, no better defence of the democratic deficit is available than that presented in the 1993 verdict of the German Constitutional Court (BVerfGE 1993: 155–213; English version in Winkelmann 1994: 751–99). The question put to the Court was whether the German Law of Accession to the Union Treaty – which the Bundestag passed by a large majority in 1992 – could be reconciled with the demands for democratic accountability enshrined in the German Basic Law. Not until the Court answered that question in the affirmative could the Treaty be ratified from the German side.

The suprastatism embodied in the first pillar of the Union Treaty, the Court argued, is provisional. Sovereignty is delegated rather than surrendered. Such a delegation is acceptable as long as the criteria of the Basic Law are upheld. According to these criteria, the common use of competences must be marginal in relation to the overall functioning of German democracy, and the manner in which these competences are employed on the European level must be predictable. As a general premise for these two criteria, the delegated portion of German sovereignty is revocable; that is, if the criteria of marginality and predictability are not met, the German authorities must retain the prerogative to reassume the delegated powers. The Court deemed the two criteria to have been met, and so concluded that the ratification of the Treaty was consistent with the demands for democratic accountability enshrined in the Basic Law.

In seeking out a judgement of my own on this matter, I shall consider the following five questions: (1) In what two senses is the relationship between the EU and the member states asymmetrical? (2) What intra-German problem was the Court enjoined to solve? (3) How did the Court conceive the demand for democratic accountability enshrined in the Basic Law? (4) How did the Court interpret the idea of provisional suprastatism in the Union Treaty? (5) Did the Court succeed in solving the problem of reconciling suprastatism with democratic accountability?

Double asymmetry

How can it be said that a federal state solves the problem of the democratic deficit? The federal state meets reasonable democratic requirements, provided that its governing agenda is possible to master at the level of the union *or* that of its constituent states, and provided that the constitution common to all of the states of the union contains an exhaustive catalogue of competences (Dahl 1983: 100ff.). The EU is not equipped with any competence of its own. How, then, can we reconcile the demand for democratic accountability in each member state with that for a suprastatal legal development and monetary order? It is that which, in the present context, is squaring the circle.

The EU is a multi-level political system which has evolved historically, and it is characterised by relations of asymmetry not just between a suprastatal legal development and the lack of any corresponding democratic accountability, but between positive and negative integration as well. It is these two mutually reinforcing asymmetries which are conceptually central here, and which are featured in the descriptive and explanatory efforts generally accepted by jurists and political scientists (Weiler 1991, Zürn 1992, 1995, 1996, Kielmannsegg 1996, Joerges 1996, Schmitter 1996, Jachtenfuchs and Kohler-Koch 1996, Majone 1996, Scharpf 1994, 1996a, 1996b, S. Gustavsson 1997).

How should we evaluate this doubly asymmetrical condition, and what course of action should we recommend? Does the preponderance of reasons speak for trying to abolish or to preserve these two asymmetries? Those wishing to abolish the asymmetries are either federalists or confederalists. For the federalist, symmetry is to be achieved through a democratisation of the suprastate. The confederalist is critical as well. But for him/her, balance is to be attained through the renationalisation of Community law.

Those who wish – in polemic with both federalists and confederalists – to preserve both of these asymmetries are those disposed to neo-functionalism. For them, these asymmetries represent something positive and promising. It is within the bounds of this second major viewpoint that the German Constitutional Court seeks to accomplish the squaring of the circle. The Court does not consider it its task to strike down the Union Treaty that has been negotiated. On the contrary, it focuses on saving the Law of Accession passed by the Bundestag, and indeed it succeeds in this effort.

But is it possible to justify the ratification of the Maastricht Treaty with the claim that this treaty – notwithstanding its obviously suprastatist and asymmetrical features – accords even so with the principle of a steadfastly constituted democracy, as this demand is formulated in the Basic Law?

The perpetuity clause

What solution did the Court propose to the problem under consideration, and how should that solution be evaluated in the light of normative democratic theory?

German democracy assumes a distinctive character on account of its historical background. It is constituted in perpetuity, and with a strong emotional attachment to the inviolability of its fundamental provisions. No popular referendums may take place within its framework. The Basic Law of 1949 cannot, moreover, be altered in respect to its core content.

The accession of the Federal Republic to the EU must therefore take place in a form permitted by the applicable articles. It is not possible to solve the problem through political means – as has been done in other member states – by allowing a referendum to undermine the central constitutional provisions safeguarding the right of the people to determine their fate. What was viewed in Denmark and in France as a political question to be decided by plebiscite was seen in Germany as a problem of constitutional law, to be decided by the Constitutional Court.

The constitutional appeal considered by the Court concerned the newly inserted Article 23 of the Basic Law, as well as the law then promulgated, on the basis of this new article, on accession to the EU. The question concerned whether these two laws emptied Article 38 of real content to such a degree that the requirement of democracy in perpetuity, in accordance with Articles 1, 20 and 79, could no longer be considered fulfilled.

The Court's opinion on this decisive point was that the Basic Law could not be thought a hindrance to membership in a confederation marked by suprastatist features, provided that the legitimation proceeding from the people could be viewed as secured within this latter framework as well. 'It is however a precondition for membership that a legitimation and an influence proceeding from the people is also secured inside the confederation of allied states' (Winkelmann 1994: 752).

The interesting thing is how this condition was framed. The very point of Community law lies in its suprastatal character. Decisions in the Council of Ministers can be adopted by majority rule. Furthermore, Community law not only has direct effect in the member states, but also enjoys priority in principle over provisions adopted within each nation. The Union Treaty takes the fulfilment of these three requirements as a given. At the same time, the Court states as a condition for its verdict that the provisions of the Basic Law in respect to democratic accountability be guaranteed.

Viewed intuitively and in terms of principle, a reconciliation between these two fundamental features would seem to be impossible. Common sense tells us that democracy requires that the demos to which leaders are held accountable must also be that demos with the sovereign power of decision. The two key concepts are thus revealed as incompatible. They could only be reconciled if the citizens of the EU as a whole succeeded in establishing a federal state with a strict catalogue of competences and a system of accountability at two levels founded on a combination of the principles of one-person–one-vote and one-state–one-vote. In such a case the either/or criterion would be met.

No federal state was established by the Union Treaty. Nevertheless, the Court upholds the amendment to the German Basic Law and the Law of Accession to the Union. With its energetic refutation of the appeals submitted, the Court claims to offer a way of reconciling the principle of suprastatism with that of democratic accountability. How does the Court accomplish this equivalent of the squaring of the circle?

The introduction to the verdict takes up approximately one-quarter of the space; in it the Court indicates which of the points of appeal it finds worthy of discussion. It focuses on the claim that the principle of German citizens as the ultimate supervisors and custodians of the political agenda – in accordance with Article 38 of the Basic Law – may be thought emptied of its content by the amendment to the Basic Law and the Law of Accession founded thereupon.

However, the Court finds that the ratification of the Union Treaty does not infringe the absolute right of German citizens to be able to influence the direction of policy through elections to the Bundestag.

> The scope of the functions and powers granted to the European Union and to the institutions of the European Communities and the means of forming political intentions laid down by the Treaty do not at present have the effect of reducing the content of the decision-making and supervisory powers of the *Bundestag* to an extent which infringes the democratic principle insofar as it is declared by Art. 79 para. 3 of the Basic Law to be inviolable.
>
> (Winkelmann 1994: 774)

The larger portion of the verdict (section C, pp. 774–98) is devoted to justifying the standpoint adopted. This justification takes the form of an assessment of whether the criteria laid down in the German Basic Law are met. First come seven pages (pp. 774–80) setting forth an interpretation of the democratic principle. The concluding part of the text (pp. 780–98) is devoted to examining a number of decisive points in the Union Treaty, the objective being to show that, according to the interpretation made, the requirements established by the Constitution must be considered fulfilled.

According to the democratic principle, Germany must in perpetuity remain a self-governing country, the agenda and decision making of which is controlled by its own citizens. In respect of this principle the Treaty does not, in the finding of the Court, violate the core content of the Basic Law.

Democratic accountability

The critical element for the Court is Article 38 of the Basic Law, which consists of three main points. The first sets forth the prerogatives of the members of the Bundestag. They are free, on their own responsibility and to the best of their ability, to seek to ascertain and to express the popular will. The second point pertains to the electoral law, while the third grants the requisite constitutional sanction to a more precisely formulated electoral law.

The interesting thing here is the first point, whereby the members of the Bundestag are granted the right to work as the representatives of the German people. 'The deputies to the German Bundestag are elected in universal, direct, free, equal and secret elections. They are representatives of the whole people, are not bound by orders and instructions and are subject only to their conscience.' A conclusion of importance in the present context follows from this first point in Article 38. Individual citizens can have their right ultimately to determine German policy infringed if, in too great a measure, the Bundestag surrenders its prerogatives to make decisions on behalf of the German people.

More precisely, the norm of representative democracy has an inviolable core content when it is considered in connection with Articles 1, 20 and 79, which define the immutability of the Basic Law and its perpetually applicable principles. The interesting thing is how the Court interprets this core content. For it is this interpretation, together with a corresponding interpretation of the Union Treaty, which furnishes the foundation for its verdict.

> Democracy, if it is not to remain as merely a formal principle of accountability, is dependent on the existence of certain pre-legal conditions, such as a continuous free debate between opposing social forces, interests and ideas, in which political goals become clarified and change course . . . and out of which a public opinion emerges which starts to shape a political will. This also means that the decision-making processes of the organs exercising sovereign powers and the various political objectives pursued can be generally perceived and understood, and therefore that citizens entitled to vote can communicate, in their own language, with the sovereign authority to which they are subject. . . .
>
> If, as at present, the peoples of the individual states provide democratic legitimation through their national parliaments, limits to the extension of the European Communities' functions and powers are then set by virtue of the democratic principle. Each of the peoples of the individual states is the starting point for the public authority relating to that people. The states need sufficiently important spheres of activity of their own in which the peoples of each can develop and articulate in a process of political will-formation which it legitimates and controls, in order to give legal expression to what – relatively homogeneously – binds the people spiritually, socially, and politically together. . . .

> From all that it follows that functions and powers of substantial impor-
> tance must remain for the German Bundestag.
>
> (Winkelmann 1994: 777f.)

More precisely, there are two criteria which, in the Court's view, the Union
Treaty must fulfil if the right of German citizens to democratic accountability is
not to be thought infringed. The first of these is the requirement of *marginality*.
That portion of German sovereignty which is used together with other member
countries must be smaller than the part concerning which the political majority
in Germany is directly accountable to the German electorate. What remains for
German democracy must be of substantial importance.

Judging what is marginal and what structural requires a theory. To be useful,
such a theory must be able to offer some practical guidance in the question of
the number and value of those prerogatives which must remain with the
Bundestag, as compared with those which can be lent out for the common use.
The theory formulated by the Court focuses on what is necessary to secure
German democracy over the long term.

In the view of the Court, then, what is marginal and what structural is not
ascertained through a formal enumeration of what belongs to the one or the
other category. One could imagine, for example, that monetary and foreign policies must be carried out under the aegis of the nation state, while policies
concerning such matters as tariffs and agricultural supports could be pursued in
common. The Court does not express itself in such a manner, however. The key
formulation – found in the concluding portion of the cited text – is at one and
the same time highly definite and exceedingly open. The boundary between
what is an acceptable and what an unacceptable loaning-out of decisional
prerogatives is set by the political conditions of German democracy's long-range
survival.

This key formulation is highly definite, inasmuch as it unequivocally places
the German interest in democracy before the European interest in integration.
Yet this same formulation is also exceedingly open, inasmuch as it does not say
anything about which policy areas are, from a democratic point of view, more
dubious candidates for integration, and which are less. The reference to general
political conditions assumes in this way the character of a general authorisation.
The remaining tasks must be sufficiently important as to ensure that German
democracy is not jeopardised.

The legal forms for Germany's participation should correspond, in other
words, to what binds the German people together spiritually, socially and politically. The decisive thing – as I interpret the view of the Court on this central
point – is the possibility of applying the majority principle. The operational definition of sufficient is disclosed by the prospects for applying the principle of a
simple majority. A people holds together – that is, it constitutes a demos in the
technical sense – to the extent that one-half of the citizenry is prepared to
subject itself to the will of the other half.

The preconditions for this happening do not consist only of a sufficiently secure assurance that future elections will be held. A political precondition applies as well. That group of the population which today comprises a minority must be assured that it can enjoy a contrary position tomorrow, and that this change can take place as a consequence of a successful mobilisation of opinion. If this condition is not fulfilled, democracy prevails in a formal and juridical sense only. That is the empirical meaning of what Joseph Weiler calls the 'no demos thesis' (Weiler 1995: 1655ff., 1996: 522ff., Weiler *et al.* 1995: 10ff.).

The other possible infringement concerns the requirement of *predictability*. German democracy is violated to the degree that the German legal order is subjected to a suprastatal legal development in such a manner that the consequences thereof cannot be foreseen. This takes place to the extent that the Law of Accession does not with sufficient precision state the conditions for the delegation of sovereignty. These must be laid down in a manner that is predictable with adequate certainty (Winkelmann 1994: 779). From that instant in which the use of delegated German sovereignty can no longer be surveyed and (it is thereby implied) influenced by the Bundestag, it is a question of lent-out sovereignty no longer, but rather of a general authorisation. In that case the common use of delegated sovereignty is no longer at issue. The Bundestag has then foresworn the ultimate responsibility – which is what Article 38 prohibits.

An agreement reached under the terms of international law certainly in practice cannot, the Court argues, be framed with the constitutional stringency normally characterising the German government's and Bundestag's administration of the norm-giving power. This follows from the multilateral character of such agreements. The requirement of predictability is nevertheless decisive. The consequences of membership in respect to rights and duties should be predictable with sufficient certainty. If this is not the case, it implies that 'subsequent important changes to the integration program set up in the Union Treaty and to the Union's powers of action are no longer covered by the Law of Accession to the present Treaty' (Winkelmann 1994: 779).

If the requirement of predictability is not fulfilled, Community law does not apply in Germany. The legislation that had proved impossible to predict is not binding on citizens and firms in the Federal Republic.

> The German state organs would be prevented, for constitutional reasons, from applying them in Germany. Accordingly, the Federal Constitutional Court reviews legal instruments of European institutions and organs to see whether they remain within the limits of the sovereign rights conferred on them or whether they transgress those limits.
>
> (Winkelmann 1994: 780.)

Determining what is sufficient and what insufficient also requires a theory. If this theory is to be analytically useful, moreover, it must be able to distinguish between an expected and an unexpected exercise of the norm-giving power. The Court must be able to react, it declares in reference to a standard work of constitutional law (Mosler 1992: 632f.), against a degree of integration (and a delegation of sovereignty arising therefrom) exceeding that foreseen in the Union Treaty and the Law of Accession. Simply put, integration must proceed in the manner intended when the particular change in the Treaty was ratified. Otherwise, the suprastatal legal development runs afoul of the prohibition against irrevocably surrendering German sovereignty expressed in Article 38.

These two specifications of the Constitutional Court – in respect to marginality and predictability – have one thing in common. The supreme consideration is that the Bundestag not surrender German sovereignty, but only delegate its use. Marginality means that a functioning German democracy is the prime consideration. The same applies in respect of predictability. This entails the insistence that it be possible, when sovereignty is delegated, to foresee the manner in which the common prerogatives will be put to use. That it be a question of delegation is for both requirements an absolute condition. Unless this condition is met, no provisional supremacy for Community law can be thought compatible with the core content of the Basic Law.

Provisional suprastatism

Against the background of these requirements for marginality and predictability, the conclusion of the Court that '[t]he Union Treaty satisfies the above requirements to the extent that it is being scrutinised in the present proceedings' (Winkelmann 1994: 780) would appear to be somewhat surprising. How is it possible to maintain that the element of suprastatism is so small that the German people do not meet with decidedly greater difficulties in holding their authorities accountable? How is it possible to argue that the consequences of ratification are foreseen with accuracy sufficient to enable us to conclude that the core content of the Basic Law is not violated?

If we proceed on the assumption that the Constitutional Court is a rationally deliberating body, we may find it worthwhile to direct our attention to its interpretation of Community law as *provisionally* suprastatal in character. If the final verdict is to follow from its interpretation of the core content of the Basic Law, the Court must render credible the thought that Germany does not part with any ultimate right of decision. Membership is so framed that accountability within the framework of the German Constitution is possible still. What is more, the Court must be able to maintain that the Bundestag can with sufficient clarity discern the manner in which the delegated prerogatives will be used. Suprastatism is not definitive. Its use can be predicted. If the prerogatives in question are misused, the Bundestag must be able to revoke that portion of the Law of Accession which has brought the consequences unforeseen.

The term provisional suprastatism is used neither by the Court nor – as far I have been able to ascertain – in the scientific debate on the distinctive character of the EU. This expression nevertheless captures, in my view, the sense intended by the Court in the best possible manner and in two different respects. First, Community law applies only as a consequence of delegation and the active decision of the member states to allow its writ to obtain within their boundaries.

Second, Community law only applies in the degree that its breadth does not exceed that foreseen when the powers in question were delegated. The Court expresses this first point in its characterisation of Community law. The membership in question is in a 'Staatenverbund', a confederation of allied states, and naught else. The counterpart in general German usage to the dichotomy between a federation and a confederation is that between a 'Bundesstaat' and a 'Staatenbund'. The Court thus injects a 'ver' between 'Staaten-' and '-Bund'.

> The Federal Republic of Germany is thus, even after the entry into force of the Union Treaty, a member in a confederation of allied states, whose common authority is derived from the Member States and which can have binding effect within the sphere of German sovereignty only by virtue of the German legal sanction. Germany is one of the 'Masters of Treaties', which have established their adherence to the Union Treaty 'for an unlimited period', but which could ultimately, through an act to the contrary, revoke that adherence. The validity and the application of European law in Germany depends on the application-of-law sanction of the Law on Accession. Germany thus preserves the quality of a sovereign state in its own right and the status of sovereign equality with other states within the meaning of Art. 2 para. 1 of the United Nations Charter of 26 June 1945.
>
> (Winkelmann 1994: 781)

The new word 'Staaten*ver*bund' denotes a category not included in the historically received doctrine regarding the types of association between states. With its designation, the Court has in mind an organisation of states sharing a Community law of an asymmetrical character. Such states permit themselves an element of suprastatism, despite the organisation not securing democratic accountability. By contrast, the two basic types of association between states – the federation and the confederation – are both symmetrically structured, in the sense that each embodies a balance between the elements of suprastatism and the conditions for democratic accountability.

The new expression thus denotes a third option in respect to who bears ultimate responsibility. A feature distinctive to this third category is the fact that sovereignty is neither surrendered (as in the case of the federal state) nor exercised by each state singly (as in the case of the confederation), but rather is lent out for the common use. In a 'Staatenverbund', responsibility still rests ultimately with the original owner. If the treaty is not fulfilled, the sovereignty in question can be recalled for use by its original owner. As long as the loan lasts, however, the true owner pledges to follow the directions specified by the leaseholder in his/her capacity as the provisional superior. Yet the true owner has never parted with the ultimate right of decision.

The other major sense in which the suprastatism under review is provisional follows from the requirement of predictability. Decisions taken on the basis of the sovereignty lent out must fall within the framework of the original intentions attending the Treaty's ratification. The provisional suprastatism lacks legal effect unless the policy undertaken is specified in the Treaty. The presence of supra-statism does not register the existence of the EU as a state in its own right. Community law enjoys priority only so long as the original permissions granted by the 'Masters of the Treaties' have not been overstepped.

Manfred Brunner, the petitioner, had taken the position that the EU was so designed as to be able to assume prerogatives of its own, even without specific enabling decisions having been taken. The Court replies that this charge is insuf-ficiently supported by good argument. Without a renewed decision by Parliament authorising such a legal application, the EU cannot acquire for itself any further prerogatives. In this respect, the Union Treaty entails no change from the legal conditions which have applied all along (Winkelmann 1994: 782f.). Historically established Community law is consistently subordinated to the member states' ratification of the Treaty of Rome from 1957 and their approval of the adjustments made in this treaty through the Single European Act of 1986.

As long as the discussion concentrates on the historically established Community law contained within the first pillar, the Union Treaty is seen to involve no change in principle compared with the Treaty of Rome and the Single European Act. However, a novel element is of great interest in this regard. That is, the decision to introduce a common currency. This additional step in integration is not merely of an innovative nature. It also raises, on account of its distinctive construction – with a central bank not subject even to the power of the Commission or the Council of Ministers – the question of the degree to which the suprastatal element in the construction of the EU can be considered 'provisional' also in this area. The Court devotes especial attention to this obvious objection (Winkelmann 1994: 788 ff.).

The question is the degree to which suprastatism is provisional in the case of monetary union as well. Can the member countries reintroduce their own currencies, should they discover that practical developments have taken another course than that foreseen in connection with their ratification of the Union Treaty? Or is this rather a truly irrevocable surrender of the possibility of ensuring democratic accountability in the area of monetary policy?

The Court's reply to this question varies according to which aspect of the problem is in view. As far as *the road towards* a common currency is concerned, the Court avers that Germany 'is not subjecting itself to an unsupervisable, unsteer-able automatic pilot in its progress to a monetary union' (Winkelmann 1994: 792). The Treaty is so written, argues the Court, that developments are assumed to take place in discernible steps. Each country must adopt the requisite parlia-mentary decisions if it is to accomplish its obligations under the Treaty. To this extent no automaticity obtains. Nor do the member states lose control in the sense that the Council of Ministers is empowered to make adjustments by means of majority decision in the so-called convergence criteria during the course of the journey (for it is not).

Each individual country possesses the right of veto in respect to all attempts to place the integration process outside the reach of democratic accountability in the member states. To this extent it can be said that the requirement of predictability is fulfilled. Both the citizens of the member states and their parliamentary representatives can, in other words, reclaim the sovereignty lent out by their governments in the course of the various steps taken towards the surrender of monetary sovereignty.

A distinct consideration, however, is the extent to which the withdrawal from democratic accountability can be regarded as provisional once monetary union has become an *established fact*. In the case of Community law generally, the requirement of democracy is met, because the national parliament of each member state can alter its own law of accession unilaterally. This possibility of unilateral exclusion does not, however, obtain, in the view of the Court, in the event of a monetary union which has been carried to completion according to the plans set forth in the Union Treaty. In that case an evident distinction arises between the Central Bank and other, constitutionally provisional, suprastatal organs. In so far as the Bank is concerned, the possibilities for influence by national parliaments – and thus by national electorates too – will have been removed almost completely. This is the practical meaning of the Bank being made independent *vis-à-vis* both the European Community and the member states.

Monetary policy has been excluded, writes the Court,

> from the regulatory power of sovereign authorities, and also – excluding a treaty amendment – from the lawgiver's control of areas of responsibility and means of action. Placing most of the tasks of monetary policy on an autonomous basis in the hands of an independent central bank releases the exercise of sovereign powers of the state from direct national or supranational parliamentary responsibility, in order to withdraw monetary matters from the reach of interest groups and holders of political office concerned about re-election.
>
> (Winkelmann 1994: 794 f.)

The Constitutional Court thus furnishes a negative answer to the question of whether the consummated currency union can be considered democratically legitimated in the same provisional sense as applies in other areas of Community law. For such is not the case. Nor should it be, in the view of the Court. On the contrary, the whole point of this arrangement is that the member states should not be able, having surrendered their national currencies, unilaterally to shut out the impact of the common monetary policy.

The ultimate objective set out for monetary policy does not inspire any misgivings in the Constitutional Court, since it is reminiscent, in all essentials, of the order prevailing in the Federal Republic itself. The task rather is that of constitutionally guaranteeing that the road forward to this objective does not involve any deviations.

The Bundestag – and thereby the Constitutional Court indirectly – must enjoy the opportunity step by step of making the requisite decisions on the road towards a suprastatism which, in this area, is not provisional but definitive. What is the rationale for this underlying distinction between the road forward to monetary union on the one hand, and monetary union as an established fact on the other?

The highest political and juridical organs of the Federal Republic must be able to see to it that no relaxation of the agreed-upon convergence criteria occurs. For if this should take place, the currency union cannot become the community of stability, foreseen by the Bundestag when, in the autumn of 1992, it voted in favour of ratifying the Union Treaty. In that perspective of transition, the Bundestag and the Constitutional Court are obliged to ratify and to check every single step towards monetary union from the standpoint of the joint meaning of Articles 1, 20, 38 and 79 of the German Basic Law. The community of stability as a consummated goal is another matter, however. When the monetary union has been established, the need for democratic accountability will be less (D. Gustavsson 1996).

Did the Court solve the problem?

Defending the democratic deficit means having to reconcile a suprastatal legal and monetary order with a demand for democratic accountability within a framework composed of democratically constituted nation states. Has the Court succeeded in squaring the circle, by thus combining the requirements of marginality and predictability with an interpretation of the suprastatism of Community law as provisional – in the sense of being conditional and revocable? My answer to that question is no, essentially for two reasons. One is philosophical in character and concerns the manner of reasoning itself. The other is theoretical: even within the form of reasoning chosen by the Court, it is possible to formulate a decisive criticism. The Constitutional Court thus cannot be said, in my opinion, to have solved the problem of the democratic legitimacy of Community law – even by the terms of its own reasoning.

My *philosophical* criticism of the manner of reasoning has to do with the realism of the assumption that the Bundestag can revoke the Law of Accession wholly or in part. How can this be done under prevailing historical conditions? Economically, socially and environmentally, the member states are closely bound up with one another. The financial markets can on good grounds be expected to react most powerfully should a country make use of its constitutional right wholly or in part to forbid the application of Community law within its territory. Must we not consider the possibility that a partial withdrawal from the Community would be so costly – in all three meanings of the word – that such a possibility is *de facto* excluded? Is a revocation of the Law of Accession a genuine option in that case? Can one be said to have solved a problem if one does so by reference to a manner of reasoning which is only possible to adduce on the level of principle? Must we not also ask whether it is politically feasible to pass a law partially shutting out the effect of Community law?

There is, naturally, a fictitious element in all constitutional theory. The concept of popular sovereignty itself, for example, contains a palpably unrealistic component. If democracy is to function, we must assume the will of the people is equivalent to that of the majority. In this analogy, however, a realistic (in the sense of experientially founded) possibility exists of ascertaining the character of the popular will through the holding of general elections and the establishment of a system of majority rule, the purpose of which is to administer and represent the will of the people.

The Constitutional Court departs even from such realism when it assumes the demand for democratic accountability is satisfied through the merely theoretical possibility of partial withdrawal from Community law. For the Court cannot adduce any example of a parliament which has ever dared defy the provisionally established suprastatal order. On no occasion and in no setting, to the best of my knowledge, has any national decision been made to close the borders of a member state to Community law.

This is sufficient reason for questioning the solution offered by the Court. Its proposed solution is no solution at all if it is not also grounded in experience. Only when a member state has in practice reassumed the right of decision which it has lent out will the theory qualify as credible. So long as this has not happened, sovereignty may be regarded as having been surrendered *de facto* by the national governments. In that case, the principle of democratic accountability must be regarded as having been weakened to a corresponding degree. For there is no comparable mechanism for the assurance of democratic accountability on the European level which has shown itself capable of replacing what has been lost on the national level.

My second reason for maintaining that the problem remains unsolved rests on a *theoretical* objection within the bounds of the philosophy embraced by the Court. In short, even within its own terms, the position of the Court is inconsistent.

The premise of the Court is that the ultimate right of decision may only be lent out in a manner corresponding to the requirements of marginality and (in respect to the impact of the loan) predictability and revocability. The sovereignty remaining must be sufficiently great for the processes of democratic decision making to retain their significance on the national level, and the uses to which the lent-out right of decision is put must be amenable to examination and discussion on that level.

From the very concept of a 'Staatenverbund' it is supposed to follow that it is only within the bounds of each member state that the mobilisation of democratic opinion and the holding of democratic accountability can take place. For the EU does not display so high a degree of cohesion that its citizens are prepared to submit to the rule of the majority. From a democratic standpoint, then, the EU consists in all essentials of its member states and their political systems.

How, within the framework of this theory, can the consummated monetary union be thought to meet the requirements of marginality, predictability and revocability? I disregard the strict demands put by the Court in relation to

German influence over the various steps on the road towards a consummated currency union. The problem rather concerns the state of affairs prevailing *after* such a currency union has begun to function according to the guidelines laid down in the Union Treaty.

According to Article 14.2 of the ECB's charter, the member states pledge so to alter their national laws and constitution as to prescribe that the head of their central bank be appointed for a term of five years, and that it only be possible to dismiss him/her following legal examination by the European Court. The prerogative to initiate proceedings aimed at such a dismissal shall devolve solely on the ECB Council (i.e. directing boards and those chairing other countries' central banks), or by the bank chair directly concerned, 'on grounds of infringement of this Treaty or of any rule of law relating to its application'. So, it will not be possible, with an individual chairing a central bank, to call the mandate into question on the grounds that said individual lacks the confidence of his/her principals.

The ECB Council consists of the heads of fifteen central banks, the irremovability of whom is backed by the exclusive support of the European Court. To these fifteen persons must be added the six members of the ECB's directing board, who are appointed by the heads of state and government for a period of eight years, and who cannot receive a renewed mandate. In a fashion comparable with that applying for the heads of the member states' own central banks, moreover, it is prescribed that, if a member of the ECB's directing board no longer meets the requirements for performing his/her tasks, or if the member has been guilty of serious negligence, the European Court alone shall be able, upon the request of the ECB Council, to dismiss that member.

Neither the Commission, then, nor the Council of Ministers, nor the EP will be able to question the general judgement of the members of the Bank's directing board, once its members have been appointed. The long mandate period is furthermore intended, as is the fact that members cannot be appointed to another term, to guarantee the independence of the ECB Council. The members thereof are not to be subjected to the slightest trace of democratic accountability on any grounds other than those formulated by the financial experts themselves, with the juridical support they can obtain in court with the help of the Treaty's provisions.

The idea, in other words, is that the twenty-one directors who are assigned the direction of the monetary policy of the EU are to create an institution of its own. Their joint governance of monetary policy is to be independent not merely in theory but also in practice. This independence is not just to obtain, moreover, in relation to democracy in the member states. The lengthy mandate period, the ineligibility of the members for renewed service and the fact that said members can only be dismissed with the support of the European Court together entail a qualitative increase in the independence enjoyed by the directors of the Central Bank. It is not just the national democracies here which are removed from influence on account of the double asymmetry considered above. Above and beyond this the EU as such – irrespective altogether of the degree of democratic accountability within each member state – forswears the possibility of weighing the value of a stable price level against other legitimate objectives.

To begin with, one can naturally question whether this means monetary policy can be 'predicted with adequate certainty'. The Court's reply to this objection is that Article 105, para. 1 of the Union Treaty prescribes that 'the maintenance of price stability is the main obligation of the ECB', and that the Treaty

> sets up long-term targets which impose the objective of stability as the stan-
> dard for monetary union, which seek to achieve that objective through
> institutional arrangements, and which finally – as the last resort – do not
> prevent withdrawal from the Community if the stability-oriented nature of
> the community breaks down.
>
> (Winkelmann 1994: 792)

In the view of the Court, therefore, Germany retains control in the area of monetary policy as well. Ultimate monetary sovereignty is thought still to rest with the German authorities, since they can – as a final emergency measure – shut out not just the common law of the Community, but the common currency as well.

More interesting, however, is the requirement of marginality. Questions of sufficient weight must remain with the Bundestag that German democracy retains a meaningful character. That is the basic idea. Is monetary policy not of substantial importance? The Court does not contest that the question can be raised. Yet there is cause, writes the Court, to draw the opposite conclusion – in this particular case. For it is precisely because price stability is so important that there is cause to exempt the Central Bank from democratic control.

> Placing most of the tasks of monetary policy on an autonomous basis in the
> hands of an independent central bank releases the exercise of sovereign
> powers of the state from direct national or supranational parliamentary
> responsibility, in order to withdraw monetary matters from the reach of
> interest groups and holders of political office concerned about re-
> election. . . .
>
> This modification of the democratic principle for protecting the confi-
> dence in the value of a currency is acceptable because it takes account of
> the special characteristic – in the German legal system, tested and proven, in
> scientific terms as well – that an independent central bank is a better guar-
> antor of currency value, and thus of a general economic basis for state
> budgetary policy and for private planning and transactions in the exercise of
> the laws of economic freedom, than sovereign bodies which in their possibil-
> ities and means of action are essentially dependent on the supply and value
> of the currency and rely on short-term consent of political forces. To that
> extent the placing of monetary policy on an independent footing within the
> sovereign jurisdiction of a European Central Bank, which is not transferable

to other political areas, satisfies the constitutional requirements whereunder the principle of democracy may be modified.

(Winkelmann 1994: 795)

The reasons are clearly stated. But are these reasons for modifying the democratic principle compatible with the principle of the specially protected core content of the Basic Law stated in Article 79, point 3, which proclaims that a change 'in the basic principles laid down in Articles 1 and 20, is inadmissible'?

To this the Court answers that the Bundestag, in connection with its ratification of the Union Treaty, intentionally adjusted Article 88 of the Basic Law, so that it now reads that the prerogatives of the Bundesbank can be made over to European organs. The condition for this is that the European Bank be independent, and that it have securing price stability as its primary goal.

In my view the Court's answer begs the question. For the question is not whether the ratification of the Union Treaty and the associated changes in the Basic Law were in line with the Bundestag's views. We must clearly assume that they were. What the question must rather concern – for a Constitutional Court – is whether the ratification and constitutional alteration passed by the Bundestag is compatible with the core content of the Basic Law according to Articles 1, 20, 38 and 79.

Is there thus a consideration of a substantive character – securing the value of the currency in the best manner possible – which can justify setting the protected core content of the Basic Law at naught? Is there accordingly a central policy area which is of such substantial importance, indeed of such surpassing importance, that it cannot be allowed to form a part of political debate and contestation? Evidently there is, in the view of the Court. In my view there is not.

Each of my objections – the philosophical and the theoretical – are fully sufficient taken singly to rebut the argument of the Court. Together, I would argue, they are decisive. In my view it cannot be shown that the Constitutional Court has succeeded in solving the problem of the democratic legitimacy of Community law and of the projected monetary union. It should be stressed, in conclusion, that I have reached my conclusion within the framework of the Court's assumption of a 'Staatenverbund'.

References

BVerfGE (1993) *Entscheidungen des Bundesverfassungsgerichts*, Vol. 89, 17: 155–213.

Dahl, Robert A. (1983) 'Federalism and the Democratic Process', *Nomos* 25: 95–108.

Gustavsson, Daniel (1996) 'EMU som tyskt författningsproblem', *Juridisk tidskrift* 7(3–4): 918–34.

Gustavsson, Sverker (1996) 'Preserve or Abolish the Democratic Deficit?', in Eivind Smith (ed.), *National Parliaments as Cornerstones of European Integration*, London: Kluwer Law International, pp. 100–23.

Gustavsson, Sverker (1997) 'Double Asymmetry as Normative Challenge', in Andreas Føllesdal and Peter Koslowski, (eds.) *Democracy and the European Union*, Berlin: Springer, pp. 108–31.

Jachtenfuchs, Markus and Kohler-Koch, Beate (1996) 'Regieren im dynamischen Mehrebenensystem', in Markus Jachtenfuchs and Beate Kohler-Koch (eds), *Europäische Integration*, Opladen: Leske+Budrich, pp. 15–44.

Joerges, Christian (1996) 'Das Recht im Prozeß der europäischen Integration', in Markus Jachtenfuchs and Beate Kohler-Koch (eds), *Europäische Integration*, Opladen: Leske+Budrich, pp. 73–108.

Kielmannsegg, Peter Graf (1996) 'Integration und Demokratie', in Markus Jachtenfuchs and Beate Kohler-Koch (eds), *Europäische Integration*, Opladen: Leske+Budrich, pp. 47–71.

Majone, Giandomenico (1996) 'Regulatory Legitimacy', in Giandomenico Majone, (ed.), *Regulating Europe*, London: Routledge, pp. 284–301.

Mosler, Hermann (1992) 'Die Übertragung von Hoheitsgewalt', in Josef Isensee and Paul Kirchhof (eds), *Handbuch des Staatsrechts der Bundesrepublik Deutschland*, Band VII, Heidelberg: C.F. Müller Juristischer Verlag, pp. 599–646.

Scharpf, Fritz W. (1994) 'Community and Autonomy: Multi-Level Policymaking in the European Union', *Journal of European Public Policy* 1(2): 219–42.

Scharpf, Fritz W. (1996a) 'Negative and Positive Integration in the Political Economy of European Welfare States', in Gary Marks *et al. Governance in the European Union*, London: Sage, pp. 15–39.

Scharpf, Fritz W. (1996b) 'Politische Optionen im vollendeten Binnenmarkt', in Markus Jachtenfuchs and Beate Kohler-Koch (eds), *Europäische Integration*, Opladen: Leske+Budrich, pp. 109–40.

Schmitter, Philippe C. (1996) 'If the Nation-State Were to Wither Away in Europe, What Might Replace It?', in Sverker Gustavsson and Leif Lewin (eds), *The Future of the Nation-State*, Stockholm: Nerenius & Santérus, pp. 211–44.

Weiler, Joseph H. H. (1991) 'The Transformation of Europe', *Yale Law Journal* 100(8): 2403–83.

Weiler, Joseph H. H. (1995) 'The State "über alles". Demos, Telos and the German Maastricht Decision', in Ole Due, Marcus Lutter and Jürgen Schwarze (eds), *Festschrift für Ulrich Everling*, Baden-Baden: Nomos Verlag, pp. 1651–88.

Weiler, Joseph H. H. (1996) 'European Neo-constitutionalism: In Search of Foundations for the European Constitutional Order', *Political Studies* 44(3): 517–33.

Weiler, Joseph H. H., Haltern, Ulrich R. and Mayer, Franz C. (1995) 'European Democracy and its Critique', in Jack Hayward (ed.), *The Crisis of Representation in Europe*, London: Frank Cass, pp. 4–39.

Winkelmann, Ingo (1994) *Das Maastricht-Urteil des Bundesverfassungsgerichts vom 12. Oktober 1993. Dokumentation des Verfahrens mit Einführung*, Berlin: Duncker & Humblot.

Zürn, Michael (1992) 'Jenseits der Staatlichkeit: über die Folgen der ungleichzeitigen Denationalisierung', *Leviathan* 20(4): 490–513.

Zürn, Michael (1995) 'The Challenge of Globalization and Individualization: A View from Europe', in Hans-Henrik Holm and Georg Sorensen (eds), *Whose World Order? Uneven Globalization and the End of the Cold War*, Boulder, CO: Westview Press, pp. 137–63.

Zürn, Michael (1996) 'Über den Staat und die Demokratie im europäischen Mehrebenensystem', *Politische Vierteljahresschrift* 37(1): 27–55.

Part II

Decision rules and the constitutional construction of the European Union

6 The European Union

Trends in theory and reform

Michael J. Tsinisizelis and
Dimitris N. Chryssochoou

Setting the framework

This chapter aims to establish a link between the dynamics of constitutional reform in the European Union (EU) and the extent to which the process of 'rethinking Maastricht' can be adequately explained from a new theoretical perspective, summed up in the concept of *confederal consociation* (Chryssochoou 1994). The gist of the argument is that large-scale constitutional engineering, far from leading to a diffusion of state sovereignty, maintains the ability of member governments to manage the process of building transnational bodies. Indeed, the EU continues to act as a source of state strength by enhancing the domestic power base of national leaders, allowing them to influence the articulation of territorial interests via the central institutions. In this sense, the confederal consociation thesis strikes a balance between interdependence and autonomy within a common framework of power. Like Puchala's (1972) 'concordance system', the model represents what we believe is 'coming into being "out there" in the empirical world'. By 'confederal', we refer to the structural properties of the larger management system, and in particular to the idea that the EU rests upon the separate constitutional orders of the states. By 'consociation', we refer to the means for arriving at collective binding decisions within a 'closed' system of political interactions analogous to that depicted by Dahrendorf as 'a cartel of elites' (Dahrendorf 1967: 267). The question to be addressed is whether confederal consociation provides a clear indication of the limits and possibilities of European constitutional change.

Images of integration in the 1990s

Applied to the EU of the 1990s, consociational theory lends support to the view that the strengthening of the central arrangements tends to reinforce the role of the segments (states) *vis-à-vis* the collectivity (EU). It suggests that the larger system enables the dominant governing elites of the constituent units 'to present themselves as leaders and agents of a distinct clearly defined community' (Taylor 1990: 176), thus resisting the strengthening of horizontal links among their respective publics, and preferring to promote vertical integration as a means of retaining ultimate authority within their domestic subcultures. Overall, consociationalism points to a managerial type of integration whereby 'progressive' initiatives reflecting the wider 'Community interest' are compromised in the name of achieving sufficient levels of decisional efficiency. The operational code adopted by the Council of Ministers and the European Council in reaching accommodation and taking positive decisions despite the reality of mutual vetoes provides a perfect test for this hypothesis: they both perform functions similar to those of a 'grand coalition'. Joint decision making often turns into a 'summit diplomacy forum' with consensus building at the leadership level. This accords with consociationalism as a theory of political stability and its distinction between 'elite political culture' and 'mass political culture' (Lijphart 1971: 11).

A further insight from confederal consociation points to the viewing of the EU as an ensemble of 'territorial communities', as opposed to a 'transnational civic unit', aiming at the amicable settlement of divisive issues in face of the peril of fragmentation. Here, the model highlights an important function of the system: 'the maintenance of stability in a situation of actual or potential mutual tension' (Taylor 1993: 82). Moreover, by emphasising the internal conditions under which nations decide to do certain things in common in favour of consensually predetermined objectives, it sets the bases of acceptable behaviour through multiple 'networks' of formal and informal arrangements, pointing to what Taylor had earlier described as 'government by alliance' (Taylor 1975: 346). In short, confederal consociation refers to the merging of distinct culturally defined and politically organised units in some form of 'Union' to further certain common ends, without either losing their sense of forming collective national identities or resigning their individual sovereignty to a higher central authority (see also Chryssochoou 1997).

As such confederal consociation poses no fundamental threat for the sovereignty of states. In other words, 'the condition of the last say' (Dahl 1956: 38) still rests with the states, rather than with an independent authoritative entity at the larger level. Thus sketched, the EU has an interesting analogue with a system of horizontal *Kooperative Staaten*, in that the formulation of common policies rests upon prior agreement between state and quasi-federal actors, whilst their implementation relies heavily on national administrative systems. Within this type of 'cooperative federalism', the collective power of the states is well protected, and political authority is jointly managed after intensive intergovernmental bargains. As Sbragia put it: '[German federalism] allows one to conceptualise a Community in which a "centre" is created that is not completely independent from its constituent units' (Sbragia 1992a: 13).

Under the German model, however, the central institutions are ultimately responsible to a federal demos, rather than to state governments alone. Indeed, it is the absence of one sovereign demos that makes the EU closer to a 'federal union of states', rather than to a 'federal state' (for the terms, see Forsyth 1981). More important, perhaps, the cooperative nature of European federalism makes it difficult for citizens to identify the locus of accountability 'in a process [where] the decision-making is shifted to common institutions and bodies which cannot be controlled according to traditional democratic standards' (Wessels 1994: 456). Hence Kirchner's warning that 'without adequate provisions to the contrary, the prevailing "democratic deficit" in EC decision-making would probably continue under the system of co-operative federalism' (Kirchner 1991: 14).

At the EU level, this polycentric pattern of federalism, whereby the defence of each separate interest coincides with the need to strike a deal in the context of a 'positive-sum' game, is best defined as a case of inverse federalism: a situation in which political authority tends to be diffused as much as possible to the executive branches of the constituent units, rather than to the central institutions. The growth of this mode of interaction, as the nub of the idea of confederal consociation, fits best the *ad hoc* evolutionary character of the EU. Yet, inverse federalism falls short of meeting the requirements of those who proclaim the demise of the (West) European nation state, supporting instead the immediate formation of a fully blown European demos within a larger federal polity. It is our contention that what we are currently witnessing in the EU is a system of consensus elite government in which the condition of territoriality coexists with that of non-territoriality in a symbiotic manner shaping the forms that transnational federalism is allowed or indeed prohibited from taking.

For the optimistic, confederal consociation forms part of a wider evolution in which today's quasi-federal arrangements may be replaced by a formal constitutional framework in which low-level consensus, bureaucratic management and executive elite dominance become the exception rather than the rule of EU practice. In this sense, a self-determining 'political community' might emerge, and be governed by democratic standards, adding to the dynamics of transnational demos formation (Chryssochoou 1996a, 1996b). This qualitative leap forward, by representing the culmination of an intensive process of large-scale community strengthening, presupposes that the positive feelings of the subunits springing from their common membership prevail over any potentially divisive issues that may arise as integration proceeds.

The new politics of co-determination

Confederal consociation provides a conscious attempt at instituting for distinct politically organised demoi a stable framework of mutual governance. At a minimum, it can be seen as one possible means of applying consociational principles in a dynamic *Staatenverbund*. At best, it can be used as a new pattern of interaction in which the EU and its component state/citizen parts transcend fragmentation through cooperative decision making. In either case, however, it opens a wide range of possibilities for reconciling the parallel demands for (territorial) segmental autonomy and overall systemic stability within a polyethnic society characterised by strong pluralistic tendencies. Such cooperative interplay between national and EU politics suggests a transformation of the classical concept of 'self-determination' into one of 'co-determination' through the institutionalisation of the principle of joint sovereignty. This gradual transformation has been sustained by the emergence over time of a transnational political culture among the segment elites.

In such a diverse network of interactions, there are no permanent coalitions of power, nor is there any fixed 'code of practice' regarding the role that each actor has or is expected to perform. Procedurally, the system is loose enough to allow consensual and majoritarian patterns of decision making to coexist and determine the outcome of specific policies dealt with at the central level. Put simply, there is no need for a 'zero-sum' competition of the interests of the collectivity and the ascending plurality of claims stemming from the subcultures. Equally, the process of 'macro-level loyalty building' should not be associated with the integration of the masses into a common political form that overrides citizens' 'fixed primary loyalties' (Lodge 1978: 234). Indeed, by perceiving the common system as inclusive of national repositories of sovereignty, confederal consociation mitigates the fears that integration in the 1990s is about the subordination of states in some form of a federal authority having a monopoly of law-making and law-enforcing powers. Rather, by dismissing an 'either/or' conception of EU politics, it suggests that a functional division of jurisdictional competences between state and international organisation is compatible not only with the very idea of statehood itself, but also with further national state-building processes, subnational community strengthening, and multiple identity holding.

This is perhaps why the initial concentration of law-making power to the nation state gives way to a continual structuring and restructuring of power within the shared undertaking based on the realisation that 'economic and political interests are best advanced by staying together in a sensibly arranged political union' (Boulle 1984: 31), where the outcome of the various claims is controlled by the members of the elite cartel. The persistence of this form of controlled pluralism is conditioned by the extent to which a delicate balance of interests can be struck among the constituent units (Chryssochoou 1995). Evidently, then, the 'winner-takes-all' ethos which subsists in majoritarian systems does not suit the present EU, for the wishes of some constituent demoi would have to be enacted in central legislation at the expense of others.

From *Gesellschaft* to *Gemeinschaft?*

In historical terms, confederal consociation represents neither a movement back to the intergovernmentalism of the 1970s, nor a leap forward to a formally amalgamated federation. Rather, the elasticity of EU institution building, along with an overriding concern for securing the representation of the 'institutional self-interest of governments' (Scharpf 1988: 254), have set the limits of democratisation in the larger polity. Despite the latter's remarkable evolution from a common market to a state-like entity, the divide between territory and demos has persisted, forcing Sbragia to suggest that the option available to the EU 'is to implement the political dimension of federalism without its constitutional dimension' (Sbragia 1992b: 263). In particular, she proposes a type of 'segmented federalism' allowing for a number of functionally specific treaty-based federal arrangements without being founded on a formal, constitutionally based federation (Sbragia 1992b: 262). Confederal consociation sharpens this point since it does not require the existence of a European Constitution for the management of pressing EU affairs.

For the time being, the EU exhibits more a dispersed system of democratic governments, rather than a democratic system of governance. One reason for this is that the interests of the 'territorial state' coexist with those of the central institutions in so far as they are a product of inter-elite negotiations. Moreover, if one takes into account that the *locus decidendi* of the EU continues to rest on state agents, it is easy to see why it is the constituent governments that have a particular influence in the overall framework of power. This effectively frees the participants from 'the albatross of federalism', in that the current balance of trends minimises the possibilities for a European 'federal government', as a type of government concerned with the public affairs of a single state (Taylor 1993: 108). Being a transitional stage, confederal consociation may give way, in time, to a nascent *Gemeinschaft*, via the application of the (revised) provisions of the Treaty on European Union (TEU). This, however, would require the evolution of the presently 'semisovereign' European demos into something more than the numerical aggregate of the member state demoi. Indeed, herein lies the greatest challenge facing the EU: the building of a common civic identity among the constituent publics or, alternatively, their transformation from a plurality of demoi to a pluralistic demos. The analysis which follows, by focusing on the politics of the 1996 Inter-Governmental Conference (IGC), provides the empirical trends of formal constitutional engineering in the 'new' European polity.

Reforming the system

It seems fair to suggest that what was not formally discussed in the context of the IGC is much more important than a number of allegedly conflicting and/or controversial areas concerning the 'mechanics' of the revision process. For instance, an essential part of the hidden agenda of the 1996 IGC concerned the future role of the (West) European nation state and its constitutional relationship with an emerging Euro-polity. The provisions of the TEU on Economic and Monetary Union (EMU) is also a case in point. And so too, the potentially dramatic consequences of further enlargement on EU institutions, along with the implications stemming from the inclusion of a 'flexibility clause' on both the constitutional integrity and political cohesion of the *acquis communautaire*.

In fact, it is these very issues that constituted the *raison d'être* of the IGC, more or less implicitly. In general terms, a clearer political physiognomy of the EU should be further established, although such an outcome became a distinct possibility in the discussions that took place in the Reflection Group, a body of experts set up by the Corfu European Council in June 1994. According to Wessels' analysis, the following four options were open for the IGC: (1) implement Maastricht; (2) reform Maastricht; (3) build upon Maastricht; and (4) abort Maastricht (Wessels 1996). The growing 'democratic disjunction' between the wishes of a fragmented European demos and its respective governing elites (Stravridis 1993), an abundance of interrelated problems of (structural) socio-economic adjustment, and the uncertain future of the (West) European welfare state, were among the major factors that gave the '1996 process' an air of distress.

For the groundwork leading to the IGC, the Reflection Group became the dominant forum for interstate communication but not for interstate negotiation. This reflected the cautiousness shown by the states in identifying first the various options for further integration and then negotiating its possible outcomes. The Group presented its findings in the Final Report of December 1995 that was later submitted to the Madrid European Council (Reflection Group 1995). In the meantime, all major EU institutions, as well as the member states individually, submitted their views for the negotiations in advance (Edwards and Pijpers 1997: chs 10 and 11).

In the Final Report, the Group defined its own tasks as being (1) the improvement in the workings of the EU, and (2) the expansion of the capabilities of the EU so as to enable it to face both internal and external challenges (including the new waves of enlargement towards the countries of Central and Eastern Europe). The Final Report is structured around three dimensions: flexibility, effectiveness and democracy. Although 'flexibility' is a difficult term to define, in some way or another it refers to 'variable geometry' practices in the form of the EMS/ERM, the Schengen Agreement or the Eureka programme. But the Report was also quick to recognise that this can only be a temporary arrangement, that should not lead to a Europe *à la carte*.

Flexibility becomes all the more important as an organising principle of the EU in view of 1999, the year which according to the TEU the final stage of EMU will commence. If this type of organisation prevails, *ceteris paribus*, a pattern of differentiated participation in integration schemes would inevitably emerge. Under this scenario, EU members will find themselves split into different groups according to their particular domestic or other priorities. Areas like social policy, EMU, Common Foreign and Security Policy (CFSP), common defence arrangements within the Western European Union (WEU) and so on, are easy to link with the flexibility clause. The expected result would be to enhance the intergovernmental features of the EU and consolidate its dominant confederal/consociational properties. 'Flexibility' also entails a strong dose of political pragmatism concerning the hidden agenda of convergence, economic or otherwise. The dilemma that emerged from the 1996 IGC was between a pragmatic versus a normative approach. But as the final stage of the negotiations was under way, there also emerged the possibility of preserving the consociational nature of EU governance by means of adopting a 'mixed' approach to European constitutional change.

Taking the principle of efficiency seriously, in conjunction with that of flexibility, might well accelerate the pace of EU policy making in various functional areas. Yet, the Report did not bother to hint at a single institutional set-up capable of satisfying both conditions, simply stating that the end-product of the revision process should preserve the 'single institutional framework' of the EU within which the composition of the European Court of Justice (ECJ), the European Commission and the European Parliament (EP) will be a constant, whereas that of the Council of Ministers and the procedures established therein, a variable.

The picture was further complicated with the introduction in the Report of issues relating to the democratisation of the EU and the need to bring the latter 'closer to its citizens'. Democracy emerged, therefore, as a third organising principle of EU governance. Interestingly though, the Report failed to provide a concrete framework for inserting a stronger dose of democracy in the workings of the EU, proposing instead only marginal modifications to existing arrangements. Overall, the outstanding issues in the institutional agenda of the IGC were, *inter alia*, the principles of transparency and subsidiarity, the hierarchy of Community Acts, the comitology phenomenon, the need for rationalising central decision making and, finally, the question of enlargement and institutional adjustment.

Reflections on the institutional agenda

Increased transparency is vital if the EU wishes to eliminate the chasm between its citizens and the central institutions. The term refers both to a right to information for EU citizens and to the need for a simpler and, hence, comprehensible decision making process. The Commission has stated that although there have been steps in this direction, there is ample ground for further improvements (Commission of the European Communities 1995: 110). To date, twenty-two Council meetings have been held in public – mostly during the Danish Presidency in the first half of 1993 – which nevertheless dealt with secondary, though not insignificant, matters. As for the Commission itself, it has received no less than 220 applications requesting access to its documents, 53 per cent of which were accepted, 17.9 per cent were rejected and 28.4 per cent were either already in circulation or published by another EU institution (Toth 1992: 1079).

We have commented in the past on the various shortcomings of the principle of subsidiarity, found in Article 3b of the TEU (Tsinisizelis and Chryssochoou 1995). The topic is by now well documented and it suffices to point out that there is a need for further clarification on its operational aspects. The majority of members in the Reflection Group, however, wished for Article 3b to remain unchanged. For its part, the Commission suggested that 'The concepts of the directive, of mutual recognition or that of partnership (in the case of regional policy) reflect the principle of subsidiarity'. This probably reveals a gross misunderstanding of what the principle is all about, or that its meaning is used in a way that suits the interests of the central institutions. In modern federal systems, it is worth noting that the principle refers primarily to concurrent competences, defined by Toth (1992: 1080) as 'the authority of two different bodies to intervene with the same authority at the same time'. Community law does not (as yet) explicitly recognise the existence of such competences, given that the powers of the Community are in principle exclusive in nature.

In addition, the legal community resented the inclusion of the principle in the Treaty on the grounds that its application might not be justiciable within the ECJ. Hence the need for the conception of a specific body at the central level for the allocation of decision-making competences among different levels of government as well as for controlling the sphere of applicability of the principle and its 'constitutionality' in each case separately. This is reflected in the Final Report where it is intended that a 'higher constitutional body' should be set up with the task of examining the employment of subsidiarity. As with the rest of the Treaty provisions liable to amendment, the final word on resolving this issue rested with the national governments of the member states.

Comitology refers to developments since the Council decision of 17 December 1987, according to which a strong network of committees of national representatives within the Council hierarchy was established. Such a system of technical committees (or management committee government) reshaping the content of decisions already made in the context of formal legislative procedures tends to override the formal powers of EU institutions, especially those of the EP stemming from the 'co-decision procedure', to the benefit of national governments. Doubtless, the existing comitology structures exacerbate the already problematic relationship between the operational dimension of EU governance and the fundamental principles of representative and responsible government. Not surprisingly, the Reflection Group did not manage to produce a unified stance on this dainty omission and, as with other conflict-prone issues, referred it to the IGC (Reflection Group 1995: 16).

The issue of rationalising EU decision making relates to the composite institutional structure created by the TEU resembling an ancient Greek temple based on three separate pillars. Under Article C TEU, the EU shares a 'single institutional framework' headed by the European Council. A closer examination, however, reveals that this framework falls short of being genuinely 'single'. In essence, Maastricht has created a messy institutional set-up where EU institutions and the member states intermingle in no less than twenty-nine different legislative procedures, depending on the policy area and the pillar in question. The problem was compounded after the so-called 'Ioannina Compromise' of July 1994, according to which, under certain conditions, when the Council operates under qualified majority, the minority veto is not the normal twenty-three votes but instead twenty-six.

Little doubt exists that the cooperation and co-decision procedures of Articles 189c and 189b respectively have increased the democratic properties of the system by bringing the EP closer to the *locus decidendi* in certain policy areas. At the same time, however, they represent a unique, but federally inspired, exercise in interinstitutional power sharing which is far from being comprehensible to the majority of European citizens whose varying interests are supposed to find adequate expression via the workings and 'policy outputs' of these procedures. Hence, the acquisition of new co-decision powers by the EP is at best a 'partial 'offset' to the more difficult issues of EU democratisation concerning the social legitimation of the EU as a nascent polity.

In any case, the Interim Report suggested that a near consensus was formed in the Group in favour of the status quo and only marginal modifications in the EP's role were considered. More specifically, a clear majority was recorded against any radical changes with regard to the present interinstitutional balance of power. At a theoretical level, the transformation of the EU into a federation would require the introduction of a republican system of checks and balances as an interim arrangement on the way to a system of fully developed demos control.

Finally, it had been suggested that the real task of the IGC was to provide for the necessary mechanisms to prepare for a smooth accession of Central and East European countries (and possibly others from the Mediterranean region) during the next wave of enlargement. Such a task, however, presents potentially insurmountable problems given the possibility of an EU composed of twenty-seven or thirty members. Flexibility and efficiency, as major organisational principles, become relevant to this enlargement. In other words, it is expected that a system of 'flexible geometry', this time, however, formally institutionalised, will again be established post-1999. The issue is further complicated by the fact that the vast majority of the newcomers are small states which, if added to the existing group of small states in the EU, will upset an already delicate balance in the decision making process. Thus, a new formula for arriving at collective decisions should be so devised as to ensure that in the enlarged EU neither the larger members nor the smaller ones will be alienated.

In light of the above, Vibert has suggested a system of 'double concurrent majorities' as a means of balancing the interests of small and big states in an EU of thirty members. Such a system would be based on the assumption that any decision-making arrangement that takes into account either the number of states alone, or the size of their population, would in one way or another upset the existing balance of power in the Council. Under this system, 'a two thirds majority would require both two thirds of the number of the member states accounting for two thirds of the population' (Vibert 1995: 54). Whether or not such a proposal will find a place in future treaty revisions, what seems certain is that, for some countries, the emphasis will be on the possibilities of forming a minority veto, whilst for others on the possibilities of overcoming a small minority of dissenting states. Confederal consociation, and its explicit reliance on reversible dissensus practices in joint decision taking, seems to justify its analytical validity for the student of European integration in the 1990s.

Theorising reform

If we embrace Taylor's prognosis that 'any European socio-psychological community is more likely to emerge despite rather than because of the intentions of leaders', then the persistence of consensus elite governance in the EU's decisional context clearly highlights 'some of the roadblocks that are in the way'

(Taylor 1993: 182). Although no straightforward answer exists as to whether the bonds of unity created by Maastricht will be strong enough to overcome the current *Gesellschaft*-like qualities of EU governance, the lesson to be learned from the '1996 process', as a case of forging a variety of segmental differences into a single political blueprint, is that unless there is a sufficient area of consensus at the elite level, no viable outcomes can exist. This accords with what some sceptical students of integration have implicitly assumed: over the last decade, the weight of the evidence is that the extension of both its 'scope' and 'level' has exploited a crucial property of consensual politics: the capacity to reconcile the challenges of innovation with the need for continuity.

The point being made here is that in the EU of the 1990s 'the burden of proof' seems to lie more on federalism rather than on intergovernmentalism as a method of organising both the internal and external affairs of the polity, in terms of convincing leaders and led of its validity both as a condition and a process of EU governance. Although this description fits neatly with the consociationalist terminology of our analysis, a more optimistic interpretation of the facts might lead to the suggestion that the coming into force of the TEU has signalled the beginning of a new transitional period, previously described by the term nascent *Gemeinschaft*. To put the matter in its historical perspective, just as Hallstein's 'First Europe' (1958–66) (institutional centralisation) was succeeded by Dahrendorf's 'Second Europe' (1969–74) (creative intergovernmentalism) and that by what Taylor calls a 'Third Europe' (1974–93) (symbiosis), so the last seems to be giving way to a Fourth Europe (1993–today) (co-determination). This phase, characterised by a conscious striving to redress perhaps the gravest democratic deficiency of the EU – who should ultimately be accountable to whom – can be seen as part of a wider evolution towards a European 'political community' comprised of citizens capable of being simultaneously conscious of their separate existence as distinctive cultural and political entities (or demoi) and of their collective existence as one European demos (Chryssochoou 1996a, 1996b).

Inevitably, some may claim that this path to integration will certainly challenge the 'hard core' of the member nation states. They may even argue that the effects of conscious community strengthening and formal constitutional engineering might be seen in the light of the existing equilibrium of territorial interests as an apology for confrontational behaviour. Such a development may take the form of various disjointed responses on the part of the segment elites as to which particular set of reforms might produce an optimal model for transnational democracy. Yet, one should also wonder whether these reservations amount to a rather deceptive dilemma between the essential requirements of democratic shared rule and the conditions responsible for the political viability of the EU.

In attempting to sketch some final lines of our understanding of integration in the context of the '1996 process', the following need to be set out. Against a mounting *crise de confiance* at the grassroots, the EU has found itself once more in its arduous journey to unification in a state of flux. Although determined to build on the relaunch of integration inaugurated by the Single European Act in the mid-1980s, its members had lost nothing of their anxiety to preserve the integrity of their respective polities against the tides of federalism. As a result, the mid-1990s have witnessed an increased tension between democracy and integration: the former was often taken to imply a straightforward loss of national democratic autonomy on the part of national representative assemblies to an allegedly overambitious EP, or indeed the making of a more federated EU as detrimental to the constitutional properties of states.

This antithesis between 'nationalists' and 'federalists' has marked its impact on the debate over the future direction of the EU, demonstrating that the process of uniting distinct politically organised units is neither a smooth nor an automatic political exercise, all the more so if it is a by-product of a predominantly utilitarian, cost–benefit calculus among the dominant governing elites. Further, it has shown that it is difficult to maintain the politics of democratic 'deepening' without active citizen support. Indeed, the 'permissive consensus', pinpointed by Lindberg and Scheingold (1970), cannot generate the necessary public commitment to the making of a European demos conscious of its political identity. If anything, the ratification of the TEU made it clear that the exclusion of citizens from the process of building new integrative arrangements is at the expense of popular fragmentation.

The picture is completed with the ever-pertinent divide between elites and demos, territorial and non-territorial claims and, finally, technocracy and democracy. This development has alarmingly emphasised the limits of integration since both the Maastricht experience and the '1996 process' have shown that the prospects for developing democracy among democracies are conditioned 'from above', stemming from a variety of sources aiming to reconcile the defence of territorial quests for segmental autonomy with the prospects for furthering the scope, but not necessarily the level, of integration. Likewise, the process of democratising the EU has been a reflection of an uneasy compromise struck between those stressing the advantages of collective action and those emphasising the costs of autonomous decision making. In any case, though, the move towards the Fourth Europe requires a more demos-oriented process of union, flexible enough to accommodate high levels of segmental diversity, yet solid enough to stand firm against the politics of consensus elite government.

'Stirred, not shaken . . . '

As *The Economist* (1997: 37) put it, the Amsterdam Summit 'produced more of a mouse than a mountain'. Or, as the *Guardian* (1997) reported: 'Europe is much the same this week as it was last week'. Hailed by some as a 'reasonable step', whilst criticised by others as lacking ambition, the new Treaty preserves the EU's three-pillar structure and with it the existence of two separate legal methods: the Community method and intergovernmental cooperation.

Furthermore, a new protocol is enshrined in the Treaty in an attempt to define more precisely the criteria for applying the principles of subsidiarity and proportionality. The Treaty states that 'In exercising the powers conferred on it, each institution shall ensure that the principle of subsidiarity is complied with', and that 'any action of the Community shall not go beyond any action necessary for the attainment of the objectives of the Treaty'. It is also stated that these principles shall respect both the *acquis communautaire* and the institutional balance, also taking into account that 'the Union shall provide itself with the means necessary to attain its objectives and carry through its policies'. Still, though, the 'burden of proof' lies on the Community which has to justify compliance of proposed legislation with these principles. *Ceteris paribus*, directives should be preferred to regulations and so should framework directives to detailed measures, leaving as much scope for national decisions as possible. The Commission should seek maximum consultation prior to initiating Community legislation, minimise administrative or financial burdens on the EU, the member governments, subnational institutions, 'economic operators and citizens', and submit an annual report to the other EU institutions on the application of these principles.

Flexibility was included in the Treaty though in a way that precludes the creation of a Europe à la carte by introducing strict conditions for its application. In particular, such 'reinforced cooperation' should (1) further the objectives of the EU and protect its interests; (2) respect the principles of the Treaties and the single institutional framework; (3) be used only as a last resort; (4) concern at least a majority of EU members; (5) respect the *acquis communautaire*; (6) not affect the competences, rights, obligations and interests of those members that do not wish to participate therein; (7) remain open to all members states; and (8) be authorised by the Council. In addition, it is stated that the new 'flexible' arrangements will be governed by the same decision making rules as in the TEU/ECT, adjusted accordingly for membership, and that the EP will be regularly informed by the Commission and the Council. However, the new Treaty precludes member states from initiating flexible arrangements in areas which (1) fall within the exclusive competences of the Community; (2) affect the Community policies, actions, or programmes; (3) concern EU citizenship or discriminate between member state nationals; (4) fall outside the limits of the powers conferred upon the Community by the Treaty; and (5) constitute discrimination or restrict trade and/or distort competition between member states. Authorisation for such 'flexible' schemes 'shall be granted by the Council, acting by a qualified majority on a proposal by the Commission and after consulting the EP'. Any objection by a member state on grounds of 'important and stated reasons' results in the whole matter being referred to the European Council for a decision by unanimity.

Conclusion

Almost half a century since its inception, the integrative system neither basks in the sunlight of a 'complete' *Gemeinschaft* – its citizens being 'members of the unit directly and not through membership of another political unit' (Zetterholm 1994: 73) – nor shivers in the shadowland of an 'unmanaged' *Gesellschaft* on the road to disintegration. But neither does it wander somewhere in the dusk of an unspecified 'half-way house' between the two. Rather, it approximates most closely to a complicated mixture of familiar models of governance in the form of a confederal consociation: an ensemble of *Gesellschaft* and *Gemeinschaft* elements, resulting in a fairly coordinated system of democracies.

The question that still remains concerns the appropriate institutional structure to sustain successive waves of enlargement in the next century. On the basis of the (largely incomplete) outcome of the 1996 IGC, there has clearly been a preference for a managerial type of reform to improve the effectiveness in policy output. Flexibility has been partially elevated to a *modus operandi* of the EU system, whereas the deepening of integration has been referred *ad calendas Graecas* – or, at least until a new review conference is convened. From a theoretical perspective, these moderate trends in European treaty reform reinforce the view that we are currently witnessing a reversal of the Mitranian (Mitrany 1943) logic to integration: instead of 'form follows function', the new integrationist slogan might be that 'function follows form'. That is, the structural properties of the larger management system determine both the quality (level/depth) and quantity (scope/range) of joint integrative schemes.

Interestingly, this is exactly the opposite of what neo-functionalists hoped to achieve: instead of politicisation (the process of linking the management of integration with the daily lives of EU citizens) becoming an additional weapon in the hands of pro-integrationist forces, it is increasingly used by the more sceptical actors, often by means of resorting to nationalist sentiments, making it difficult to mobilise the constituent publics in favour of further integration and, eventually, towards a 'complete equilibrium' among different levels of governmental authority. Such a development, by contesting the idea that European polity formation is a linear process towards a federal end, may lead to a condominium type of organisation, characterised by 'multiple flexible equilibria': a historically unprecedented arrangement in which 'both territorial as well as functional constituencies would vary' (see Abromeit, this volume).

Whatever the future Euro-polity may eventually come to resemble, we claim that the present EU is better understood as a confederal consociation. As already noted, the model refers not only to the defining properties of the regional system, but also to the politics of European constitutional choice, still determined by a 'cartel of elites' under conditions of tightly controlled pluralism. Thus, it is highly plausible that any proposed changes to the functioning of the system that may disrupt the existing equilibrium of forces within the elite cartel and its ability to exercise managerial control over integration must be considered a distant possibility. The insistence of the member states on preserving the status quo and deferring any decision on institutional reform until the next enlargement actually takes place sharpens this point.

The lesson to be learned from Amsterdam is that European integration in the late 1990s is not about the subordination of states to a higher central authority which possesses a monopoly of law-making and law-enforcing powers, but rather it is about the preservation of those state qualities that allow the participating entities to survive as separate collectivities, whilst engaging themselves in a polity-formation process that increasingly transforms the traditional patterns of interaction amongst them. In conclusion, it is likely that the new EU will allow for an economic and monetary union, but not for a federally inspired political union guided by the overarching will of a single and undifferentiated European demos.

References

Boulle, L. J. (1984) *Constitutional Reform and the Apartheid State: Legitimacy, Consociationalism and Control in South Africa*, New York: St Martin's Press.

Chryssochoou, D. N. (1994) 'Democracy and Symbiosis in the European Union: Towards a Confederal Consociation?', *West European Politics* 17(4): 1–14.

Chryssochoou, D. N. (1995) 'European Union and the Dynamics of Confederal Consociation: Problems and Prospects for a Democratic Future', *Journal of European Integration* 18(2–3): 279–305.

Chryssochoou, D. N. (1996a) 'Europe's Could-Be Demos: Recasting the Debate', *West European Politics* 19(4): 787–801.

Chryssochoou, D. N. (1996b) 'Rethinking Democracy in the European Union: The Case for a "Transnational Demos"', in S. Stavridis *et al.* (eds), *New Challenges to the European Union: Policies and Policy-Making*, Aldershot: Dartmouth, pp. 67–85.

Chryssochoou, D. N. (1997) 'New Challenges to the Study of European Integration', *Journal of Common Market Studies* 35(4): 521–42.

Commission of the European Communities (1995) 'Report on the functioning of the Treaty on European Union', SEC (95) 731 Final, 10 May.

Dahl, R. A. (1956) *A Preface to Democratic Theory*, Chicago: University of Chicago Press.

Dahrendorf, R. (1967) *Society and Democracy in Germany*, London: Weidenfeld.

The Economist (1997) 'Mountains Still to Climb', 21 June: 37.

Edwards, G. and Pijpers, A. (eds) (1997) *The Politics of European Treaty Reform: The 1996 Intergovernmental Conference and Beyond*, London and Washington, DC: Pinter.

Forsyth, M. (1981) *Unions of States: The Theory and Practice of Confederation*, Leicester: Leicester University Press.

Guardian (1997)'The Real Lesson of Amsterdam', 18 June.

Kirchner, E. J. (1991) *Decision Making in the European Community: The Council Presidency and European Integration*, Manchester: Manchester University Press.

Lijphart, A. (1971) 'Cultural Diversity and Theories of Political Integration', *Canadian Journal of Political Science* 4(1): 1–14.

Lindberg, L. N. and Scheingold, S. A. (1970) *Europe's Would-Be Polity*, Englewood Cliffs, NJ: Prentice Hall.

Lodge, J. (1978) 'Loyalty and the EEC: The Limits of the Functionalist Approach', *Political Studies* 26(2): 149–53.

Mitrany, D. (1943) *A Working Peace System*, London: Royal Institute of International Affairs.

Puchala, D. J. (1972) 'Of Blind Men, Elephants and International Integration', *Journal of Common Market Studies* 10(3): 267–84.

Reflection Group (1995) *Final Report of the Reflection Group*, 5 December, SN 520 REV.

Sbragia, A. M. (1992a) 'Introduction', in A. M. Sbragia (ed.), *Euro-Politics: Institutions and Policymaking in the 'New' European Community*, Washington, DC: The Brookings Institution, pp. 1–22.

Sbragia, A. M. (1992b) 'Thinking about the European Future: The Uses of Comparison', in A. M. Sbragia (ed.), *Euro-Politics: Institutions and Policymaking in the 'New' European Community*, Washington, DC: The Brookings Institution, pp. 257–91.

Scharpf, F. W. (1988) 'The Joint Decision Trap: Lessons from German Federalism and European Integration', *Public Administration* 66(3): 239–78.

Stavridis, S. (1993) 'Democracy in Europe: West and East', in *Conference Proceedings on People's Rights and European Structures*, Manresa: Centre Unesco de Catalunya, pp. 129–33.

Taylor, P. (1975) 'The Politics of the European Communities: The Confederal Phase', *World Politics* 27 (April): 336–60.

Taylor, P. (1990) 'Consociationalism and Federalism as Approaches to International Integration', in A. G. R. Groom and P. Taylor (eds), *Frameworks for International Co-operation*, London: Pinter, pp. 172–84.

Taylor, P. (1993) *International Organization in the Modern World: The Regional and the Global Process*, London: Pinter.

Toth, A. G. (1992) 'The Principle of Subsidiarity in the Maastricht Treaty', *Common Market Law Review* 29: 1079–1105.

Tsinisizelis, M. J. and Chryssochoou, D. N. (1995) 'From "Gesellschaft" to "Gemeinschaft"? Confederal Consociation and Democracy in the European Union', *Current Politics and Economics of Europe* 5(4): 1–33.

Vibert, F. (1995) *A Core Agenda for the 1996 Inter-Governmental Conference (IGC)*, London: European Policy Forum.

Wessels, W. (1994) 'Rationalizing Maastricht: The Search for an Optimal Strategy of the New Europe', *International Affairs* 70(3): 445–57.

Wessels, W. (1996) 'The Modern West European State: Democratic Erosion from Above or Below?', in S. S. Andersen and K. A. Eliassen (eds), *The European Union: How Democratic Is It?*, London: Sage, pp. 57–69.

Zetterholm, S. (1994) 'Why is Cultural Diversity a Political Problem? A Discussion of Cultural Barriers to Political Integration', in S. Zetterholm (ed.), *National Cultures and European Integration*, Oxford: Berg, p. 73.

7 Legitimacy dilemmas of supranational governance

The European Commission between accountability and independence

Thomas Christiansen

Political integration, institutional reform and the crisis of legitimacy

In the 1990s we have witnessed a major transformation in the nature of European integration: the gradual emergence of an agenda for the 'constitutional reform' of the European Union. After the ratification debates which followed the signing of the Maastricht Treaty, the Reflection Group helped to set the agenda for the 1996–7 Inter-Governmental Conference (IGC). The Amsterdam Treaty essentially deals with the fundamental structural arrangements for future EU decision making. This, in itself, is no small matter: it indicates that we are witnessing not only a quickening of structural reform in the EU – indeed a trend towards continuous reform – but also a move away from the preoccupation with *policy* (Single Market, EMU) in past IGCs, towards genuinely *institutional* reform. It seems as if the EC/EU has gone full circle: after the 1955 EPC/EDC failure there was a move away from political integration and a concentration on the laborious process of market integration (customs union, '1992' programme, EMU), only to return in the 1990s to confront the accumulated back-log of 'political' and institutional issues.

Market integration has been extremely successful. The success of progressive tariff reduction and deregulation, it has been argued, was in part made possible because a parallel movement towards the establishment of accountable, political structures was lacking (Moravcsik 1993). But the very success of 'indirect' integration – reaching an 'ever-closer union' through market and legal integration – has forced the 'political', institutional questions back onto the centre stage of EU reform.

There are a number of ways in which the legitimation of the European construction can be approached. This chapter examines the legitimation of one key institution, the European Commission. Much of the 'democratic deficit' debate is directed at the operation and involvement of the Commission. Its relationship to Parliament (Westlake 1994), its degree of openness and transparency, its link with private interests (Mazey and Richardson 1994) are increasingly the subject of academic interest. Yet, the Commission has not undergone any fundamental structural change since its inception. Its role and charter are largely unchanged, even though the Council, Parliament and Court have metamorphosed significantly. The Commission is, therefore, a key aspect in reflections about the constitutional choices the EU has to face.

In pursuing this theme, this chapter seeks to show that for the legitimation of its complex institutional structure the EU cannot rely on one-dimensional domestic analogies. The chapter thus provides a critique of some of the conventional writings on the EU's 'democratic deficit'. The chapter is structured in three parts. First, the normative basis underlying the discussion of constitutional choice is spelled out. A second part examines the requirements of legitimising European governance against the background of problems with standard theories of majoritarian democracy. The model of legitimation of European integration developed here is then applied to the specific institutional arrangements which concern the Commission. Finally, the conclusion considers proposals for a resolution of this dilemma against the background of the Amsterdam Treaty.

Normative foundations of European integration

Debating European constitutional choices necessarily involves certain value-judgements about European governance. Any discussion of the legitimacy of European governance ought to spell out its assumptions with regard to the normative basis of integration. It is only by following such a clarification that a discussion of the EU's reform debate can be sensibly engaged and that 'better' constitutional solutions can be proposed. This section discusses three basic premises about the nature of integration which are guiding the subsequent discussion. First, European integration is of independent normative value above and beyond the benefits it provides to specific states, groups and individuals. Second, integration must be understood as an open-ended process rather than the emergence of a specific set of institutions and policies. Third, European integration is not only the expression of, but also the response to, processes of globalisation. Each of these assumptions has important repercussions for the subsequent discussion of legitimacy in the EU.

The first of these points, the independent value of European integration, is perhaps the most contentious. Yet looking at the origins and early history of the European Community it is evident that West European integration was, for a significant period of time, regarded as something more than merely a maximisation of national interests. The idea of European integration was one of superseding competition and conflict between nation states by replacing the state system with a qualitatively different system. Many saw this as a federal project, but as this proved to be far reaching, recourse was made to functional integration. Subsequently, the normative aspect of the European idea – indeed the European idea itself – was largely lost from view as the emphasis was on functional logic and national interests. Yet it is crucial for this understanding of integration that the functional path has merely been the method rather than the aim of European integration.

Elevating the process of integration to such a normative position is not to say that the EU is superior to the nation state as a framework for problem solving, or that its output is inevitably good. Indeed, later parts of this chapter will discuss in some detail both the continuous significance of states in Western Europe and the pathologies of European policy making. But neither can the value of integration be judged solely by looking at the short-term benefits which states seek and derive from membership. During the functional, 'non-political' phase of the Community, the value of closer integration was presented in such utilitarian terms. Membership in the Community, and the further development of its policy instruments, would increase trade, economic growth and global competitiveness. While this might, on the whole, well be the case, it has made the justification of further integration difficult when, or where, these benefits have not been forthcoming.

If integration is justified in purely utilitarian terms, the fundamental value of an enduring and stable framework of interstate cooperation based on the rule of law is largely lost. To point out that the initial function of integration was to foreclose the potentiality of renewed war between Germany and France seems almost nonsensical in the 1990s. Yet the issue of German unification in 1990 has emphasised the significance of a strong and stable European architecture capable of absorbing the shocks of change in Central and Eastern Europe. There are probably many examples of the way in which the process of integration has helped to pacify domestic or interstate conflicts (such as Belgian territorial politics or the conflict in Northern Ireland), but the fixation on functional integration and the preoccupation with national interests has helped to obscure the long-term significance of European integration.

The stability which integration has brought to European politics is not so much the consequence of current agreement among member states as a result of the accumulated experience of a legal and institutional framework that has been built up over the past forty-five years. The specific characteristics of European integration – the degree of transparency it has brought to international politics, the rule of law it has established in interstate relations, the scale of administrative and commercial interaction it has generated – make this a normatively valuable framework for political decision making.

Clearly, there are limits to the transparency and the rule of law in the EU, as there are serious limits to democratic participation. But a normative judgement must be based on comparison with a credible alternative to the path of integration which has been followed. The most likely alternative to functional integration is the persistence of a state-centred system in which decision making would be much less democratic, transparent, justiciable and efficient. Seen in this light, the critique of the EU's 'democratic deficit' for a further democratisation of the EU is only credible if it is based on an affirmation rather than a rejection of the integration process. Dismissing the European project because of a perceived lack of democratic procedures is, consequently, misplaced.

The normative value of European integration can therefore be derived from arguments about the accountability, transparency and effectiveness which the process has brought to the international relations of the region. These are moral categories which are usually invoked by those who criticise the democratic credentials of the European integration. Yet, even though a normative defence of integration based on liberal ideals is possible, this must remain a matter of assertion rather than reasoning. This is because the arguments provided here will not convince those for whom the nation state is a value in itself. To those who consider nationality rather than democracy the normative foundation of government, there is nothing in the process of European integration which will persuade them that the EU has a normative quality of its own.

A second premise of this chapter – that European integration is a process rather than a set of institutions, policies and procedures – will be more easily acceptable to most observers. It will suffice here to point to the spatial and institutional dynamics which are likely to keep this process going for the foreseeable future. This is no small matter since, in the conventional understanding, constitutionalisation is by definition aimed at the design of a fixed framework for political decision making. Constitutionalisation itself might be a process, but its result – a constitution – is meant to limit rather than facilitate changes in political structures and procedures. Legitimising a process rather than a static entity therefore requires constitutional choices that are fundamentally different.

It is difficult to design structures which conform to the values of democracy and effectiveness and it requires the kind of value trade-offs every federal-type system has to face (Kincaid 1995). But in the current EU debate, many view the IGC as facing a further constitutional choice: the trade-off between 'widening' and 'deepening' the EU. This widening versus deepening debate, now that applications for membership from Mediterranean and East European countries are piling up, and that elaborate 'pre-accession strategies' have been devised, is clearly more than a catalyst for policy reform. Enlargement certainly calls into question the viability of the CAP and other redistributive instruments, but, more fundamentally, enlargement raises questions about the very identity of the EU. Asking 'where does Europe end?' is inseparable from asking 'what is Europe?' The fact that the EU's borders are not finally set – never have been, and will not be for the foreseeable future – means that its constitutionalisation is fundamentally different from otherwise comparable reform processes in national settings. European integration has created institutional structures and constructed a lasting arena for public policy making, yet it remains essentially a process of integration. However federal it may turn out to become, it is not, and cannot be, a state.

European constitutional choice has to take account of this procedural nature of integration. It is, at best, futile to try and define a process in static, and statist, terms. But doing so might also do damage to the integration process. What is needed is a framework which is open ended enough to allow future enlargements, while at the same time addressing the issues of concern and of interest to the current members. It must also be grounded in past choices. There is no *tabula rasa* from which a 'European Constitution' could be designed. Reform needs to be based on past choices and present institutional realities – at both the national and European level. Proposals for radical reform ignoring this basic principle – such as the 1955 Treaty for a European Political Community and the European Parliament's 1984 Draft Treaty for European Union – are bound to be studied by historians as instances of utopianism.

A final point here concerns the relationship between processes of integration and processes of globalisation. Part of the problem in reforming the EU has often been that it is seen as an expression of globalisation and, by inference, as a sign of governments 'giving in' to globalising social and economic forces which erode national sovereignty and national identity. This is unsurprising considering the amount of trade liberalisation the EU has been engaged in, and the way in which this has been justified as a response to global competitiveness. Yet it is crucial in the understanding of European governance presented here that integration is a dynamic reaction to globalisation. What is, on the one hand, a loss of national autonomy in social and economic regulation is, on the other hand, the emergence of a system in which states can collectively regain some regulatory control over otherwise untrammelled processes of globalisation. The development of the EU is, in this sense, not the capitulation of nation states in the face of global markets and other transnational forces, but their rescue (Milward *et al.* 1992). Beyond that, the emergence of a specific policy-making arena at the European level is an expression of structural differentiation in the international system – transnational and supranational organisations are becoming increasingly significant structures for collective action. Liberalist theory

In this perspective, European integration is a process in which the translation of abstract democratic ideals needs to respond not just to citizens' ability of participating in decision making (which is diminishing in the EU), but also to the system's capacity to facilitate public control over transnational economic and social processes (which is intensifying in the EU). As a consequence, there is a need to reformulate democratic theory – in a manner comparable with its transformation from city state to nation state – if we are to make normative sense of European integration (Dahl 1994).

Legitimising European governance: beyond majoritarian democracy

The public debate in recent years has converged around the notion that the EU's problem with legitimacy is essentially its 'democratic deficit'. There are additional problems, such as a Court frequently regarded as 'activist' (Rasmussen 1988) or the apparently limitless extension of competences (Pollack 1994). Yet the essence of the problem is the limitations placed on the use of the national veto in the face of still rudimentary parliamentary powers. As a result, the bulk of legislative decisions in the EU are taken by qualified majority vote (QMV) in closed session by a collectivity of executives who are, at best, indirectly elected representatives. This, in a nutshell, sums up the EU's democratic deficit.

There are many variations and further developments of this problem that need to be addressed – the distance between Parliament and electorate, the size of constituencies, the problem of language, the relationship between national parliaments and the EP, the use of referendums – but the general acceptance is that in order to legitimise an EU operating on a regular QMV basis, a healthy injection of representative democracy is needed. Alternatively, those who object to an extension of the powers of the EP, such as the British government under John Major, also demand reductions in the use of QMV.

Yet, on a closer examination, the democratic legitimacy of the EU is increasingly seen as a highly complex issue, in which the 'majoritarian avenue' might do damage to the European project (Dehousse 1995). The underlying problem here is the conceptual history of liberal democracy. If we look at their origin and early practice, we see that the structures and procedures of representative government are not simply the instruments of liberal democracy as which they are usually regarded. They have functioned also as elements in the construction of nation states. Indeed, in the liberal era, the conferral of democratic and other citizenship rights has been one of the most important instruments for state building. From the French Revolution onwards, the extension of parliamentary democracy was essential in the creation of strong central states based on a common national identity.

The conferral and the guarantee of citizenship rights requires final authority. There must also be a boundary to the community upon which democratic rights and obligations are bestowed. Democratic theory itself cannot give any satisfactory answer to these questions (Barry 1989). In this respect liberal democracy and representative governments necessarily rest upon existing state or communal boundaries, or else use what Barry calls 'arguments of persuasion' to create new boundaries. Borders and hierarchy are the hallmarks of the modern state. And while the establishment of democratic regimes has not always created states, and while many states remain undemocratic, there are no examples for state-less forms of democracy.

But it is a particular sequence of historical events which has created this apparently inherent link between democracy and state building. It certainly ought not to stop us looking for and thinking about 'state-less' forms of democracy, something which a growing number of scholars have undertaken (Held 1992, Tassin 1992, Weale 1995). In the particular context of a discussion about European constitutional choice, there must also be recognition that the linkages that have developed between liberal democracy and the modern state are, in part, contingent developments.

Historically, the establishment of liberal democracy came to be tied to, first, popular sovereignty and, later, national self-determination. Popular sovereignty demands that 'the people' have ultimate control over the institutions of state. National self-determination demands that each nation be recognised as 'a people' with the right to determine their own affairs. These two principles have been fused in the powerful combination of ideas and values that is the nation state. The revolutions of the eighteenth, nineteenth and twentieth centuries each had their part in establishing the fusion of 'people's power' with 'national liberation', joining citizenship with nationality. Thus, we are now faced with a generalised perception that the acquisition of democratic rights requires the establishment of a state –

possibly a state within a federation, but preferably an independent state. This is the message transmitted by the experience of post-1945 decolonisations as much as from post-1989 democratisation in Central and Eastern Europe.

In this context, the German Constitutional Court spelled out the limits of further integration in terms of 'national democracy'. Part of the argument was based on the idea that sovereignty in Europe lay with the various state-peoples (*Staatsvölker*). If democracy is thus grounded in the ethnic make-up of the continent, then it would be, by definition, impossible to democratise the EU. Without people no state, without state no democracy, without democracy no people – this reading of the constitutional situation in Germany and the wider Western Europe caused much criticism (Weiler 1995, Joerges 1996a), precisely because it foreclosed the opportunity to increase the progressive democratic reform of the EU itself. Sverker Gustavsson discusses some of the problematic aspects of this judgment in this volume.

The debate surrounding this judgment, as well as the general critique of the linkage between ethnicity and democracy, have attempted to show that it would be misleading, indeed even dangerous, to view the linkage between liberal democracy and the nation state as inherent or automatic. Yet the fact that 'national democracy' is a social construction does not mean that it is easily toppled by secular processes such as globalisation or integration. Indeed, as we observe in the world after the Cold War, such processes induce 'societal insecurity' in populations which increasingly have to confront the challenges of transnationalism without the protective shelter of 'their' state (Wæver *et al.* 1993). A revival of ethnic nationalism in the 1990s has been one of the consequences.

The force of social constructions is such that their consequences are 'real'. The social and political practices which help to maintain social constructions, including the conceptual foundations of 'national democracy', must therefore also enter into the equations of constitutional engineering. Such recognition of historically constructed linkages such as the one between identity and democracy certainly limits the prospects for significant progress towards further integration and further democratisation. But emphasising this is not the same as saying – as the German Constitutional Court has appeared to do – that there cannot be legitimate government outside the framework of democratically constituted nation states. The limits imposed by pointing to the force of social constructions are less about the extent of change than about the speed. There is thus a strong argument in favour of introducing novel, democratic procedures only gradually while remaining sensitive to the normative significance of 'integration' and 'nationality' in the legitimation of supranational governance.

Ignoring the implications of nationality for the legitimation of emerging polities is bound to lead to more serious problems than unsatisfactory policy implementation or a 'bad press' for EU institutions in member states. On the global scale, the experience of democratisation of multinational polities has regularly led to bloody and costly fragmentation processes. The history of decolonisation – from the foundation of India to the current conflict in Chechnya – is rich in examples. In Western Europe, the spectre of fragmentation does not raise fears of bloodshed, yet it is clearly antagonistic to the goal of integration which had the original aim of overcoming war and bloodshed on the continent. The basic dilemma that any constitutional choice of the EU needs to address is the way in which supranational governance can be democratised, without jeopardising the integrative process. This is why the abstract ideal of a polity based on majoritarian parliamentary democracy needs to be adapted to the special requirements of EU governance.

What follows from this general discussion is that the legitimacy of the EU is based on three distinct values: democracy (the demand for public accountability), integration (the search for institutionalised solutions to transnational policy making), and member state autonomy (the maintenance of national diversity). Such a triangular conception of EU legitimacy is a reflection of the 'contradictions between intergovernmental bargaining, functional administration and democracy [which are] embedded in the treaties establishing the European Communities' (Wallace and Smith 1995: 140). We have indicated how the values of democracy, integration and national autonomy are in potential conflict with each other. A European Constitution aimed at enhancing the legitimacy of the system of supranational governance will therefore need to balance these carefully. The potential of democracy and public accountability for the legitimacy of the EU is apparent. The significance of system effectiveness and of national diversity in legitimating the EU requires some clarification.

European integration, having turned to the path of functional integration, requires positive results in the economic realm for its justification. Providing welfare benefits and economic growth is generally seen as a way of legitimising emergent polities. Lipset writes that to 'attain legitimacy, what new democracies need above all is efficacy, particularly in the economic arena, but also in the polity. If they can keep the high road to economic development, they can keep their political houses in order' (Lipset 1994: 1). While this statement is directed at new democracies – those emerging from colonial or dictatorial rule – it rings true also with respect to the EU.

The dilemma of European constitutional choice, then, results from in-built contradictions among the values of democratic government, effectiveness of supranational decision making and maintenance of national diversity. Significant progress on each of these values is bound to jeopardise the realisation of the other two, and as a result of one-dimensional reform the legitimacy of the system will be threatened. A one-dimensional extension of parliamentary procedures – giving full co-decision-making powers to the EP – might well lead to a centralisation of power at the European level. Increasing the participation of national – and regional – parliaments carries the risk of slowing down or stalling effective decision making in the EU. Either solution, or a combination of both, would enhance the EU's democratic legitimacy. But it would jeopardise, at the same time, the legitimacy which the system derives from producing effective policy outputs or the way in which it maintains recognition of national diversity and autonomy (Dehousse 1995). It might act, in other words, as the catalyst towards the kind of systemic fragmentation that democratisation has shown itself to be in other historical or geographical contexts.

This is not to say that there ought not to be an extension of parliamentary powers or democratic rights. Clearly, the democratisation of the EU is an unfinished project, and other chapters in this volume make convincing cases why and how this project needs to be carried forward. But to point to the particular dilemma of European governance developed above implies that – unless we are prepared to see the EU system turn into a state – it cannot be legitimised entirely through majoritarian democratic procedures. Reforms and constitutional choices will need to adapt the ideals of liberal democracy to the specific conditions of supranational governance. What this means in practice is that calls for a 'democratic Europe' ought to be replaced by a debate about balancing integration and democratisation. An important element in the debate about continuous and gradual reform is the examination of the role and functioning of each institution, the management of its relationships with other supranational institutions, with national governments and with individual citizens. Such a comprehensive examination of individual institutions is one way of establishing the constitutional needs of European governance. An outline of such an analysis of the European Commission follows below.

Multiple accountability of the European Commission

The triangular conception of EU legitimacy so far developed neatly reflects the discrete normative contribution of each of the main institutions: the Council of Ministers as the guardian of national autonomy, the EP as the guardian of democratic governance, and the Commission, together with the ECJ, as the guardian of effective integration.

This interinstitutional model of EU legitimation is easily supported by a conventional institutional perspective. The EP derives its legitimacy and authority from direct elections which to some extent bypass the national political circuit (even if this is still more a formality than an applied rule). Party federations are the main aggregates of political power within the chamber, and the resultant political groups cut across national boundaries. While the EP supports a maximalist integrative agenda, it is prepared to jettison integrative progress as much as national sentiments when it comes to the achievement or protection of democratic procedure and parliamentary status. Disputes over the budget have, in the past, been the clearest example of that. In equal measure, the Council of Ministers is an organ concerned with advancing integration and political representation (if aggregated at a very high level), while at the same time it is the arena in which individual state representatives seek to protect what they regard as 'national interests'. It is the latter aspect of its work which has turned it into an often sceptical, defensive and occasionally even uncooperative actor in the integration process.

The Commission, finally, does pursue communitarian goals and is charged with the administration of common policies and the supervision of implementation in the member states. As a result, it has come into close contact with actors at the regional and local level, as well as with non-state actors in Brussels. Regularly it has been in conflict with the member states, not in the least before the ECJ, but it is also frequently charged with violations of the principles of transparency and openness in the EU. Its allegiance it less to the specific interests of either member states or 'the people', but rather to the much more abstract *acquis communautaire*. Together with the Court, the Commission produces legislation and supervises its implementation, independent of member state interests or popular pressure.

But while this perspective shows that each of the central institutions of the EU – Council, Parliament and Commission – does, at a superficial level, perform a specific legitimising function, it in practice harbours reflexes and organisational logics which are in contrast if not in conflict with these. The image of a 'division of labour', then, does make some sense of the high degree of consensualism and inter-connectedness of the European institutions – in order to maintain overall legitimacy all the institutions simply have to respect each others' specific normative role – though it still is a mighty simplification. Constitutional 'divisions of labour' are never that neat, and the EU system is no exemption. Indeed, if anything, it demonstrates the opposite.

The reproduction of this interinstitutional logic can also be identified in the intrainstitutional setting. In fact, each of the institutions can be shown to possess democratic and integrative and national logics. Consequently, the balancing act of legitimation is performed not only at the level of the interinstitutional rela-tions, but also, and perhaps more crucially, within each of the institutions. In maintaining its own institutional legitimacy against the frequent desire of creating a hierarchical, simpler and perhaps more democratic regime, the Commission has consistently defended a functionalist structure that, it could be argued, has pursued integration at any cost. At the same time there are frequent claims that units within the Commission, and even the institution as a whole, fall under the spell of individual governments when it comes to the pursuit of specific policies. Clearly, the Commission is different things to different people.

In looking at the Commission in slightly more detail, it is important to recognise at the outset that the role of guardian of the integration process remains the oldest and most important tasks of the Commission. Despite a lot of action and commitment to other values (such as democracy and the respect of national autonomy), the pursuit of 'ever-closer union' remains the primary object of the Commission. But a closer look reveals that within the Commission other forces are at work, which are often hidden from view by the image of the Commission as a unitary actor. These three aspects of Commission activity can be identified as: a 'parliamentary', a 'technocratic' and a 'diplomatic' Commission. While the presence of such contradictory agendas clearly bodes ill for institutional coherence, the conclusion here is not that greater uniformity is called for. Instead, the continuation of these rival legitimation agendas within the Commission is necessary, since it is the balance between all three of them, rather than the preponderance of any one, which constitutes the institution's overall legitimacy.

The 'parliamentary' Commission (Fitzmaurice 1994) does in fact exhibit a strong and growing tendency to act as a representative government, with public access to internal Commission activity, the existence of party links and the significance of parliamentary scrutiny having grown massively in the 1990s. After Maastricht, when during the difficult ratification process it became clear that the functional nature of the European project of the 1980s had left the people behind, all the institutions have sought to remedy the 'democratic deficit'. In the intervening period, the Commission, in particular, has felt the need to respond to the critique of technocracy and democratic deficit. An elaborate programme of greater openness, transparency and subsidiarity has been the result (Preston 1995).

This state of affairs demonstrates that the development of a direct Commission–public relationship is accelerating. The various channels – the EP, the intermediary social groups and organisations, the provision of access to, and certainty about, administrative procedures within the Commission – are combined attempts at making the Commission more accountable to citizens. But this is not an easy process, and the Commission still has a long way to go before not only relating directly to the public, but actually transmitting the impression that citizens are in any meaningful way able to hold the Commission to account. For the time being, a large gap remains between what would be a comprehensive system of citizen participation and the current opportunity structure. The critique of the unsatisfactory degree to which the EU deals with the issue of citizenship is echoed in the contributions by Nentwich, Kostakopoulou and Kuper to this volume. But, as we see in this chapter, the search for remedies to address this questionable situation raises problems at the level of institutional legitimacy.

By contrast, the presence of an 'intergovernmental' Commission is demonstrated by a number of unique features. One is that the appointment structure in the upper echelons of the Commission appears to be dominated by concerns about nationality more than political affiliation. The appointment of the Commissioners themselves is, of course, explicitly based on nationality. Hardly less explicit is the role of Commissioners as a link between national political systems and the EU bureaucracy. While on the one hand operating as something like ambassadors of the EU when they return to the national political circuit, they are also widely regarded as the most appropriate entry point for political interests from the member state level when they seek influence in Brussels. The increasing incidence of voting in the college of Commissioners regularly sees the Commission divided along national lines to the point where the line-up of ministers in the Council and the Commissioners in the college behind declared national positions is taken for granted. A further aspect of the Commission's internal intergovernmentalism is that much of the EU's regulatory policy making is conducted in the ambit of comitology, in which the Commission participates, but which is strongly guided by member states' interests in maintaining control over the policy-making process.

At the same time, the technocratic character of the Commission has not really subsided. In a number of areas, the Commission has tried to enhance its independent character. While some areas of Commission activity have been opened to the influence of party politics, others have been removed from partisan politics. One aspect here is the growth and rising intensity of scientific advice on which the Commission relies (Joerges 1996b). Another is the Commission's activity in the fields of monetary or competition policy which are based on institutional independence. With respect to the latter, one observer has complained that the Commission appears as 'the master of its own procedural destiny' (Brent 1995). At the same time, the Commission finds the transition from its more traditional role as 'policy entrepreneur' to that of a 'policy manager', rather a difficult move to make (Laffan 1997).

Since the Commission cannot hope to satisfy fully the demands of democratic legitimacy and member state interests, there is merit in the search for alternative models. As a way of escaping the contradictions of multiple accountability, greater institutional independence is being considered as a 'third way' of legitimising the Commission's activity. In a sense, it means turning the potentially paralysing effect of having to account to two 'masters' into a virtue. The aim would be to remove the Commission's regulatory activity from the floor of partisan politics, and to achieve legitimation through greater independence rather than greater accountability (Majone 1994). In that respect, the Commission forms the core of an EU that can be seen as the 'independent fourth branch of government' (Majone 1993).

Recent developments indicate this path as one of potential in the future design of the Commission. A number of independent 'Decentralised Agencies' were set up in 1993, even though this was mainly for low-key tasks like the licensing of medicinal products and the exchange of governmental information in a variety of sectors. There are demands for parts of the Commission to be turned into independent agencies. There have been repeated calls, for example, for taking merger control out of what is seen as too political a process of decision making (Ehlermann 1994). Others go further and demand that the Commission be split up into various such independent agencies: a European Trade Commission, a European Environmental Agency, a European Cartel Office, etc. (Vibert 1995). The case for such an 'un-bundling' of the Commission is argued with reference to the increasing diversity of tasks, and – again – the need to remove delicate decisions from political influences.

This does not seem to find much sympathy with most national delegations and the Commission itself (Council of the European Union 1995, European Commission 1996). Clearly, greater institutional independence, linked to a more explicit administrative code of conduct, can only be one element in the legitimation of Commission activity. Greater use of comitology, a structured relationship to the EP and more direct contact and communication with individual citizens will also have to be features of the future Commission. In other words, the Commission will continue to be a hybrid organisation, combining supranational and intergovernmental elements.

Conclusion: squaring the triangle?

In all its complexity, the Amsterdam Treaty appears at first sight to have pushed the Commission along the 'parliamentary' avenue. With the EP achieving greater co-decision powers *vis-à-vis* the Council and enhancing its powers *vis-à-vis* the Commission as part of a revised investiture procedure, the expectation is that the Commission will become more accountable to the EP (Nentwich and Falkner 1997). That is certainly the impression of those within the Commission who are responsible for parliamentary liaison and who have seen their workload increase exponentially in the past few years. Yet, at the same time, the clauses in the new Treaty which govern the number of Commissioners tell a different story. The larger countries have linked the reduction in the number of 'their' Commissioners from two to one to the reform of voting in the Council – a clear sign (if any was needed) that the future legitimacy of the Commission hinges on the element of member state representation that goes on within it.

There is, in fact, very little to suggest that the conflict between 'parliamentary' and 'intergovernmental' modes will not continue to coexist within a Commission that is becoming more internally diverse and divided as its responsibilities widen. The 'third way' – a Commission that is more 'independent' in relying on its unique procedural expertise and its central position as a broker among the multiple policy networks of the EU – will therefore also be necessary to balance the tension between overall centralisation, which is induced by the move towards majoritarianism, and fragmentation, which results from the importance of national positions within the Commission. A degree of independence from either of these forces is what might provide some slight relief for an institution that might otherwise be tempted (or forced) down one or other of these slippery slopes – with potentially disastrous results for the legitimacy of the EU as a whole, as discussed in the first part of this chapter.

Even as it is, the presence of these three very different organisational modes within the same institution will lead to internal contradiction and to inconsistencies in policy output. But to the extent that European regulatory activity in the future will always require member state support, wider public acceptance and a degree of independent authority, internal contradiction and the lack of coherence are the price the Commission will have to pay to remain the key actor in the development of European governance and to contribute positively to the legitimation of the EU as a whole.

References

Barry, B. (1989) *Democracy, Power and Justice*, Oxford: Clarendon Press.

Brent, R. (1995) 'The Building of Leviathan – The Changing Role of the European Commission in Competition Cases', *International and Comparative Law Quarterly* 44(2): 255–79.

Council of the European Union (1995) *Reflection Group's Report*, Brussels.

Dahl, R. A. (1994) 'A Democratic Dilemma: System Effectiveness versus Citizen Participation', *Political Science Quarterly* 109(1): 23–32.

Dehousse, R. (1995) 'Institutional Reform in the European Community: Are there Alternatives to the Majoritarian Avenue?', *West European Politics* 18(3): 121–36.

Ehlermann, D. (1994) 'Zur Wettbewerbspolitik und zum Wettbewerbsrecht der Europäischen Union', in E. Kantzenbach *et al.* (eds), *Hamburger Jahrbuch für Wirtschafts- und Gesellschaftspolitik*, Tübingen: J.C.B. Mohr, pp. 255–80.

European Commission (1996) *Opinion for the 1996 Intergovernmental Conference*, Luxembourg.

Fitzmaurice, J. (1994) 'The European Commission', in A. Duff *et al.* (eds), *Maastricht and Beyond*, London: Routledge, pp. 179–89.

Held, D. (1992) 'Democracy: From City-States to a Cosmopolitan Order?', *Political Studies* 40(Special): 10–39.

Joerges, C. (1996a) 'Political Science and the Role of Law in the Process of European Integration', *European Law Journal* 2(1): 115–33.

Joerges, C. (1996b) *Integrating Scientific Expertise into Regulatory Decision-Making*, EUI Working Paper RSC No. 96/10, Florence: European University Institute.

Kincaid, J. (1995) 'Values and Value Tradeoffs in Federalism', *Publius* 25(2): 29–44.

Laffan, B. (1997) 'From Policy-Entrepreneur to Policy-Manager: the Challenge facing the European Commission', *Journal of European Public Policy* 4(3): 422–38.

Lipset, S. M. (1994) 'The Social Requisites of Democracy Revisited', *American Sociological Review* 59(1): 1–22.

Majone, G. (1993) *The European Community: An 'Independent Fourth Branch of Government'?*, EUI Working Paper SPS No. 93/9, Florence: European University Institute.

Majone, G. (1994) *Independence v. Accountability? Non-Majoritarian Institutions and Democratic Government in Europe*, EUI Working Paper SPS No. 94/3, Florence: European University Institute.

Mazey, S. and Richardson, J. (1994) 'The Commission and the Lobby', in G. Edwards and D. Spence (eds), *The European Commission*, London: Longman, pp. 169–201.

Milward, A. *et al.* (1992) *The European Rescue of the Nation-state*, London: Routledge.

Moravcsik, A. (1993) 'Preferences and Power in the European Community: A Liberal Intergovernmentalist Approach', *Journal of Common Market Studies* 31(4): 473–523.

Nentwich, M. and Falkner, G. (1977) 'The Treaty of Amsterdam: Towards a New Institutional Balance', *European Integration online Papers* (EIoP), Vol. 1, No. 015; http://eiop.or.at/eiop/texte/1997-015a.htm.

Philip Morris Institute for Public Policy Research (ed.), (1995) *What Future for the European Commission* Brussels: PMIPPR.

Pollack, M. (1994) 'Creeping Competence: The Expanding Agenda of the European Community', *Journal of Public Policy* 14(2): 95–145.

Preston, C. (1995), 'Obstacles to Enlargement: The Classical Community Method and the Prospects for a Wider Europe', *Journal of Common Market Studies* 33(3): 451–63.

Rasmussen, H. (1988) 'Between Self-Restraint and Activism: A Judicial Policy for the European Court', *European Law Review* 13(1): 28–38.

Tassin, E. (1992) 'Europe: A Political Community?', in C. Mouffe (ed.), *Dimensions of Radical Democracy – Pluralism, Citizenship, Community*, London: Verso, pp. 169–92.

Vibert, F. (1995) 'The Case for "Unbundling" the Commission in Philip Morris Institute for Public Policy Research', *What Future for the European Commission*, Brussels: PMIPPR, pp. 16–20.

Wæver, O. *et al.* (1993) *Identity, Migration and the New Security Agenda in Europe*, London: Pinter.

Wallace, W. and Smith, J. (1995) 'Democracy or Technocracy? European Integration and the Problem of Popular Consent', *West European Politics* 18(3): 137–57.

Weale, A. (1995) 'From Little England to Democratic Europe?', *New Community* 21(2): 215–25.

Weiler, J. (1995) 'The State "über alles" – Demos, Telos and the German Maastricht Decision', *European Law Journal* 1(3): 219–58.

Westlake, M. (1994) *The Commission and the Parliament – Partners and Rivals in the European Policy-making Process*, London: Butterworth.

8 How to democratise a multi-level, multi-dimensional polity

Heidrun Abromeit

The problem

The European Union is a puzzle for political scientists. It is an elusive thing, escaping classification: neither a federation nor a confederation (whatever the difference between both may be),[1] neither (solely) territorially nor sectorally defined; nor is it a mere (cooperative) addition of states. Above all – and so far there seems to be unanimity among scholars – it is no 'state', nor will it ever be one. Instead the EU qualifies as something *sui generis*, a multi-level and 'multiperspectival polity' (Ruggie 1993: 172) and as such a 'post modern' entity (Ruggie 1993, Diez 1995).

Such reasoning is less removed from reality than one might think. In fact the European polity is made up of the formal institutions of the Community, of the member state governments, of subnational units (in some cases; see Marks 1993), as well as of sectoral policy networks including not only governments on the various layers but organisations of various types and various degrees of 'europeanization' (see Héritier *et al.* 1994). The outcomes of their complex interactions are European laws and policies, which means that this 'non-state' exerts state-like powers with direct impact on the peoples of the member states. What characterises this institutional–organisational mêlée above all is (1) the lack of 'constitutional' order – whether it be hierarchical or horizontal or otherwise – and transparency, as well as (2) the lack of legitimisation: the existing formal–informal setting does not envisage any active role for the people. The latter deficiency, of course, cannot be repaired without the former: effective democratic participation as well as control hinge on the clarity of responsibilities and the transparency of decision making. At the same time (as even the notoriously optimistic *Eurobarometer* tells us), both deficiencies have already given rise to considerable disillusionment and discontent.

What is needed, since Maastricht I, is not so much a proper definition of this new type of polity (state or non-state), but the proper identification and assignment of its elements, with the aim of detecting the hidden order underlying the EU's 'emerging political disorder' (Marks 1992: 221) – which in fact Maastricht II did not help to clarify. The task is, in other words, one of modelling a multi-layer/multi-perspectival political system, depicting the structure of the existing mixture of decision-making institutions and policy networks, of 'statist' elements and intergovernmental as well as intersocietal cooperation, in this way clarifying it and indicating the places – the crucial 'intervention points' – where participatory elements can and should be introduced. Hence, the conceptual task meets practical needs.

Inadequate solutions

At 'official' European level, three main solutions to the constitutional problem have been debated so far: (1) the upgrading of the European Parliament to a chamber with real legislative powers; (2) the participation of the (subnational) regions in the EU legislative process by means of a third chamber; (3) progress towards a federation modelled after the German, 'cooperative' fashion. Whatever arguments may be brought forward in favour of these solutions (and there are some at least for the first two of them), on the whole they seem inadequate to tackle the problem of multi-level, multi-dimensional decision making, even if combined with each other.[2]

Upgrading the Parliament

An upgrading of the EP, for example as proposed by Føllesdal in this volume, presents itself, at first sight, as the likeliest remedy for the democratic deficits of the EU. Democracy, however, is not identical with parliamentarianism (and to think in these categories represents a misconception of the non-state, *sui generis* character of the EU, anyhow). If parliaments are to act as guarantors of democracy, certain conditions have to be met. A parliament has to be based on some sort of 'collective identity' as well as on a modicum of cultural homogeneity; it has to be embedded into intermediate structures (see Grimm 1994: 38ff.) – parties, groups, 'public opinion' – which run horizontally through the respective society (and unite it, in a way, although they represent societal conflicts); and there has to exist a strong link with the government, to make the latter 'responsible to the people'. Where these conditions are absent, parliaments may, on the one hand, be reduced to merely symbolic quality, whether they have some legislative powers or not. Where, on the other hand, homogeneity is lacking, they may be 'dictatorial' instead of democratic in so far as the normal parliamentary procedure of majority rule generates structural minorities and is unable – or, more likely, unwilling – to deal with their problems. And finally, in a case such as that of the EU, strengthening the EP means centralisation. Even if there were European parties worth speaking of, majority rule at the centre would, as a matter of course, leave regional interests out of account. To date, the main cleavages in 'European society' are territorial and a parliament is not the place to represent them. As a consequence, European parliamentarians deal with either symbolic or superficial issues which are of little interest to the peoples they should represent. Or they engage in log-rolling and package deals themselves, like the governments and the member states' representatives in the other

European institutions do, which makes them unfit to control the latter. It is very much to be doubted that the EU type of government could ever take the form of 'parliament supremacy' after the 'Westminster' fashion (see Hogan, as early as 1967: 205ff.). Should the EU ever develop into a federalist state (which is also to be doubted), a well-working, strong parliament would never be more than a part of the solution.

The Committee of the Regions

In order to tackle the problem of democratic legitimisation whilst recognising the territorial basis of European politics a Committee of the Regions has been invented to develop eventually into a third chamber (in the event that the Council of Ministers should ever mutate into a second one). At present one might say that the Committee of the Regions is a body in search of a job: it may be 'heard', but it does not participate in legislative decisions; it may not even apply to the European Court of Justice. If it were upgraded, however, it would be necessary for its members to have equal legitimisation – that is, to be 'true' representatives of their regions – as well as equal standing, meaning that those regions would be equally recognised by their respective nation state governments. Since most of the EU member states are unitary states, this precondition is flatly unrealistic. Representatives of non-existent subnational units can be expected to act either as (additional) delegates of their national governments or as parochial politicians; either way they would find it hard to gain any political importance, to say nothing of filling a democratic deficit. Hence, this device is another case of symbolic politics – as indeed the CoR's practice so far shows.

A federal solution?

Some sort of (con-)federalism is clearly indicated when it comes to conceptualising the future Europe. Somewhat lopsidedly, the European debate in this respect centres around the German variant which has rightly been dubbed a 'unitary federalism' (Hesse 1962) or even a 'hidden unitary state' (Abromeit 1992). Its most conspicuous feature is a lack of (legislative and fiscal) autonomy of the *Länder* (mainly due to the constitutional device of 'concurring legislation', i.e. competing legislative competences), for which their governments are compensated by their participation in central decision making via the Bundesrat (which is not a parliamentary second chamber in the strict sense but an assembly of governments). The resulting 'joint policy-making' (Scharpf 1988) has been much criticised as being both undemocratic and inefficient; there is no need to recapitulate the criticisms here. Unfortunately, European practice has gone some way in the same direction already: by institutionalising a sort of 'concurring powers' in the shape of the (mostly misunderstood) principle of subsidiarity;[3] by shifting unnecessarily detailed legislative powers to the European level; by practising *in extenso* 'joint policy-making' between governments, including even those on the communal level (see Scharpf 1994). This, in fact, has created the existing muddle out of which constitutional remedies are now sought.

Elements of a multi-level, multi-dimensional polity model

A contractarian approach

In trying to find adequate solutions to the constitutional problem, it is advisable to go back to contract theory which is the common root both of democracy and of federalism. Historically as well as ideally, the 'classical' federations were created by treaties; not historically but ideally democracies rest on the fiction of the social contract. The core of contracts is less the notion of 'exchange' (as rational choice theory suggests) than the notion that participants in a contract have to agree; otherwise contracts would not come into existence. The main point in a contractarian approach is, consequently, the insistence on every participant's *right to give or withhold consent*, the reverse side of which is the ban on outvoting minorities. Any departure from this rule produces external effects; such externalities grow with the size of the minorities outvoted. Hence, any digression from *unanimity* rule needs special justification (see Buchanan and Tullock 1962: 70ff., 81). If previously agreed decision-making rules, other than unanimity, prove in practice to be damaging to one or various minorities' aims or interests (i.e. if externalities turn out to be too high), these minorities ought to have the right to revoke their consent.

Actually, this specific contractarian approach reaches further than Buchanan's 'marginalist' interpretation of contract theory (Buchanan and Tullock 1962: 319f.), which envisages the right to withhold consent only in the case of changes in the existing set of (procedural) rules. Arguably this marginalist view cannot adequately meet the needs of a loose, non-state super-structure like the EU, over-arching rather heterogeneous (and even partly unwilling) societies. For in this case we are not dealing with *one* type of contract only, the constitutional one, but with at least three: (1) the original treaty between the member states which was agreed 'vicariously' by their governments (mostly without asking their peoples); (2) the constitutional contracts of the member states (as well as of the organisations taking part in EU decision making in their own right), since these can be violated by decisions on the European level; (3) the 'every-day' contracts resulting from negotiations between member states (and groups), gradually expanding the field of European policies and again apt to violate the peoples' rights arising from 'type 2' contracts. It would render the right to withhold consent purely fictitious if it were to be restricted to the 'type 1' contract.

Contract theory is strictly individualistic. In contrast, federalist theory deals with territorial units, while in reality decisions are made by group representatives. Hence, a contractarian approach has somehow to bridge the gap between individual and group consent. As will be seen below, I propose to do so by direct-democratic 'outlets': the right of (territorial or sectoral) group members to contradict their representatives.

In order to conceptualise the decision making of federal systems in particular, the theory of fiscal federalism is a helpful tool. It is closely related to contract theory in so far as it makes use of the unanimity rule in allocating decision-making powers to various state levels. Decisions can only be taken at central state level when at that level unanimity can be reached; they have to be taken at regional level if at that level unanimity can be reached; and they may not be taken at all when there is no unanimity at all (Neumann 1971: 500ff.). Again, this implies that legislative powers can be won only with the consent of all participants in the process and that such powers may be annulled if unanimity is lost.

Territorial and sectoral representation

The existing decision-making set of the EU consists of (1) institutions with legislative and executive powers (the Commission and the Council of Ministers as well as, in part, the European Court), (2) institutions of symbolic value (the EP, the Committee of the Regions and the Economic and Social Council), (3) policy networks composed of the Commission (always) and various as well as varying (collective) actors such as state governments, regional authorities and interest groups. Decision-making procedures include the widest possible range of rules: simple majority (in the EP and – as yet very rarely – in the Council), absolute majority (in the EP), qualified majority (in the Council where in those cases state votes are weighted) and unanimity (as yet in the Council in quite a number of cases and as a matter of fact in the policy networks where 'bargaining' instead of straight voting is the rule). In fact, if not in theory, the latter decision-making rule still dominates the status quo. This ought to please contractarians, at first sight.

However, various snags intrude. Generally speaking, bargaining systems are suspected of being inefficient and unduly expensive: in order to win the consent of all participants in a network (as well as to pay due respect to the varying intensities of their preferences) log-rolling takes place and 'pork barrel' solutions come to be normal practice, producing as likely as not vast externalities for all those who do not participate. At the same time, such systems are said to be undemocratic: they operate clandestinely, their outcomes may differ widely from the interests of those whom the bargainers represent, and no one takes responsibility for the results. Not only in practice but in theory as well policy networks seem to cause democratic deficits; as yet one looks in vain for a convincing normative theory of political responsibility and democratic participation in complex bargaining systems (Scharpf 1992: 108). The third flaw in the EU's policy-making set is that at least at official level all non-EU actors are dependent on the nation states. From this it follows that even if unanimity rule is practised in the Council, European decision making continually leaves out a considerable number of minorities which will, as likely as not, gradually develop into structural ones.

The dominant position of the nation state governments is a problem particularly for the regions in federalist member states. Of course direct links between the regions and the Commission exist, at least since the reform of the European Structural Funds of 1988 prescribed a 'three-sided partnership of the Commission, member states, and regional authorities in drawing up, financing, and monitoring Community Support Frameworks' (Marks 1992: 211). But as Marks so rightly observes (Marks 1992: 215): 'To the extent that subnational units of governance exist in the Community, they do so at the behest of the member states. They have no legal standing independent of the states of which they are a part.' (For various countries, see Jones and Keating 1995.) Furthermore, it is only the regions' governments/executives with which the Commission deals, and only with respect to economic disparities. They are recognised as lobbyists of their regions, not of any other – let alone constitutional – status. At the same time, this implies that several local authorities can join to form a 'region' and may outflank and outdo (for instance) the *Länder* in the Commission's lobbies.

Obviously one of the structural features of European policy making is its regional dimension; what is lacking, however, is the 'proper' regional representation. Considerations of democratic legitimacy as well as of efficiency (see the final subsection below) suggest that representing regions solely by government executives is not sufficient. On the other hand, we have already seen that the newly created Committee of the Regions is no adequate solution either, especially since Committee members are not nominated by the regions themselves, but again by member state governments; to make matters worse, their numbers do not even roughly correspond to the number of existing subnational units (see Article 198 TEC). If justice shall be done to regional identities and diversities as well as to the constitutional status of subnational units in federal states, it is necessary to break up the 'constitutional monopoly' of the nation states (Marks 1992: 217) and look for devices of direct regional representation.

The other structural feature of European policy making is the sectoral dimension, so far embodied in informal policy networks. Here proper representation is lacking as well. What has been said about the Committee of the Regions may be said, *cum grano salis*, of the Economic and Social Council: as a whole it has but a symbolic role, and its members are appointed by the Council of Ministers, i.e. by the member state governments, with different vote weights attached to nations instead of allotted according to the importance of sectors (Article 194). At the same time, the link between European lobbyists and (potential) members of sectoral groups is rather dubious, at any rate definitely more so than that between the citizens and authorities of regions. Hence, in order to legitimise European policy making, some sort of effective as well as direct sectoral representation is called for, too.

To sum up, the EU's existing decision-making structure as a whole is marked by a high degree of complexity which partly results, in fact, from the laudable aims (1) to take into account the various levels and dimensions of its polity and (2) to make allowances for the varying intensities of its members' needs and preferences. In addition to its being complex, this (super-)structure lacks transparency (and hence is uncontrollable), has lost touch with regional or sectoral 'grassroots', and is probably overcostly. Furthermore, it weakens parliamentarism and democratic legitimacy within member states: the decisive actors in all networks and at all levels are governments and administrators who, in pledging their words, render inner-state parliamentary debates pointless.

A system of veto rights

What we are looking for is a decision-making *structure* combining the regional and the sectoral dimension, producing democratic legitimacy but avoiding pitfalls such as lack of transparency, independence of agents from their 'principals', log-rolling and other decision-making pathologies. As for the decision-making *rule*, contract theory as well as the theory of federalism teach us that the more heterogeneous the society is, the closer the rule has to get to unanimity. Yet the greater the majorities needed the likelier are, normally, either log-rolling or non-decision. This lands us with a dilemma which is never easily to be solved (see Dahl 1994) but is of particular poignancy in a complicated 'emerging polity' like the European one.

One way of approximating unanimity is to add more chambers to the legislative process. Assuming for the moment that the EU would develop into a federalist state, a second chamber would have to be reserved for the representation of the member states, the more so since most of them are unitary states. Additional regional and sectoral representation would then call for third and fourth chambers. It is difficult to imagine four-chamber systems working. Since both regions and organised interests of European societies differ widely in character, status and power, the likeliest result would be the domination over the third and the fourth by the second chamber. So not much would have been gained in additional legitimacy, but a lot lost in decision-making effectiveness.

If the creation of additional chambers, and if qualified or 'super-majorities' in the existing ones do not produce the desired results, these may be achieved the other way round. Unanimity can be defined as the absence of dissent; hence near-unanimity can be reached *ex negativo*, by vesting groups or units with direct-democratic veto rights. This device allows for regional and sectoral 'representation' (a representation without representatives, one might say) as well as for flexibility; it legitimises Community decision making while avoiding the need to establish a distinct state and 'state-like' institutions beforehand.

The general idea is that when an EU policy has been agreed upon by the existing policy-making set, previously defined groups/units (see below) will have the right to contradict it if a (qualified) majority of their members decide against it in a referendum. In such a case the region or group would not 'opt out'; instead the policy would not be adopted at EU level, but whatever issue it was would be dealt with separately by the member states. A negative referendum would be a fairly effective blockage too; while 'pork barrel' solutions might still occur, log-rolling would hardly be feasible.

Various questions will, of course, have to be answered to make such a direct-democratic device appear plausible. Three of them will be debated subsequently:

(1) How can the respective units be defined? (2) What sorts of decisions will be subject to the referendum? (3) Who may initiate such referendums and which majorities should be needed at which levels? (For details see Abromeit 1998: ch. 5.)

1   On the regional dimension, the question of which units are to be endowed with the veto right poses comparatively little difficulty. It is an innate right of federalist states' subunits. They are 'states' themselves; and they are so not least because their people feel like minorities to be protected against nation state majorities. Such protection ought to be retained against majorities at even higher levels. All other regions, that is those without autonomous status, could qualify for the veto only if granted the right by their respective state. For some time, this would constitute a 'two-class' system of regions. Just this asymmetry, however, might trigger off further decentralisation in heretofore unitary states.

It is more difficult to distinguish sectoral units. Systematically, the definition is simple: like regions the sectoral units should be marked by their 'collective identity'. The problem is to find out empirically who 'identifies'. One advantage of including the sectoral groups formally in the decision-making structure (apart from making the proceedings of policy networks more transparent) lies in their multinational character, their potential independence from nation states; they are the actors who are most liable to reduce the latter's dominance. But the same amorphousness which allows such independence is a definite disadvantage when it comes to identifying the members which may then be called to participate in the referendums. Certainly it would be unwise to restrict the quality of being a sectoral unit member to those who are organised in the sector's interest groups. As a starting point, I suggest the inclusion of (a) not just one single interest group, but whole networks (in so far as they are sectoral) or 'markets', embracing, as a rule, an 'opposite side' (which will in many cases be that of consumers), and (b) the reference (or 'latent') groups of the respective organisations, that is those whom the latter can mobilise.

2   It would be equally unwise to apply unanimity rule – or veto rights – to each and every decision. The minimum subjected to it, as defined by contractarians, is any decision altering decision-making rules. In federations one further type of decision at least qualifies for the strict rule: any decision which alters the allocation of powers between state levels. In a multi-level community such as the EU this can be put more precisely as any decision which touches upon the regions' spheres of autonomy. In practice this means that any attempt to expand the EU's legislative powers would be put to a very severe test indeed. In order to block clandestine expansion by way of an 'implied powers' doctrine (as already embodied in Article 235 TEC), as well as to redress developments which have proven detrimental to some regions' interests, referendums concerning the allocation of powers should always be possible. On principle, that is, the much talked-about *acquis communautaire* is not to be conceptualised as untouchable.

Again, to define the 'intervention points' is more difficult in the case of sectoral units. Wherever sectoral spheres of autonomy exist (as for instance in industrial relations), any alteration in these should qualify for a referendum. Sectoral groups, however, are usually not distinguished by 'entrenched rights'; instead they will frequently be united by rather intense preferences, or else strong feelings of 'shared risks', both of which should entitle them to veto adverse policies. This may or may not have the effect of protecting the status quo, but will of course imply a strong bias against EU regulation. Yet such a bias may turn out to be a small evil compared with the external costs imposed on others by groups successfully demanding regulations in their own favour.

3   As for procedures, the petition for those blocking referendums in the case of the regional units could be initiated by anybody who can mobilise a quorum still to be defined. Since membership in sectoral units is considerably less obvious, it is probably sensible to leave it to organised groups (or parts of those), including NGOs, to try to mobilise a sufficient part of their reference group(s). The latter, however, should principally be conceptualised as one transcending nation state borders. If the need to mobilise a sectoral 'public' of various languages puts sectoral units at a disadvantage, this is made up for by the organisational advantage interest groups have, for instance, over regional *ad hoc* groups.

Of course one will have to think carefully about the quorum for the petition and for the referendum proper as well as about the respective levels at which majorities are to be won. On the one hand there is the principle of not outvoting those with preferences of higher intensity; according to that, no quorum should be required for the referendum proper. On the other hand there is the fear that groups that are too small might acquire completely disproportionate blocking power. A first suggestion is the following: (a) if petitions of sectoral groups are to lead to cross-national referendums, a simple majority of participants ought to be sufficient for the veto – provided the majority is in fact multinational; (b) in case of the veto of subnational units it seems to be reasonable to ask for a qualified majority to make it successful; it should then be followed up by a second referendum, this time successful with the simple majority of participants, in the member state the regional unit belongs to. The rationale behind this procedure can be stated as follows: by this method the region would be obliged to prove that its entrenched rights had been violated and that people felt keenly about it; this keen minority would then have a fair chance to prevail over a lukewarm national minority.

The problem of decision-making efficiency

The model sketched here allows for democratic participation on a regional as well as on a sectoral basis, thus reflecting the multi-dimensionality of EU policy making; it meets the requirements of a 'non-state' with incongruent territorial and functional domains. Without prescribing a 'statist' development of the EU, it would as well allow for progress from the nineteenth-century model of the 'nationalities' state' (Lepsius 1991). To prevent misunderstanding, note that the model does not require any alteration in the existing decision-making set, let alone its abolition. The decision set would simply be complemented by non-governmental veto rights.

The first and main objection raised against it will be that of lacking decision-making efficiency: (1) this way too few (if any) problems would be soluble at European level; (2) the indirect unanimity rule would cause asymmetries; (3) the whole procedure would be much too time consuming.

1   In fact it is to be expected that direct-democratic veto rights would permit 'Brussels' less detailed regulation than it has come into the habit of issuing up to now.[4] However, not only Euro-sceptics feel that the 'Eurocrats' are overdoing it; the discontent in the member societies is tangible. Veto (instead of opt-out) rights would induce the EU to play a less active role, to confine regulation to fewer policy areas and, above all, to restrict regulation only to frameworks.

2   The indirect unanimity rule of the direct-democratic veto will in some respects prove less inefficient than the existing form of unanimity in the Council and in policy networks. Referendums, if they do occur, may break up package deals; instead, with the aim to win voters European politicians might be induced to develop plausible concepts for single policies. At the same time, it is difficult to imagine log-rolling going on between voters in referendums. The inefficiencies ascribed to unanimity rule and 'super-majorities' do apply when delegates and especially when government members are the ones to give their consent and bargain for it (see Scharpf 1988; see also Weale, this volume); they do so much less when people are asked directly.

All the same, the 'default condition' is valid in both cases, which means that the envisaged decision-making model would in fact cause at least one asymmetry, which is the protection of the status quo. But 'progress' can be defined in various ways, and progress in European 'harmonisation' may, for a considerable part of Europe, mean a step backwards in, for instance, social policy or environmental protection. The veto rights would protect the status quo only in the formal sense of – possibly – slowing down the pace of Europeanisation.

3   There is little to be said about the time factor: the amount of time needed to reach decisions at European level will not be much increased; with the introduction of co-decision it is high already. The suggested veto would, however, introduce an additional element of uncertainty into decision making, since agreements reached by European institutions could be revoked.

On the whole, it is not to be expected that the model outlined would cause any more inefficiencies than the existing policy-making set; in effect, it is likely to produce one or two inefficiencies less, not least due to the higher degree of acceptance resulting from the possibility of direct participation. Democracy creates its own kind of efficiency. Yet democracy takes its time, and it takes more time the more heterogeneous the society is. This is the main point: any argument about decision-making efficiency has to start from the character of the society, the amount and sort of conflicts dividing it, and the nature of the problems to be solved. The more complex the situational factors are, the more complex central decision-making structures will have to be; otherwise they will produce externalities and with them inefficiencies, no matter how streamlined they are and how little time they consume. But while in heterogeneous societies composed of units with different cultural identities acceptable decision making at central level is inevitably difficult, the need for central decision making is limited here as well (see Blöchliger and Frey 1992). The need for 'harmonisation' felt by bureaucrats at the centre may be felt much less by people on the peripheries. And what is valid for federal states must be even more so for a loose, as yet mainly sectorally defined, community like the EU. If the lesson to be learnt from democratic theory and practice is that democracy 'takes its time', the lesson from federalist theory and practice is that diversity has to be endured.[5]

Open questions

Democratic decision-making systems have to meet three demands: (1) depict the relevant conflicts of the respective unit; (2) be effective in the sense of producing 'relevant' decisions that are accepted by and implemented in that unit while avoiding undue external costs; (3) allow for participation of unit members. The model sketched here has been concerned mainly with the third demand; it deals with the first demand in so far as its aim has been to combine representation of the three main sources of conflict in Europe: nation state interests, regional interests and sectoral interests. As for the request of decision-making efficiency the argument has been – somewhat perfunctorily – chiefly the negative one that existing decision-making structures are rather inefficient, anyhow.

Not only in this latter respect do a lot of questions remain open. Many of these centre around the problem of sectoral representation. The theoretical as well as empirical difficulties of distinguishing sectoral units and identifying their members are obvious. The foremost question in the minds of readers will be: why bother about it? Why not go ahead at once with Europe-wide referendums, setting aside the tricky problem of defining subgroups? There are three reasons for not doing so:

1   The salience of the sectoral dimension of European politics. Potent sectoral policy networks do exist, and it is high time their bases are made visible.
2   The lack of genuine 'European majorities'. European society consists of a great number of minorities; every majority found in any of its institutions is artificial in the sense that to reach it bargaining and coalition building have to take place and minority interests have to be sacrificed. The model

outlined here is based on the notion that all minorities have rights that deserve protection; but how are they to be protected if direct-democratic vetoes have to be backed by an all-European majority?

3   The fundamentally European character of sectoral groups. Unlike the regions in federal states the sectoral groups are principally independent of nation states. In the shape of the European issue networks a new 'transnational' actor has entered the political arena; high time for this actor to find a legitimisation of his/her own.

Unfortunately the threefold need for sectoral representation clashes with the contractarian stipulation to avoid externalities. A sectoral veto will unavoidably cause external costs, a problem which will be exacerbated by the indisputable fact that organised groups differ widely in power, resources and mobilising chances.

The regional veto poses some questions, too. For what will happen with/within the unitary states? Their governments and parliaments will not be easily convinced that it might be a good idea to grant veto rights to regions. And what about the – as yet very few – 'Euro-regions'?

The major justification for the veto rights is the minorities' supposed high intensity of preferences which ought to be respected by lukewarm majorities. But another of the open questions is how to operationalise the intensity of preferences. Will it suffice to take (as the Swiss do) the actual participation in referendums as the one and only indicator?

More questions of this sort can easily be listed. But one of the most important ones is that of finding actors in national as well as European arenas who are ready and willing to deal with the task of democratisation.

Notes

1   For the German Constitutional Court the EU qualifies as something in between: a 'Staatenverbund ohne Kompetenzkompetenz' (BVerfGE 1993: 155–213).

2   The 'Reflection Group' preparing the Turin Intergovernmental Conference, however, was more modest in its proposals. In so far as the proposals were structural, they centred on the object of attaining a modicum of 'clarity' in simplifying some of the EU's decision-making procedures and in reducing their number (see Report of the Reflection Group, 1995: 84ff.). The outcome of the 1996 IGC which came to its close in June 1997 in Amsterdam was even more modest in this respect, with the one exception of the move to extend the EP's legislative powers.

3   After Maastricht II this principle by no means will be clearer: it took the drafters of the Amsterdam Treaty two pages to explain what Article 3b TEC might mean.

4   This may be questionable in the long run. European politicians might, in anticipation of possible vetoes, try to respect the interests of even small groups and risk detailed regulation even further. However, these might run the risk of being blocked even more frequently.

5   It has become popular among European politicians to warn of 'the slowest ship determining the speed of the convoy' (thus Helmut Kohl in a speech of January 1996). However, if the fastest ship is to determine the speed, there won't be any convoy.

References

Abromeit, H. (1992) *Der verkappte Einheitsstaat*, Opladen: Leske+Budrich.

Abromeit, H. (1998) *Democracy in Europe. Legitimising Politics in a Non-State*, Oxford: Berghahn Books.

Blöchliger, H. and Frey, R. L. (1992) 'Der schweizerische Föderalismus: Ein Modell für den institutionellen Aufbau der Europäischen Union?', *Aussenwirtschaft* 47(4): 515–48.

Buchanan, J. M. and Tullock, G. (1962) *The Calculus of Consent*, Ann Arbor, MI: University of Michigan Press.

BVerfGE (1993) *Bundesverfassungsgericht, Entscheidungen*, Vol. 89.

Dahl, R. A. (1994) 'A Democratic Dilemma: System Effectiveness versus Citizen Participation', *Political Science Quaterly* 109(1): 23–34.

Diez, T. (1995) *Neues Europa, altes Modell*, Frankfurt a.M.: Haag+Herchen.

Grimm, D. (1994) *Braucht Europa eine Verfassung?*, München: Carl Friedrich von Siemens-Stiftung.

Héritier, A. *et al.* (1994) *Die Veränderung von Staatlichkeit in Europa*, Opladen: Leske+Budrich.

Hesse, K. (1962) *Der unitarische Bundesstaat*, Karlsruhe: C. F. Müller.

Hogan, Willard N. (1967) *Representative Government and European Integration*, Lincoln, NE: University of Nebraska Press.

Jones, B. and Keating, M. (eds) (1995) *The European Union and the Regions*, Oxford: Clarendon Press.

Lepsius, M. R. (1991) 'Nationalstaat und Nationalitätenstaat als Modell für die Weiterentwicklung der Europäischen Gemeinschaft', in R. Wildenmann (ed.), *Staatswerdung Europas?*, Baden-Baden: Nomos, pp. 19–40.

Marks, G. (1992) 'Structural Policy in the European Community', in A. M. Sbragia (ed.), *Euro-Politics*, Washington, DC: Brookings Institution, pp. 191–224.

Marks, G. (1993) 'Structural Policy and Multilevel Governance in the EC', in Cafruny and Rosenthal (eds), *The State of the European Community: The Maastricht Debate and Beyond*, Harlow: Longman, pp. 391–410.

Neumann, M. (1971) 'Zur ökonomischen Theorie des Föderalismus', *Kyklos* XXIV: 493–510.

Report of the Reflection Group (1995) *Report* SN 520/95, Brussels.

Ruggie, J. G. (1993) 'Territoriality and Beyond: Problematizing Modernity in International Relations', *International Organization* 47: 139–74.

Scharpf, F. W. (1988) 'The Joint Decision Trap: Lessons from German Federalism and European Integration', *Public Administration* 66(3):239–78.

Scharpf, F. W. (1992) 'Die Handlungsfähigkeit des Staates am Ende des Zwanzigsten Jahrhunderts', in B. Kohler-Koch (ed.), *Staat und Demokratie in Europa*, Opladen: Leske+Budrich, pp. 93–115.

Scharpf, F. W. (1994) *Optionen des Föderalismus in Deutschland und Europa*, Frankfurt/New York: Campus.

9 Opportunity structures for citizens' participation

The case of the European Union

Michael Nentwich[1]

Introduction

Hitherto, the political rights of European citizens with respect to the European system have been limited to the right to vote and to stand for European elections (Articles B, TEU and 8ff., ECT). But recently, a growing number of authors have discussed the pros and cons of elements of direct democracy though with very different approaches (see e.g. Abromeit, this volume, Allais 1991, Bogdanor and Woodcock 1991, Bohnet and Frey 1994, Buchmann 1993, Christiansen 1995, Esposito 1997, Grande 1996, Murswiek 1993, Neunreither 1995, Opp 1994, Schneider 1994, Svensson 1994, Wallace 1993, Weiler *et al.* 1996, Zampini 1996, Zürn 1996).

Public debate in Europe has also been influenced by the relatively high number (ten!) of national referendums on European issues since 1992. The Treaty of Amsterdam will again be subject to referendums in at least some states. The European Parliament even proposed (although without success) a Europe-wide referendum on the results of the conference to take place the same day in all member states of the EU 'on the grounds that a collective decision affecting the whole of Europe is at stake' (European Parliament 1995: 44). During the 1996/7 Inter-Governmental Conference, the Italian and Austrian governments proposed (also without success) a Europe-wide initiative process: the signatures of 10 per cent of the electorate of at least three EU member states would make a valid proposal for EC legislation forwarded to the EP (*Agence Europe* No. 6823, 02/10/1996). Yet, the 'fathers of the Amsterdam Treaty' were not prepared to change the status quo. Only indirect, non-binding and largely informal channels for the participation of citizens have been put into place so far.

In order to prepare the ground for a meaningful debate on these developments, and more far-reaching proposals for the inclusion of direct-democracy devices in the EU Constitution, I first outline the concept of 'opportunity structures for citizens' participation'. I then take a closer look at the current position on citizens' participation in the EU. On the strength of this analysis, some democratic innovations are suggested in the last section.

Opportunity structures for citizens' participation

The concept and theory of the 'political opportunity structure' was developed in the late 1960s and early 1970s to describe and explain the conditions in which people engage in collective action (Tarrow 1989: 32 ff., 1995: fn. 29, Kriesi *et al.* 1992). Kitschelt defines the political opportunity structure as 'specific configurations of resources, institutional arrangements and historical precedents for social mobilisation, which facilitate the development of protest movements in some instances and constrain them in others' (Kitschelt 1986: 58). He distinguishes between three different aspects of the political opportunity structure (1986: 61–2): first, coercive, normative, remunerative and informational resources; second, the institutional opportunity structure or 'political regimes', involving both formal and informal rules; and third, the relatively inert character over time of such structure.

Recently this concept of the political opportunity structure has been used and developed in the wider area of participation research. Taken in the singular, the notion has been used mainly in respect of the whole political system. In the plural, the notion has been applied only in analyses comparing several states, but it has been recognised that there may be considerable variations among policy arenas within the same political regime (Kitschelt 1986: 63), making it possible to speak about 'opportunity structures' which differ in different policy areas. In order to bring out the fact that there may be several possible 'channels' of participation, some authors use the term 'structure of political opportunities' (Eisinger 1973: 12, Tarrow 1995: 231).

In general, the use of the singular 'structure' indicates that there is a structure common to all channels, however diverse they may be, and that one has to consider the important links and relationships between the different opportunities. More recently, 'opportunity structures' has been used while stressing that the number and range of these structures has increased considerably in modern democracies (Mazey and Richardson 1994: 13). The use of the plural 'structures' thus means that every opportunity to participate, every channel into decision making (and implementation) is associated with specific (structural) properties which differ from channel to channel. This terminological shift is related to the broadening of the concept in the sense that the main focus on protest movements has been replaced by more general research into all forms of political participation. Mazey and Richardson, for instance, developed a market analogy for political participation reminiscent of Kaase and Marsh's concept (1981: 137) of a 'political action repertory' consisting of both unconventional and conventional political involvement (Mazey and Richardson 1994: 14).

Here I shall use both the singular and plural versions of the concept. When describing the many different channels of citizens' involvement, I analyse their different structures but I also look at the more aggregated level of the quality of the opportunity structure of the EU political system as a whole. The single structures of participation will be called 'opportunity structures for citizens'

participation', the aggregated level will be called the 'political opportunity structure'. In order to capture the many ways of getting involved in a political system,
I use the term 'opportunity structures for citizens' participation' in a rather
broad sense, comprising conventional and unconventional, direct and indirect,
formal and informal, active and passive, policy- and polity-related, implemented
and not yet implemented (i.e. innovative) involvement or participation of (groups
of) citizens. I therefore define 'opportunity structures for citizens' participation
(OSCPs)' as the various sorts of channels of access to the public sphere and to
the policy-making and implementation processes which are available to citizens;
and 'political opportunity structure (POS)' as the aggregated structure of OSCPs
in a given political system (cf. Kitschelt 1986: 58 and 61).

OSCPs of the European Union

In this section, I consider the OSCPs currently within the EU. A discussion of
the full theoretical background to this analysis can be found in Nentwich (1997).

Voting at the European level

European citizens are entitled to elect their MEPs (Article 8b.2, TEC). This is
the only 'direct' form of participation from all Euro-OSCPs. However, its significance depends very much on the political importance of the elected body (and
here, despite the reforms by the Amsterdam Treaty, considerable deficits in
comparison with all national parliaments are evident).

Voting at the national level of the member states might be considered as an
act of participation in the European polity as well. First, the composition of the
national legislature influences considerably the transposition and implementation
of legislative acts of the EU. With respect to the implementation of EC directives, national voting can be classified as a form of 'decision making'. Second,
national elections influence the composition of two central EU institutions,
namely the Council of Ministers and the European Council. Consequently,
national voting is a 'polity-related' OSCP, in the sense that it affects the composition of policy institutions. It is perhaps the most important channel by which
public opinion affects EC policy via member state governments (Young 1995: 9).
Third, national voting is also a 'control mechanism' in the sense that a strong
political mandate at the national level may induce a government to hold a particular view on a European issue leading to the use of the veto in the Council of
Ministers or the filing of complaints to the European Court of Justice.

Petitions to the European Parliament

The right to petition the legislature was formally granted to European citizens
only by the Maastricht Treaty (Article 8d TEC), although it was accepted and
even encouraged before. However, a major obstacle to use of the petition as a
device might be the new *locus standi* rules (Marias 1994). The new Article 138d

TEC restricts the right to petition for any individual to matters 'which affect him, her or it directly'. This means that petitions as an opportunity structure for political participation (as opposed simply to defending one's rights) might no longer be within the scope of the right to petition. Petitions are, however, an indirect OSCP, particularly in the European context. As long as the role of the EP is not that of a primary legislative chamber, any citizen's influence via this body remains handicapped. Nonetheless, Parliament frequently forwards petitions to the Commission: in 1993, twenty-three suspected infringements cases (out of 1,340) were brought to light by petitions and led directly to changes in national legislation or, in some cases, to infringement procedures before the Court (Commission of the European Communities 1993a, Newman 1995, Nentwich 1995). Only fewer than 10 per cent of the petitions address general political affairs, mainly environmental issues or animal protection. Yet, as many as 3 million European citizens supported some of these petitions.

Hearings and conferences organised by the European Parliament

Committees of the EP only occasionally organise hearings or conferences with experts. Recently, the EP organised a large public hearing with respect to the subjects of the 1996 IGC. Representatives of a hundred non-government organisations were invited by the EP in October 1995 and in February 1996 in order to make their views known to the MEPs (see European Parliament 1996). 'Ordinary' citizens have not been involved on a larger scale so far.

Direct contacts with MEPs

Many citizens contact their MEP when they think a problem needs Europe-wide attention. Previous research suggests that a sharp distinction has to be made between those MEPs who are elected on a local and personal basis, such as the British, and those who are elected on the basis of a member-state-wide party list (Bowler and Farrell 1991, 1993). While the British MEPs have a much closer relationship with their local electorate – the 'constituency' – most continental citizens do not even know the name of their MEP. In a list-based electoral system it is very unlikely that citizens directly contact an MEP. Rather, they address the national parties or the EP directly (via a petition). When addressed personally, MEPs have two possible ways of reacting: either to try to amend the EP agenda appropriately or to formulate a written or oral question to the Commission or the Council. To this extent EU citizens may influence the agenda not only of the EP but also of the other institutions as well. However, it has to be stressed that this OSCP is rather weak since, so far, the EP as a whole and single MEPs in particular have in many cases no decisive impact on EU politics. This is even more true for contacting other representatives at the European level, such as members of the Economic and Social Committee or the Committee of the Regions, since their position in the EC policy-making structure is even weaker than the EP's.

Addressing the Ombudsperson

Based on the new Articles 8d.2 and 138e TEC any physical or legal person (not only EU citizens!) has the right to apply to a European Ombudsperson, whose task is to deal with specific instances of maladministration of institutions or bodies. Thus, as an opportunity structure for political participation, the role is rather limited. Among the first cases, only a few have political content (access to the Council's minutes; lack of action of the Commission regarding French nuclear testing). Thus, it seems that this OSCP will not develop a high political profile.

Letter writing to the Commission

There are roughly three categories of letters received by the Commission: complaints about the non-implementation of EC law; requests for information and documents; and general statements. According to the Commission (1993a), the number of complaints from European citizens is more or less constant (slightly over 1,000 per year). Although the Commission favours the mass media as the principal means of communication between the EU and its citizens, it has stated that the improvement of personal contacts, both on the telephone and in writing, between citizens and the Commission is a priority (1993a: Annex III). With a view to increasing transparency, a special Citizen's Desk has been set up in DG X which is responsible for answering citizens' general enquiries. Furthermore a decision on public access to Commission documents and a code of conduct concerning public access to Commission and Council documents have been adopted in 1994 (Commission 1994). However, the relationship between the Commission and citizens seeking information has to be seen as a precondition rather than an OSCP in itself. By contrast, contacting the Commission in order to influence its policies is an indirect OSCP which, in some areas, can possibly be quite effective. In his study on EU water policy, Richardson reports on 'whistle blowing by ordinary citizens' and suggests that

> [w]hatever policy networks and policy communities might now be in existence or might develop, they all have to operate in the context of rather wide and unregulated participation by individuals. In that sense, policy making discussions are always conducted with an additional but empty seat at the table – representing the threat of individual citizens who regard [something] as of high salience.
>
> (Richardson 1994: 146)

This idea of an 'empty chair' seems to be helpful in understanding not only the indirect influence of citizens on the Commission, but on policy making in the EU as a whole.

Green and White Papers

In order to come to 'a more open participation' (Commission 1992), the Commission wishes to involve all interested parties by giving them the opportunity to present their opinions. The Commission increased the number of comprehensive discussion papers (twenty-one in 1996–7; see Commission 1995: 82). They outline the background of a problem, the main arguments as perceived by the Commission, and the suggested solution(s). Everybody is entitled to respond to a White/Green Paper by written statement to the Commission. The Commission has also announced its intention to introduce a system of notification and consultation similar to the general legislative consultation procedures known at the national level.

Hearings and conferences organised by the Commission

The Commission (1992) also announced its intention to organise more conferences, hearings or information seminars which might be another tool to initiate a discussion on policy projects. So far, they have involved interest group representatives, experts and national/regional/local delegates, whereas the ordinary citizen has so far not been part of such activities. However, the Commission has assigned the task of providing feedback and stimulating debate on Europe to its representations in the member states. This should also be done by organising hearings, seminars and conferences. The Commission stresses that the aim of these activities is not only to present the point of view of the Commission but to stimulate transborder debates (Pinheiro 1993).

Participation in EC committees

Committees are a typical feature of the European policy process. So far, there are no examples of participation by lay citizens; as a general rule members of EC committees are experts or officials. The Consultative Council of Users (CCU) within DG X, the Consumer Consultative Council (CCC) and the Consultative Forum on Environmental Matters provide some examples of committees which deal with typical citizens' issues. Although the ordinary citizen may not sit in these consultation committees set up by the Commission, they seem to be one of the more important opportunity structures for participation. However, they illustrate the overall tendency of the EU in seeking to channel its contacts with the 'citizens' by involving organised interests, for example consumer or environmental groups. Therefore, I classify the existing opportunities to participate via EC committees as 'indirect', since citizens' interests and opinions are mediated by associations. However, even though it has been admitted that these committees are more about associations than single citizens, they fall short even of the needs of indirect involvement of citizens in EU policy-making processes because the committees 'are failing to keep pace with the speed of the decision-making process and . . . do not provide any real place for single issue groups' (Venables 1990: 23).

Being active in small interest groups

The Commission has a reputation of being extremely accessible to interest groups (Commission 1993b, Mazey and Richardson 1993, Peters 1994: 11; Greenwood *et al.* (1992) show sectoral differences). Basically, there are two forms of dialogue: advisory committees and expert groups (see above) on the one hand, and through contact on an unstructured, *ad hoc* basis on the other. In respect of the latter, the Commission is 'committed to the equal treatment of all special interest groups, to ensure that every interested party, irrespective of size or financial backing, should not be denied the opportunity of being heard by the Commission' (Commission 1993b). In practice, however, size and financial backing matter a lot. Strength and influence also depend on the type of interest which should be represented. Less than 2 per cent of all Brussels lobbyists work for non-commercial interests (Venables 1990: 22). A project outside and not financed by the Community framework was launched in 1990: the European Citizen Actions Service (ECAS), an independent international non-profit association whose members are over 300 NGOs, which promote civil liberties, culture, health and social welfare. ECAS is an information and advocacy service – the lobby for those associations which cannot afford having their own representative in Brussels. The existence of ECAS illustrates a deficit of the EU political system: citizens along with their voluntary and community sector associations have only limited access to the policy-making processes. Only highly professional institutions such as ECAS are able to offset this deficit at least partly.

Membership in large interest groups, parties or federations

As in any democratic system, this OSCP is also present at EU level. However, most of the lobbies active in Brussels are head federations of national organisations and, hence, without individual membership. Therefore and because of the specific features of the EU system (centralisation, geographical remoteness), this opportunity structure is dominated by professionals and it is an even more mediated (indirect) OSCP for the 'credit card member' than in the national context. In particular, there is no European party system; that is, the political groups active at the European level do not act independently of the national levels and there is no individual membership of citizens either (see Gaffney 1996). Given the Amsterdam reforms regarding the EP, the importance of European party politics might increase in the long run (Nentwich and Falkner 1997).

Proceedings before the ECJ

Proceedings before the ECJ can be interpreted as a Euro-OSCP because the Court's function is that of a constitutional court of the EU. Forcing the EU institutions or a member state to change their policy by means of the Court's declaration that the measure originally adopted is unlawful under that EU Constitution, could be seen as an act of political participation. Indeed, there are many examples where actions raised by ordinary citizens (not only by commercial enterprises) had a direct impact on member states' and Community policies. There are three relevant types of proceedings, but they constitute considerable problems of access. Article 173 TEC on annulment of Community acts, on the one hand, seems to be a powerful tool, but the conditions of active legitimation ('right of standing') are not very workable. There are only a few cases where a legislative act directly affects the individual in a manner sufficient to allow direct access to the ECJ (cf. Everson 1996). On the other hand, Article 175 on failure to act has only a very limited area of application in political terms since legislative acts fall outside the scope of Article 175. As far as the preliminary ruling procedure (Article 177) is concerned, all depends on the goodwill of the national judge, because a court which does not decide in the last instance is not obliged to refer a question of Community law to the ECJ. Furthermore, this indirect OSCP is rather expensive and time consuming.

Protest in the European context

There have been some examples of Euro-level protest actions (Tarrow 1995). However, protest is a rather exceptional way of 'participating' in EU politics. The main reasons seem to be the difficulty of organising it on a European scale and the fact that protest at the national level has only very limited and indirect influence at the EU level. Furthermore, a policy's origin at the EU level is often simply not known by the wider public. This makes it particularly difficult for political entrepreneurs to mobilise a substantial part of the population for protest against the EC in general and against specific decisions in particular (Opp 1994: 393). Even if the organisers are successful to some extent, protest at the EU level only matters provided a series of additional conditions are fulfilled. For example, if a protest movement wants to prevent a specific decision, it may be helpful if there is a unanimity requirement for the Council. However, a specific government is only likely to block a measure if a significant proportion of protesters come from within its borders, and if no other 'national interests' are at stake. By contrast, where citizens want to push through a specific policy at the European level, they have in many cases to convince each and every single Council member. In a nutshell, there are several structural obstacles for a widespread use of this indirect Euro-OSCP. However, Tarrow (1995) predicts a rich and turbulent future for social movements at the national level with regard to European issues.

European mass media

So far, there are only very limited attempts to launch Europe-wide or at least transborder media. The only newspaper is *The European* along with the TV channel 'Euro-News' operating on a large scale. The obvious reason for this are the difficulties met by such enterprises by the diversity of languages and media traditions in Europe. However, with the widespread interconnection of news agencies (and the existence of a specialised European news agency 'Agence Europe' as well as the server 'Europe' of the European Commission on the World Wide Web), there is a shared base of information in Europe. But European public forums for political debate exist at present only for a slim elite (e.g. readers of *The Financial Times*). Therefore, this OSCP is virtually absent at the European level.

Eurobarometer

Regular surveys are carried out throughout the member states in order to ascertain European citizens' attitudes *vis-à-vis* the EU and specific policy areas such as EMU. Since the questions are, as a rule, very general and do not ask for dis/approval of specific policy measures, it is hard to see how EU officials and European politicians could take these surveys into account.

The political opportunity structure of the European Union

Citizens have not been at the centre of the European political system for the greater part of its history (Neunreither 1995). Only with the first election of MEPs in 1979 did the European citizenry become directly involved. In the mid-1980s the Adonnino Committee (1985) submitted proposals on improved citizens' participation in the political process of the Community. In many respects, 'European citizenship' as introduced by the Maastricht Treaty (see Articles B.3 TEU and 8 to 8e TEC) only spelled out *de jure* what had been granted *de facto* before. However, there are also a few new OSCPs (e.g. the Ombudsperson). Yet, it has to be added that the TEU also diminished political scrutiny and judicial control on matters directly affecting the rights of individuals by establishing a third, intergovernmental, pillar (Wallace 1993: 102), which will persist after the implementation of the Amsterdam Treaty.

Summarising the analysis so far, we may describe the European status quo as follows. The POS of the EU does not know any element of direct democracy in the narrow sense. Apart from European elections every five years, there are no direct ways to participate in European politics. The citizens therefore do not have an opportunity either to play a direct role in agenda setting or to directly influence the actual decision making; nor can they directly control the whole process. Nevertheless, in common with other representative systems, there are some points of access to the political system which, however, are indirect and informal and require a lot of activity by the citizens to make them work at all. In addition, we have found that the Commission's underlying strategy favours contacts with highly organised interests, that is with special interest groups, especially with transnational associations. 'Citizens' Europe is very much about citizens' associations, more than the individual citizen' (Venables 1990: 22).

Direct contacts with the 'ordinary citizen' are dominated by a hierarchic, unilateral approach. The Commission–citizen relationship is rarely interactive. There are only very few channels for feedback, and these mainly serve the Commission's interest in fine-tuning its information activities in order to make them more efficient. Furthermore, the strongest indirect OSCP (i.e. the right to petition the EP) as well as other OSCPs targeting at the EP such as contacts with MEPs still depend for their actual value on the specific competences of this institution in the relevant policy field.

Thus, the Euro-POS is not very open for citizens, and the direct responsiveness of European governance to citizens' input is rather low. The bias for organised interests and the hierarchic top-down approach when it comes to direct contacts with citizens may be described as a 'predominantly exclusive' strategy (Kriesi *et al.* 1992: 222–3). In contrast to most political systems of its member states, the EU's POS totally lacks elements of direct democracy, and is conservative in the sense that only very limited attempts have been made to implement non-traditional OSCPs.

Citizens' involvement in EU politics: status quo and innovative proposals

The OSCP/POS approach as chosen in this chapter adds an additional argument to the debate on how to overcome the widely perceived democratic deficit of the EU: a comparison of the POS between the successful federally organised states (e.g. Switzerland, Canada, Australia, Austria, Germany) as well as most EU member states, on the one hand, and the EU, on the other, reveals that the political system of the EU not only falls short of standards in terms of a representative democracy, but is also comparatively closed to direct participation of its citizens. Although the increased role of the EP in the future will also strengthen some of the existing Euro-OSCPs and therefore open up the European structure to some extent, it is obvious that only introducing new opportunities in the European context could counterbalance the loss of participatory opportunities for the citizens of several EU member states due to the shift of many competences to the supranational level. In particular, I propose the following improvements of the existing Euro-OSCPs and some innovative procedures to be added to the European system:

1   One of the major shortcomings of the Euro-POS is the lack of sufficient means to get information on the EU's policy processes and of any institutionalised mechanism to receive citizens' input. Based on American experience with political participation via the Internet, and on preliminary attempts to use these new technologies also in the European context, a promising project would be to establish *a powerful Europe-wide interactive communication network for political information and participation*. This network could facilitate access to information on European issues (e.g. legislative proposals, policy documents, voting records, etc.) and be accessible from

public points (in every European municipality) as well as from PCs via the Internet. To become a real OSCP, an important feature should be its inter-activity: the network should not only serve as an informational tool, but, equally important, as a means of communication between the citizens and the European political system. Because of the geographical remoteness of the European polity, this telecommunicative device seems specifically apt to overcome the deficits experienced so far by citizens' groups in gaining access to Euro-politics. (For a similar proposal see Weiler's 'Lexcalibur – The European Public Square' (Weiler *et al.* 1996, Weiler 1997).) In addi-tion, the establishment of an own TV channel of the EU should be discussed.

2   The interactive network focusing on individual and group contacts could be complemented by an opportunity structure securing valuable mass input on a regular basis. In order to enhance public awareness and media coverage of European issues, on the one hand, and to enable substantive popular input into the European policy-making process, on the other, Fishkin's idea of deliberative opinion polls (Fishkin 1991) should be adapted to the European context: several times a year *European Deliberative Opinion Polls* should be organised in every member state on the same day. The representative sample of citizens should be briefed intensively on specific issues which are on the European agenda, be given the opportunity to discuss them with national and European experts, and be asked for their 'deliberated opinion' at the end. The results of the polls in all member states should be summarised and published throughout the EU.

3   In order to stimulate further debate on European policies and legislative acts it is suggested that the Commission enhances the frequency and improves the distribution of White and Green Papers. Widespread use of *European formal notification and consultation* with all interested associations, interested groups, etc., as well as interested members of the public in general should be established. With respect to the citizens, the Commission might publish announcements in major mass media all over Europe as well as on the World Wide Web with a short summary of the legislative proposal and an (e-mail) address or phone/fax number to contact in order to get detailed information. It should be obligatory to provide Parliament and Council and the media with an extensive summary of and statistics on the contributions of the general public.

4   Stimulating debate and opening the policy process for citizens should be an issue not only for the Commission, but also for the Parliament. Therefore, enhancing the frequency and range of *EP hearings* on European issues could be at the heart of another 'soft' (i.e. indirect) OSCP. As in the latest experiment of the EP, also the potential of the World Wide Web and/or the proposed interactive network should be explored in the future.

5   Taking into account the opinions of the EU citizens may also be promoted via expanding the range of issues of the *Eurobarometer* surveys. At the

moment, with a few exceptions, only questions of general and long-term interest are being asked. Enriching these periodical opinion polls by – 'policy-related' – issues of the current European agenda and – 'polity-related' – to the assessment of office holders might be a valuable additional input to the European political system.

6   The extension of the *rights of standing before the European Courts* could be an appropriate means, compatible with the present system, in order to open up an important controlling OSCP at the EU level. Considering the growing importance of independent agencies and, thus, of delegated administration and even legislation, this seems particularly important.

7   In order to promote the evolution of a genuine European party system instead of the present party federations without any direct relationship to the European citizenry, *trans-European parties* should be founded and individual membership allowed. This might be a necessary precondition for establishing this classical OSCP, known from all national levels, at the European level as well. This might be amended by a specific line of the EU budget in order to help these trans-European parties in their attempt to EU-wide mobilisation.

The complete lack of 'direct' and 'policy-related' OSCPs in the European context is striking. Clearly, the appropriateness of many specific forms of direct democracy in the EU context cannot automatically be taken for granted.[2] However, the current tide of anti-European feelings and the many cries for democratic reform make a thorough debate on improving the Euro-POS definitely worthwhile. The following proposals for new OSCPs could serve as a starting point for discussion:

8   The lack of a direct agenda-setting capacity at the EU level is probably best remedied by a *European indirect popular initiative*. A voters' petition should be submitted to both 'chambers' of the European legislature (i.e. Council and Parliament) before the issue is placed on the ballot. They could have six or nine months to enact the proposal. If they fail to do so a Europe-wide facilitative referendum has to be held. An essential condition for an initiative process is 'a petition requirement high enough to prevent ballot clutter, and low enough to enable grassroots groups to qualify an initiative for the ballot' (Schmidt 1989: 181). A double requirement seems to be most appropriate in the European context: first, 3 or 4 per cent of the total number of European voters (or of the ballots cast in the previous European election) and, second, the same proportion of voters in at least five states. A similar proposal was recently made by Weiler *et al.* (1996) and Weiler (1997).

9   When we turn to the decision-making phase, a *mandatory constitutional referendum* seems conceivable. It would have to take place whenever the 'constitutional texts' of the EU (the 'primary law') are altered (e.g. to ratify the results of the 1996 IGC). Thus the necessity of popular approval existing in some member states would be generalised and Europeanised – which might confer additional social legitimacy. It might also be envisaged

to establish a list of other important questions which should be treated the same way as 'constitutional issues' (own resources, major treaties with third countries; see also Schneider 1994). As in the Swiss example, a double majority of both votes cast in the whole of the EU and of agreeing member states might best fit the needs of the EU.[3] This could be either supplemented with a turnout criterion (e.g. a minimum turnout of, say, 30 per cent in every single member state and of 50 per cent of the total Europe-wide number of voters), or the number of votes cast in the previous European election.

10   Also in connection with decision making in the narrow sense, a *voluntary referendum* could be launched by a minority, for example one-third of the MEPs, or the blocking minority in the Council. This could help to overcome deadlocks in the decision-making process.

11   In order to give the citizens also a chance to control the European legislature directly, a *controlling petition referendum* seems appropriate. Europe-wide referendums could be launched by a Europe-wide qualifying popular initiative with a view to cancelling a legislative act (EC directive or EC regulation) that has already been enacted by the European legislature.[4] See in this context also Abromeit's proposal of direct-democratic 'veto rights' elsewhere in this volume.

12   Finally, the *recall of single Commissioners* might be a valuable tool to enhance the public accountability of the Commission. The recall would be launched by a public petition. If the petition reaches a certain threshold (e.g. 3 or 4 per cent of the total number of European voters), the EP should be required to have a vote of confidence in that Commissioner.

The Amsterdam Treaty reforms continued along the path of improving the representative elements of EU democracy rather than introducing policy-related OSCPs. In particular, the EP's standing as a second legislative chamber was enhanced considerably and thus those OSCPs which are dependent on the EP's political weight were improved as a reflex (Nentwich and Falkner 1997). Furthermore, transparency has gained some ground and thus the information base for politically interested citizens was enlarged. However, the political opportunity structure of the EU remains closed to direct participation of the citizenry at large.

Notes

1   This article is part of a research project financed under the Human Capital Mobility Programme by the European Commission and the Austrian Research Funds, FWF. I would also like to acknowledge the support of Jeremy Richardson, Gerda Falkner, Thomas Christiansen, Elinor Scarbrough, Elizabeth Meehan, Patrick Fafard, Ian Budge, Amy Verdun and Richard Kuper, all of whom commented on earlier versions of this paper.

2   As a general rule, only those issues which fall within the field of competences of the EU should be potential candidates for direct decision. The same controlling

instruments as 'normal' legislative procedures should be applicable and the ECJ should be given the power to cancel a referendum if the issue was *ultra vires*. Thus, European referendums on, for example, abortion or the death penalty are not proposed here.

3 That is to say, 50 per cent plus of the Europe-wide electorate is not sufficient, since the result of the referendum in at least eight states has also to be in favour of the proposal. Neither a broad majority of the most populous states nor popular agreement in the smaller states would be sufficient.

4 Drawing on the American discussion on a national referendum and initiative, as well as on current practice at the US state level and in Switzerland, the question of the fairness in media access and of adequate voter information (official ballot leaflets) should be laid down by EU legislation for all proposed direct OSCPs.

References

Adonnino Report (1985) 'People's Europe', *Bulletin of the European Communities* Suppl. 7/85, Luxembourg: Office of Official Publications.

Allais, M. (1991) *L'Europe face à son avenir – Que faire?*, Paris: Robert Laffont/Clément Juglar.

Bogdanor, V. and Woodcock, S. (1991) 'The European Community and Sovereignty', *Parliamentary Affairs* 44(4): 481–93.

Bohnet, I. and Frey, B. S. (1994) 'Direct-democratic Rules for a Future Europe – the Role of Discussion', *Kyklos* 47: 341–54.

Bowler, S. and Farrell, D. (1991) 'Representation and the European Parliament in 1990: Electoral Systems and Constituency Service', European Policy Research Unit Working Paper 3/91, Department of Government, University of Manchester.

Bowler, S. and Farrell, D. (1993) 'Legislator Shirking and Voter Monitoring: Impacts of European Parliament Electoral Systems upon Legislator-Voter Relationships', *Journal of Common Market Studies* 31(1): 45–69.

Buchmann, M. C. (1993) 'The Relevance of the Swiss Experience for a European Constitution', Paper presented at the COST A7-workshop on 'Democratic Rules for a Future Europe', Lucerne, Switzerland, December 1993.

Christiansen, T. (1995) 'Gemeinsinn und Europäische Integration – Strategien zur Optimierung von Demokratie- und Integrationsziel', *Zeitschrift für Parlamentsfragen*, Special issue 'Demokratie in Europa: Zur Rolle der Parlamente'.

Commission of the European Communities (1992) *Communication on Transparency*, SEC(92) 2274.

Commission of the European Communities (1993a) *Eleventh Annual Report on Monitoring the Application of Community Law*, COM(94) 500 final.

Commission of the European Communities (1993b) *Communication on 'An open and structured dialogue between the Commission and special interest groups'*, OJ 93/C 63/2.

Commission of the European Communities (1994) *Decision 94/90/ECSC, EC, Euratom on public access to Commission documents of 8 February 1994 with a Code of conduct concerning public access to Commission and Council documents*, OJ 94/L 46/58.

Commission of the European Communities (1995) *Report on the Operation of the Treaty on European Union from 10 May 1995*, SEC(95) 731 final.

Eisinger, P. K. (1973) 'The Conditions of Protest Behaviour in American Cities', *American Political Science Review* 67: 11–18.

Esposito, F. (1997) 'Le référendum européen: un outil démocratique pour une Europe démocratique?', Paper prepared for the IPSA Seminar on 'Amsterdam and Beyond:

The European Union Facing the Challenges of the 21st Century', 9–12 July 1997, Brussels.

European Parliament (1995) *Resolution on the functioning of the Treaty on European Union with a view to the 1996 Intergovernmental Conference – Implementation and development of the Union*, A4–0102/95 of 17 May 1995.

European Parliament (1996) *Summary Report on the Public Hearing 'The Intergovernmental Conference 1996: The European Parliament – A Heaven for the Concerns of the Citizens'*, A4-0068/96 of 3 and 27 March 1996.

Everson, M. (1996) 'Non-Majoritarian Governance, the Courts and Citizenship Participation in the European Union: Towards a European Polity?', Paper presented at the IPSA-Research Committee on European Unification Seminar, 3–5 July 1996, Brussels.

Fishkin, J. S. (1991) *Democracy and Deliberation. New Directions for Democratic Reform*, New Haven, CT, and London: Yale University Press.

Gaffney, J. (ed.) (1996) *Political Parties and the European Union*, London and New York: Routledge.

Grande, E. (1996) 'Demokratische Legitimation und Europäische Integration', *Leviathan* 3: 339–60.

Greenwood, J., Grote, J. R. and Ronit, K. (eds) (1992) *Organized Interests and the European Community*, London: Sage.

Kaase, M. and Marsh, A. (1981) 'Political Action Repertory Changes Over Time and a New Typology', *Political Action*, Beverly Hills, CA: Sage.

Kitschelt, H. P. (1986) 'Political Opportunity Structures and Political Protest: Anti-Nuclear Movements in Four Democracies', *British Journal of Political Science* 16: 57–85.

Kriesi, H., Koopmans, R., Duyvendak, J. W. and Giugni, M. G. (1992) 'New Social Movements and Political Opportunities in Western Europe', *European Journal of Political Research* 22: 219–44.

Marias, E. (1994) 'The Right to Petition the European Parliament after Maastricht', *European Law Review* 19(2): 160–83.

Mazey, S. and Richardson, J. J. (eds) (1993) *Lobbying in the European Community*, Oxford: Oxford University Press.

Mazey, S. and Richardson, J. J. (1994) 'Interest Groups and Representation in the European Union', Paper presented to the Workshop 'Democratic Representation and the Legitimacy of Government in the European Community', ECPR Joint Sessions Workshops, 17–22 April 1994, Madrid.

Murswiek, D. (1993) 'Maastricht und der pouvoir constituant – Zur Begründung der verfassungsgebenden Gewalt im Prozezder europäischen Integration', Der Staat 11(3): 161–90.

Nentwich, M. (1995) 'Citizens' Involvement in European Union Politics. Towards a More Participatory Democracy?', Paper presented at the Fourth Biennial International ECSA Conference, 11–14 May 1995, Charleston, SC, Maastricht: Ellis (on CD-ROM).

Nentwich, M. (1997) 'Opportunity Structures for Citizens' Participation: The Case of the European Union', *Essex Paper in Politics and Government* 116; also available in *European Integration online Papers* (EIoP) (1996) Vol. 0, No. 1; http://eiop.or.at/eiop/texte/1996-001a.htm.

Nentwich, M. and Falkner, G. (1997) 'The Treaty of Amsterdam: Towards a New Institutional Balance', *European Integration online Papers* (EIoP) (1997) Vol. 1, No. 15; http://eiop.or.at/eiop/texte/1997-015a.htm.

Neunreither, K. (1995) 'Citizens and the Exercise of Power in the European Union: Towards a New Social Contract?', in A. Rosas and E. Antola (eds), *A Citizens' Europe. In Search of a New Order*, London: Sage.

Newman, E. (1995) Interview given to the author by E. Newman MEP, the Chairman of the Petitions' Committee, on 6 April 1995 in Strasbourg.

Opp, K.-D. (1994) 'The Role of Voice in a Future Europe', *Kyklos* 4(3): 385–402.

Peters, B. Guy (1994) 'Agenda-setting in the European Community', *Journal of European Public Policy* 1(1): 9–26.

Pinheiro, J. (1993) *Communication to the Commission from 30 June 1993*, SEC(93) 916.

Richardson, J. J. (1994) 'EU Water Policy: Uncertain Agendas, Shifting Networks and Complex Coalitions', *Environmental Politics* 3(4): 139–67.

Schmidt, D. D. (1989) *Citizen Lawmakers: The Ballot Initiative Revolution*, Philadelphia: Temple University Press.

Schneider, F. (1994) 'A Constitution For Federal Europe', *European Brief* 2(1): 30–1.

Svensson, P. (1994) 'The Danish Yes to Maastricht and Edinburgh. The EC Referendum of May 1993', *Scandinavian Political Studies* 17(1): 69–82.

Tarrow, S. (1989) 'Struggle, Politics, and Reform: Collective Action, Social Movements, and Cycles of Protest', *Cornell Studies in International Affairs, Western Societies Paper* No. 21, Ithaca, NY.

Tarrow, S. (1995) 'The Europeanization of Conflict: Reflections from Social Movements Research', *West European Politics* 18(2): 223–51.

Venables, T. (1990) 'European Citizens Action Service', in C. McConnell (ed.), *Citizens' Europe? Community Development in Europe Towards 1992*, Colchester: Community Development Foundation.

Wallace, H. (1993) 'Deepening and Widening: Problems of Legitimacy for the EC', in García (ed.), *European Identity and Search for Legitimacy*, London and New York: Pinter.

Weiler, J. H. H. (1997) 'European Citizenship: The Selling of the European Union', in E. Antalovsky *et al.* (eds), *Integration durch Demokratie – Neue Impulse für die Europäische Union*, Marburg: Metropolis.

Weiler, J. H. H. *et al.* (1996) 'Certain Rectangular Problems of European Integration Empowering the Individual: The Four Principal Proposals', http://www.iue.it/AEL/EP/fpp.html.

Young, A. R. (1995) 'Participation and Policy Making in the European Community: Mediating between Contending Interests', Paper presented at the Fourth Biennial International ECSA Conference, 11–14 May 1995, Charleston, SC, Maastricht: Ellis (on CD-ROM).

Zampini, F. (1996) 'Démocratie et avenir de l'Union', Paper presented at the IPSA-Research Committee on European Unification Seminar, 3–5 July 1996, Brussels.

Zürn, M. (1996) 'Über den Staat und die Demokratie im europäischen Mehrebenen-system', *Politische Vierteljahresschrift* 1: 27–55.

Part III

Citizenship and constitutional choice

10 The many democratic deficits of the European Union

Richard Kuper[1]

Introduction

That there is a 'democratic deficit' at the heart of the European Union has become part of the conventional wisdom over the last decade or so. Most of the discussion of this deficit, however, takes place in rather narrow terms, where democracy is defined as 'an institutional arrangement' with a focus on government structures and their interrelationship. By the test of certain liberal democratic principles, the EU is then identified as deficient in a number of respects.

In this chapter I argue that this approach, valuable so far as it goes, ignores many realities that undermine the extent and the depth of democracy in the EU. By spelling these out I hope to enlarge the concept of the democratic deficit by demonstrating that the deficits are multiple, ranged across many axes. Democracy is multi-faceted and the concept of democratic deficit something that can be applied to individual democratic states, not just to the EU. So, the issue of central concern here is not the divide between democratic and non-democratic (Spain before and after Franco, South Africa under and after apartheid), it is, rather, the degree and quality of the democracy in the EU which, however one characterises the form of governance emerging, is a cooperative venture among unambiguously democratic states. Having detailed four democratic deficits, I end with a brief discussion of the criticisms most likely to be levelled against such an approach.

The conventional account of the EU's democratic deficit identifies its shortcomings as a lack of accountability and transparency. The Council of Ministers is answerable to no one, and meets in secret – the only legislative body in the democratic world to do so. The Commission, heavily influenced in its construction by Monnet's roots in the elitist and technocratic French state tradition, combines political and administrative functions, but, unlike national cabinets, it lacks the legitimacy to provide the political direction for the Community with which it is notionally charged. Technically dismissible *en bloc* by the European Parliament (EP), it is effectively unaccountable. The EP, in its turn, lacks adequate powers to make laws, to set a budget, raise taxes or control the Commission. As a result there is popular apathy in relation to the EU as a whole.

It is perceived as remote and citizens feel they are unable to influence it or become involved in its development.

On this basis, it is clear where the problem lies. Shirley Williams, for example, defines the 'democratic deficit' as 'the gap between the powers transferred to the Community level and the control of the elected Parliament over them' (Williams, 1990: 306). Similarly, for David Martin (1991: 60) the democratic deficit 'results from the fact that powers transferred by national parliaments to the European Community are not being exercised by the democratically elected representatives of the people of the Community'. Thus proposals to remedy the deficit usually hinge on extending the powers of the EP.

Not the least committed advocate of increased powers for the EP has been the EP itself. Since its deliberations in the early 1980s which culminated in the February 1984 Draft Treaty on European Union, the EP has been arguing for the right to initiate legislation and to have powers of co-decision with the Council. The Single European Act and then the Maastricht Treaty saw definite expansions in its powers but came nowhere near to meeting its demands.

In the run-up to Amsterdam the EP's submission to the Reflection Group called for the extension of parliamentary powers, increased accountability of the executive and the bureaucracy, and the opening up of the Community to its citizens both in terms of accessibility and transparency, to go hand in hand with the development and extension of coherent EU policies in relation to foreign policy, security, environment, cultural diversity and social disparity.

The key, the EP argued, to establishing both legitimacy and efficiency was to merge gradually the three pillars giving the EP similar powers in all areas and to vest democratic accountability for matters which remain outside the first pillar jointly in the EP and the national parliaments. What the EP proposed at the institutional level, therefore, was 'stronger and more democratic Union institutions' (European Parliament 1995: 8). The Council's role would be clearly defined as one of representing states, just as the EP represented peoples. Both would have equal status in all fields of legislative and budgetary competence. Greater democratic control was also envisaged as a result of cooperation/coordination between the EP and national parliaments and ensuring that the latter debate major issues prior to Council meetings.

Some advances were made at Amsterdam, especially in the area of co-decision and in the public investiture of the Commission. In an early analysis Nentwich and Falkner (1997: 17) conclude that 'the state of democracy of the Union was indeed improved by shifting the balance towards the EP, but only in a rather formal sense'. At the same time, after Amsterdam, many areas still remain beyond the remit of the EP (setting the budget, for example); the problem of comitology remains unaddressed, the remoteness of the EU from its citizens untouched.

Yet, even if the EP proposals were to be adopted in their entirety, they might bring the Community no closer to the ordinary citizens of Europe than at present. There are many objections to envisaging democracy at EU level as simply a replication of national state forms, even those of federalist states (see the chapters by Abromeit and Weale in this volume). My analysis here, however, focuses on four major problem areas which are not usually voiced so centrally – if voiced at all – in discussions of the democratic deficit.

First, there is the question of trying to build an effective democracy on a treaty rather than a constitutional basis. Second, there are the democratic limitations of liberal democracy itself. Third, there are the issues of citizenship in a democracy and who is entitled to the claims of citizenship. Fourth, there are the much underrated issues of economic control, in particular the rights of a democracy, in the interests of political equality and social justice, to control the economic activities taking place within its borders.

The need for a constitution

That the EU's legitimacy is fragile is acknowledged by a wide variety of commentators. The notion of involving the peoples of Europe more directly in fashioning an EU of the future might therefore have some appeal. The experience of the mass movements within civil society which were so important in undermining the legitimacy of the autocratic regimes of Eastern Europe in the 1980s and helping to shape an alternative consensus might also have been expected to leave some mark.

Little of this kind emerges in the debates on the democratic deficit, however. Instead, most discussions of the development of European law talk about a steady process of 'constitutionalisation' brought about by European Court of Justice decisions. One example is provided by Mancini (1991: 178) who argues that the 'main endeavour' of the Court had been to 'remove or reduce' the differences between treaties and constitutions, with three principles being particularly important: supremacy of EC law, direct effect and preemption. All three of these have been increasingly established over time, recognised by national courts in the member states. Similarly, in a discussion of citizenship, Rey Koslowski (1994) shows how a series of Court decisions, in a process of legal spillover, has extended integration by conferring rights on individuals.

All this is true, and important. But this line of argument obscures a fundamental point: none of these Court decisions and the resulting integration have generated any popular commitment or enhanced legitimacy. (On democracy and legitimacy see Beetham and Lord, this volume.) Indeed, the complexity of some of the arguments is testimony to the fact that they are not part of a democratically rooted legitimacy, a democratic *acquis communautaire* as it were. If the EU has a constitution it is fair to say that its citizens are not aware of it. Any constitution worthy of the name should encapsulate – and contribute to – the construction of some common sense of identity. To secure open, democratic, pluralistic and secular values, what Europe needs is a popular mobilisation in favour of just such values, expressed in a living constitution which derives its legitimacy from its citizens (Kuper 1997).

Joseph Weiler and his colleagues point to the process through which the

Community has expanded its competences at the expense of the member states, which, though to date has been beneficial overall, they see as a 'ticking constitutional time bomb' (Weiler *et al.* 1995: 35) that could yet blow the Community apart. They pose the question sharply: 'By what authority, if any – in the vocabulary of normative political theory – can the claim of European law to be both constitutionally superior and with immediate effect in the polity be sustained?' (Weiler *et al.* 1995: 10). Yes, the ECJ has made its pronouncements and yes, to date, they have been accepted by national courts. But Weiler *et al.* detect some stirrings of resistance in, for example, the German Constitutional Court's reasoning in reaching its judgment that the Maastricht Treaty did not violate the German Constitution. It was 'a flagrant act of defiance vis-à-vis the European Court of Justice, in direct contradiction with its jurisprudence on the power of national courts to declare Community law invalid' (Weiler *et al* 1995: 37), and it has compromised 'the constitutional integrity of the Community', with its argument that 'the limit to Community legislative powers was as much a matter of German constitutional law as of Community law' (1995: 36). (See Gustavsson in this volume.)

The solution proposed – the setting up of a Constitutional Council with jurisdiction only over competences – reads very much like a wheeze to get round the problem so eloquently identified. At its heart is the issue of legitimacy; and in a situation where advanced industrial societies are increasingly characterised by a disenchantment with traditional politics, it seems unlikely that a purely institutional reform can recreate it at a supranational level. On the contrary, current integration logic, according to Andreas Gross (1995: 10) of the aptly named citizens' organisation Eurotopia, 'leads to a widening gap between the EU and its citizens, who find its creation progressively removed from them'. It is in relation to this that the second, substantial, weakness of a purely institutional solution to the democratic deficit can be best located.

Broadening the concept of democracy

The last two decades have seen attempts to redefine 'the boundaries of the political' on both right and left (Maier 1987). The whole thrust of the new social movements, for instance, has been to broaden both what counts as political and the legitimate arenas through which political aims may be pursued. In Offe's view (1987: 72) the counterposing of the two spheres of the public (equals the political) and the private of liberal democratic theory

> has been superseded by three spheres: the private, the noninstitutional political, and the institutionalised political. So too the contrast of state and civil society is superseded as the new movements claim the space of 'political action within civil society' as the terrain from which to challenge both private and institutional-political practices.

These new social movements may be seen as the more or less effective 'bearers' of the whole range of critiques of liberal democracy. The argument, at one level, is about the limited, tenuous access to the political process which 'thin' liberal democracy affords (Barber 1984, Red–Green Study Group 1994). In its place is developed a view of democracy as empowering, rather than merely protective, based on the centrality of some form of participation with an emphasis on decentralisation and on grassroots self-activity. At a deeper and more profound level, the argument moves on to the very nature of democracy itself, which is viewed as a process rather than a set of formal institutions (Kuper 1994).

From this perspective, the problem is less about making the Commission/Council accountable to the EP than about changing the nature of the political process itself, bringing the citizens directly into politics. Politics would be transformed by providing for far more direct access to resources and recognised spaces within the political process to facilitate activity within civil society (see e.g. Barber 1984, Wainwright 1993, Abromeit this volume). Indeed, the more power is given to a democratically elected EP in which, after enlargement, each MEP will 'represent' over 700,000 people, the greater the need for a vast array of alternative sites and processes of democracy. Otherwise central governing bodies will be experienced as infinitely distant from the ordinary citizen.

These limitations are well captured in Michael Nentwich's contribution to this volume. His wide-ranging analysis of the political opportunity structure of the EU concludes that the frequently affirmed belief in the remoteness of European politics from the citizens is all too well founded – something that remains as true after Amsterdam as it was before.

Citizenship: what and for whom?

The third weakness of the traditional notion of the democratic deficit is its neglect of any notion of citizenship. The writings of Elizabeth Meehan (1990) and others on citizenship in the context of the EU are not generally taken up by writers on the democratic deficit. Ever since T. H. Marshall (1950), there has been a recognition of three aspects of citizenship: civil, political and social. And while Marshall has been extensively criticised (see Mann 1987, Turner 1992, Fraser and Gordon 1994), his work, nonetheless, ought to make it impossible for us ever to look at the quality of democracy without looking at the quality of the citizenship on which it rests. Indeed some would argue for adding a fourth – cultural – dimension to Marshall's list, on the basis of Canadian and Australian experiences of multiculturalism (Castles 1994).

So there is plenty that needs spelling out to give substance to the Maastricht commitment 'to strengthen the protection of the rights and interests of the nationals of its member states through the introduction of a citizenship of the Union'. Here, however, in the words of Duff *et al.* (1994: 29), 'the Maastricht Treaty takes no risks'. Citizenship of the EU is acquired by virtue of being a citizen of a member state, and the rights acquired relate almost exclusively to electoral rights – the right to vote and to stand in local and European elections.

The EP and others have argued for an extension of these citizenship rights, and the Reflection Group (1995: 19) believes there is a majority view that European citizenship is 'an essential aspect of making the Treaty acceptable to European public opinion'. But the proposals under discussion are not of the same order as those involved in Marshall's view of social citizenship as entailing a right 'to a share in the full social heritage and to live the life of a civilised being according to the standards prevailing in the society' (cited in Fraser and Gordon 1994: 92). This is not to suggest that a democracy without social rights is unworthy of the name, merely that one without such rights suffers from a democratic deficit of a high order. The situation in the EU is anomalous, to say the least. Certain social rights within the Community have been established both as a result of directives and of Court of Justice decisions, especially in the area of sex discrimination (Meehan 1993). But other areas, where an extensive but varied range of citizens' social rights exist in the member states (especially in education, housing and welfare), are generally seen as tangential when European citizenship is discussed.

It might be said that this is not a real problem, because it is covered by the doctrine of subsidiarity, but this really will not do. Subsidiarity is an important principle but cannot be used to justify differential rights and entitlements in the long term in areas which are central to the citizenship – and thus the empowerment, autonomy and equality – of members of the democratic polity in process-of-becoming which is the EU. Of course there are important issues to resolve in practice as to how to combine the universality of citizenship rights with a respect for diversity and difference which it is also essential to foster on democratic grounds. But here Stephan Leibfried (1993) is surely right when he argues that the development of European social citizenship requires positive integration (the creation of a common social space), rather than the negative approach (the removal of barriers) on which the Community has been founded.

But then Community social policy has always been an adjunct to economic policy, not an instrument of citizenship. The first Social Action Programme in the 1970s, for example, was already clearly seen in this light (Meehan 1993: 59–77). While it is true that the Commission's 1994 White Paper on Social Policy talks of establishing 'the fundamental social rights of citizens as a constitutional element of the European Union', there is still 'little concrete evidence that European social policy is perceived by the Council as other than a handmaiden to economic objectives' (Hantrais 1995: 15). If anything there has been a narrowing of focus over time. Linda Hantrais (1995: 19–37) shows clearly how the language in which social policy is discussed has changed since the 1950s, moving from a goal of 'harmonisation' of social protection, through 'approximation' to 'convergence' which, in reality, means little more than cooperation around different national systems.

There is another vital aspect of the democratic deficit which relates to citizenship or, rather, to the non-citizenship of a large number of residents in the EU. There are some 14.1 million resident aliens in the EU of which 4.9 million are members of other member states, that is EU citizens, leaving 9.2 million with rights of residence but not citizenship, a category of people sometimes described as 'denizens'. Although they only constitute 2.8 per cent of the total population (*Eurostat* 1993), they constitute in simple numerical terms a sixteenth member state larger than Luxembourg, Ireland, Finland, Denmark, Austria and Sweden. In addition, there is an unknown number of people with a variety of statuses from accepted (temporary residents, legal residents or workers), to tolerated ('margizens' – many refugees and undocumented aliens) all the way to outright illegals (Martiniello 1994).

The discrimination which even the best-off of these groups, the resident aliens, suffer in terms of legal rights is extensive, not just within the countries in which they reside (and this varies not just between country and country and between ethnic group and ethnic group) but also in relation to the EU as a whole. At this level they have, in particular, no rights of free movement nor any protection against racial discrimination. The inequities of this situation are attested to in innumerable ways (Layton-Henry and Wilpert 1994, Miles 1994, Bauböck 1994), and many proposals have been made to remedy them, particularly strong ones coming from the EP (European Parliament 1991, Geddes 1995).

The democratic deficit, implicit in the exclusion from citizenship of members of the Community who contribute to its economic and social life as fully as many of those included, is obvious. But it is not only resident aliens who face discrimination. Sivanandan (1989: 90), anticipating 1992, wrote that:

> Citizenship may open Europe's borders to blacks to allow them free movement, but racism which cannot tell one black from another, a citizen from an immigrant, an immigrant from a refugee – and classes all Third World peoples as immigrants and refugees and all immigrants and refugees as terrorists and drugdealers is going to make such movements fraught with difficulty.

Such issues are not to be dealt with at the European level, but left rather to the individual member states under the doctrine of subsidiarity. It is, unfortunately, not necessarily in the interests of these governments to act either. If the entry of immigrants into deprived areas 'brings home to indigenous classes the fact that they do not control their jobs or their neighbourhoods' (MacLaughlin 1993: 37) the *de facto* toleration of racism and discrimination provides a convenient way in which national governments can avoid taking responsibility for their own failures in these areas. As integration undermines the ability of nation states to resuscitate deprived communities, it may indeed, unwittingly, fuel ethno-nationalism and xenophobia. The need for European-level policies to counter disadvantage thus becomes all the more important. Instead, the doctrine of subsidiarity is left to face 'a post-Cold-War agoraphobia and the feeling that the European

Community is now open to an unprecedented invasion from both East and South' (MacLaughlin 1993: 36–7). Making 1997 the European Year Against Racism and even establishing a European Monitoring Centre on Racism and Xenophobia (finally agreed by Council in June 1997), however welcome in themselves, risk being a substitute for effective EU action.

Economic integration, the democratic deficit and the role of regions

When discussing the democratic deficit the fact that the European Economic Community started life as a common market is generally ignored even though every major step in its development has been fuelled by economic concerns of various kinds. Over the last four decades the environment in which the Community has grown has changed substantially; over the last one, dramatically. The shift from Fordist standardised mass production to a new, more flexible, system, however characterised, has been part of a process of economic globalisation. The collapse of the East European system was in part a result of this widespread economic change to which those countries were unable to adapt sufficiently rapidly. It is quite clear that the nation state today has a greatly reduced control over economic activity within its territorial boundaries than, say, forty years ago. The growing transnationalisation of economic activity undermined the national systems of regulation on which Keynesian economic (and social democratic political) strategies had come to depend. The bonfire of controls which attended the deregulation of the City of London has not happened in quite such a dramatic way at EU level. But the slow and sometimes tortuous movement towards the single market has represented just such an effective reduction of national controls over large swathes of economic activity.

This has profound democratic implications. The greatest democratic deficit of all is encapsulated in the peoples of Europe lacking effective political control of either the economies of their own states or the economy of the EU as a whole. Helpful here is a regulationist school perspective in which every regime of accumulation is associated with a corresponding mode of regulation (Lipietz 1992). The latter is in effect a social compromise which brings the contradictory behaviours of individuals into line with some collective principles which can sustain the process of accumulation. The Keynesian welfare form has become increasingly unviable since the 1970s and a new compromise has to be more or less painfully constructed – so far with little success. What is at stake is how democratic or how authoritarian, how outward looking or how inward looking a new viable – yet to be concluded – compromise will be. Indeed, the very quality of the democracy of Europe is at issue, for there are transitional periods when choices about the economic ordering of society have profound implications for democracy.

These choices, at the level of the individual European state, are greatly circumscribed compared with the fairly recent past. These states are generally reduced to jockeying for competitive advantage in a global economic environment from which they really can no longer aspire to protect themselves individually. The EU provides one level on which to reconstitute that 'minimum degree of coordination of state regulation necessary to permit the international reproduction of capital' (Piccioto 1991). At the same time, however, as these processes of Europeanisation and globalisation are occurring, we are witnessing a 'new significance of territorial diversity and difference' from below (Amin and Thrift 1994: 6), as nation states lose their pre-eminence.

What makes for success today is disputed. But what has been called 'institutional thickness' (Amin and Thrift 1994: 14) seems to be a vital, if not sufficient, determinant of regional economic success in a globalised world. This concept is a rich one, combining a multiplicity of social and economic institutions, active sets of relationships amongst them resulting in shared collective rules and representations and a mutual awareness of being involved in a common enterprise: 'It is', as Amin and Thrift put it (1994: 15), 'a "thickness" which both establishes legitimacy and nourishes relations of trust.'

Such legitimacy and trust are not, of course, incompatible with hierarchical relationships (whether bureaucratic or kinship based) but there are reasons for believing that they sit more easily with relatively democratic modes of economic organisation. Job enrichment, quality circles and the like are all aspects of a recognition that the active involvement of workers in collective enterprise is the key to productivity in the new knowledge-based industries. And the fostering of networks and provision of collective services attuned to local needs creates an active industrial role for local and regional public institutions.

Such analyses provide an economic underpinning for the dream of a Europe of the Regions, and suggest why, as the economic powers of intervention of nation states decline, a focus on regions as economic centres and as arenas in which new, democratic, social identities can be constructed, is likely to be a fruitful one (Murray 1991). Tendencies towards regionalisation have characterised many European countries since the 1970s – Spain, Italy, France, Belgium. There is no doubt that the cultural specificity of regions like Scotland or Catalonia provides a basis for a regional identity which is harder to construct in Rhône-Alpes, say, or South-East England. But then nations were not always easy to construct either and the demand that one be prepared to die for one's country before being allowed to vote in it does not have to apply to regions (or, indeed, any longer to nations).

The emphasis, anyway, is on the term 'construction'. Regions, no less than nations, are artefacts, 'imagined communities'. And one can imagine them as exclusivist, ethnically cleansed, communities rather than democratic, open and inclusive (witness the disintegration of the former Yugoslavia). Or, less apocalyptically, but also worryingly, there are the dangers of 'bourgeois regionalism', a regionalism of the affluent at the expense of the poor, encapsulated in the chauvinism of Umberto Bossi and the Northern Leagues (Harvie 1994). In and of themselves, regions are a panacea for nothing. But as part of a democratic project for Europe in the twenty-first century they can come into their own.

It is in this context that a divorce between citizenship and nationality becomes easier to envisage. That there are competing traditions of citizenship in the various member states is obvious, ranging from a republican conception (citizenship derived from participation in a community of equals) to a *volkisch* one (citizenship a matter of blood). The more the rights and obligations of citizenship are elaborated at the European level and exercised at the regional level, the more the tensions between different state traditions can be avoided. Indeed, Weiler *et al.* elaborate a reading of Article 8 of the Treaty on European Union which sees the potential strength of the notion of citizenship of the EU lying precisely in the fact that it belongs to citizens who by definition do not share the same nationality (Weiler *et al.* 1995: 20–4). Closa and Kostakopoulou, too (this volume), develop variants of this approach, seeing the development of European citizenship as a process and a possible political project.

Current EU economic policy, competition driven as it is, has not proved a universal recipe for economic growth, still less for the effective distribution of its fruits. There seems little doubt that regional inequalities in the Community have increased since the mid-1970s (Dunford 1994). Equally it has been cogently argued, most recently by Amin and Tomaney (1995: 11), that 'cohesion will be undermined by the inherent bias of the EU's measures for promoting growth and productivity towards the economic interests of the advanced regions and the major corporations of Europe'.

Thus a pure Europe of the Regions could result merely in a proliferation of small, non-sovereign units in a beggar-my-neighbour competition for a niche in the transnational division of labour. An EU developing on present lines, towards maximal economic union but with no expansion of the current limited social and regional dimension and no other effective measures of redistribution, is likely to be deeply fractured, regionally as well as nationally.

It is not that the danger has gone unrecognised, but the forces that were willing to cooperate on delivering the single market are themselves divided on the issue of the social compromise they are prepared to accept. It is important to stress that the choices facing Europe are inherently political. A single market and a single currency in an EU genuinely committed to eliminating disparities of life-chances which depend on social or regional location will demand an expansionist macroeconomic policy, active industrial intervention, a high level of solidarity, and transfer payments – at least as transitional measures and quite possibly as long as a capitalist market system survives (Holland 1993).

Objections

What does this imply in terms of wider democratic theory? It no longer makes sense in the late twentieth century – if it ever did – to define democracy in narrow political terms. What counts as political is itself the subject of discussion and debate and the new social movements have forced a recognition of the political dimension of all aspects of life – social, economic, environmental, even personal.

Many commentators feel that this approach is stretching the notion of democracy and the democratic deficit too far, making of it a repository for all goods or simply a 'garbage-can' concept. At stake is what can and should be linked definitionally to democracy, what is left to be empirically determined as outcomes. And while a decision to abolish the right to vote, even if positively supported by a majority of the citizenry, might be recognised as undemocratic at least in its implications for the (formerly) democratic community, can the same be said of a decision, for example, to cut welfare benefits?

I do not find the question as easy to answer as some seem to. Of course, in and of itself, democratic decisions can be legitimately made, by majority vote, to cut welfare benefits, close state schools and hospitals, privatise public enterprises without any single one of them being undemocratic, in form or in substance. But if the cumulative result is to undermine the ability of citizens to participate in democratic decision making, then surely we have a right – and a duty – to reconsider how democratic they can conceivably have been. The argument here rests on the assumption that while democracy 'is a political concept . . . [which] embraces the related principles of popular control and political equality' (Beetham, 1994: 28) there are a number of logically necessary conditions for such principles to be able to operate fully, and that if they are not satisfied, the democracy is in deficit. Indeed these conditions can now be recognised as broader than has traditionally been conceived. Traditional liberal concerns with basic freedoms like freedom of speech or of assembly have to be complemented by a wide range of other concerns which can be conceptualised as preconditions for effective democracy. Increasingly, and I believe correctly, social rights are being taken seriously as falling into this category. For instance, if autonomy is a necessary condition for political equality, it is hard to see how rights to an adequate education and adequate health care can be excluded from the necessary preconditions for a full democracy (Doyal and Gough 1991, Saward 1994: 16–17). In other words, democracy cannot be simply about procedures, not outcomes; for outcomes react back on and influence the conditions of existence of democracy itself.

Conclusion

One cannot be too sanguine about the prospects for success in the short term in reducing the democratic deficits of the EU. A full democracy is not something that can (or will) be handed down to the not-quite-citizens of the EU. The history of democracy shows it as something which has emerged out of conflicts and struggles in which class and other social movements have wrested concessions and control from powerful elites. Such powerful elites continue to exist today, whether organised within nation states or transnationally. Democratisation threatens what are no doubt perceived by many of them as 'vital interests' and its effective extension will continue to be resisted or subverted at every turn, in the name of subsidiarity (identified with national identity) or market freedom.

At the same time, there are real possibilities for intervention. The very desperation with which many nation states are clinging on to their 'sovereignty' is, I believe, an indication of the extent to which it has already been eroded – from above and below as well as by the emergence of non-state forms of authority, heralding the emergence of what Goodman (1995: 2), following Ruggie, calls a 'multiperspectival polity'. This view is not shared by everyone. Mann (1993), for instance, takes an altogether more cautious view of changes in the nation state, seeing it as 'diversifying, developing, not dying'. But in dissecting the various functions which became fused in the nation state (war-making; communications infrastructure; site of political democracy; guaranteeing social citizenship; and macroeconomic planning) he points out that for most of history they were not located in the same agency, and need not be so located in the future. In Western Europe, but not yet elsewhere, he finds them now partially separated.

There are good reasons to suggest that conditions in Europe can provide for their further separation and simultaneous democratisation. As Meehan (1993: 159) points out, the 'complex multi-dimensional configuration' of forces that make up the reality of European politics today 'can provide many openings for challenging authority, for expressing our various loyalties associated with our various identities, and for exercising our rights and duties in more than one arena'. While the difficulties of responding to these opportunities are great, it may be said that the dangers of not doing so are even greater. The prospect of a Fortress Europe is particularly frightening – of an open racism towards the Muslim world and a more covert racism within Europe itself, of a Europe of the haves versus an Eastern Europe and a North Africa of the have-nots superimposed on a divide within the Community of a rich North and a poor South, of rich regions and poor regions (see Lipietz 1993).

Fortunately, such a prospect is not on the cards in the immediate future. But the failure to resolve the European economic crisis or to provide Europe with an outward-going sense of direction and social purpose provides the conditions on which forces of chauvinism, ethno-nationalism and economic and social reaction can flourish. In that eventuality, European integration would be under severe pressure and the very existence of the EU called into question. It is as well to contrast such a future with what Alain Lipietz (1993: 512) has called the 'dream scenario':

> A different Europe is possible – one that is ecological, social and democratic in its overall decisions, but regionally diverse in its life-styles; tames blind market forces through a common base of social rights and ecological duties and mobilises its financial and technical resources to make standards of living equal in different regions.

Any analysis which takes the democratic deficit seriously in all its dimensions is bound to take us in the direction of that dream.

Note

1 This paper has been revised in the light of its very refreshing – and critical – reception at the ECPR conference in Oslo on 29 March 1996. To respond fully to the various objections raised, which were essentially to the approach and not the detail of the analysis, would really require an additional paper. I hope, however, that I have sketched the framework for such a response. In addition to thanking Michael Nentwich, my discussant, and the rest of the workshop participants, I would also like to acknowledge my indebtedness to John Palmer, Irene Bruegel and Mike Newman.

References

Amin, Ash and Thrift, Nigel (1994) 'Living in the Global', in Ash Amin and Nigel Thrift (eds), *Globalization, Institutions, and Regional Development in Europe*, Oxford: Oxford University Press, pp. 1–22.

Amin, Ash and Tomaney, John (1995) 'The Challenge of Cohesion', in Ash Amin and John Tomaney (eds), *Behind the Myth of the European Union: Prospects for Cohesion*, London: Routledge, pp. 10–47.

Barber, Benjamin (1984) *Strong Democracy: Participatory Politics for a New Age*, 4th printing, Berkeley, CA: University of California Press.

Baubóck, Rainer (ed.) (1994) *From Aliens to Citizens: Redefining the Status of Immigrants in Europe*, Aldershot: Avebury.

Beetham, David (1994) 'Key Principles and Indices for a Democratic Audit', in David Beetham (ed.), *Defining and Measuring Democracy*, London: Sage, pp. 25–43.

Castles, Stephen (1994) 'Democracy and Multicultural Citizenship. Australian Debates and their Relevance for Western Europe', in Rainer Baubóck (ed.), *From Aliens to Citizens: Redefining the Status of Immigrants in Europe*, Aldershot: Avebury, pp. 3–27.

Doyal, Len and Gough, Ian (1991) *A Theory of Human Need*, Basingstoke: Macmillan.

Duff, Andrew, Pinder, John and Pryce, Roy (eds) (1994) *Maastricht and Beyond: Building the European Union*, London: Routledge.

Dunford, Mick (1994) 'Winners and Losers: The New Map of Economic Inequality in the European Union', *European Urban and Regional Studies* 1(2): 95–114.

European Parliament (1991) *Report drawn up on behalf of the Committee of Inquiry into Racism and Xenophobia* (The Ford Report), Luxembourg: Office for Official Publications for the European Communities.

European Parliament (1995) *Draft Report of the Committee on Institutional Affairs on the development of the European Union*, 14 March 1995, PE 211.919/B.

Fraser, Nancy and Gordon, Linda (1994) 'Civil Citizenship against Social Citizenship?', in Bart van Steenbergen (ed.), *The Condition of Citizenship*, London: Sage, pp. 90–107.

Geddes, Andrew (1995) 'Immigrant and Ethnic Minorities and the EU's "Democratic Deficit"', *Journal of Common Market Studies* 33(2): 196–217.

Goodman, James (1995) 'Sovereignty and Capital Accumulation in the European Union: Theoretical Interpretations', PSA Conference paper, York, April 1995.

Gross, Andreas (1995) 'Why Europe Needs a European Constitution as a Foundation for a Transnational Democracy', PSA Conference Roundtable, York, April 1995.

Hantrais, Linda (1995) *Social Policy in the European Union*, Basingstoke: Macmillan.

Harvie, Christopher (1994) *The Rise of Regional Europe*, London: Routledge.

Holland, Stuart (1993) *The European Imperative: Economic and Social Cohesion in the 1990s*, Basingstoke: Macmillan.

Koslowski, Rey (1994) 'Intra-EU Migration, Citizenship and Political Union', *Journal of Common Market Studies* 32(3): 369–402.

Kuper, Richard (1994) 'Democracy as Process and the Green and Socialist agendas', *Contemporary Politics* 1(4): 73–91.

Kuper, Richard (1997) 'The Making of a Constitution for Europe', Loughborough: UACES Research Conference.

Layton-Henry, Zig and Czarina, Wilpert (1994) *Discrimination, Racism and Citizenship*, London: Anglo-German Foundation for the Study of Industrial Society.

Leibfried, Stephan (1993) 'Towards a European Welfare State? On Integrating Poverty Regimes into the European Community', in Catherine Jones (ed.) *New Perspectives on the Welfare State in Europe*, London: Routledge, pp. 133–56.

Lipietz, Alain (1992) *Towards a New Economic Order* (first published 1989), Cambridge: Polity.

Lipietz, Alain (1993) 'Social Europe, Legitimate Europe: The Inner and Outer Boundaries of Europe', *Environment and Planning D* 11: 501–12.

MacLaughlin, Jim (1993) 'Defending the Frontiers: The Political Geography of Race and Racism in the European Community', in Colin H. Williams (ed.), *The Political Geography of the New World Order*, London: Belhaven, pp. 20–45.

Maier, Charles S. (ed.) (1987) *Changing Boundaries of the Political: Essays on the Evolving Balance between State and Society, Public and Private*, Cambridge: Cambridge University Press.

Mancini, G. Federico (1991) 'The Making of a Constitution for Europe', in Robert O. Keohane and Stanley Hoffman (eds), *The New European Community*, Boulder, CO: Westview, pp. 177–94.

Mann, Michael (1987) 'Ruling Class Strategies and Citizenship', *Sociology*, 21: 339–54.

Mann, Michael (1993) 'Nation-states in Europe and Other Continents: Diversifying, Developing, Not Dying', *Daedelus* 122(3): 1–23.

Marshall, T. H. (1950) *Citizenship and Social Class*, Cambridge: Cambridge University Press.

Martin, David (1991) *Europe: An Ever Closer Union*, Nottingham: Spokesman.

Martiniello, Marco (1994) 'Citizenship of the European Union. A Critical View', in Rainer Bauböck (ed.), *From Aliens to Citizens: Redefining the Status of Immigrants in Europe*, Aldershot: Avebury, pp. 29–47.

Meehan, Elizabeth (1993) *Citizenship and the European Community*, London: Sage.

Miles, Robert (1994) 'Explaining Racism in Contemporary Europe', in Ali Rattansi and Sallie Westwood (eds), *Racism, Modernity and Identity: on the Western Front*, Cambridge: Polity, pp. 189–221.

Murray, Robin (1991) *Local Space: Europe and the New Regionalism*, Stevenage: CLES & SEEDS.

Nentwich, Michael and Falkner, Gerda (1997) 'The Treaty of Amsterdam: Towards a New Institutional Balance', *European Integration online Papers* (EIoP) Vol. 1, No. 015; http://eiop.or.at/eiop/texte/1997-015a.htm.

Offe, Claus (1987) 'Challenging the Boundaries of Institutional Politics: Social Movements since the 1960s', in Charles S. Maier (ed.), *Changing Boundaries of the Political: Essays on the Evolving Balance between State and Society, Public and Private*, Cambridge: Cambridge University Press, pp. 63–105.

Picciotto, Sol (1991) 'The Internationalisation of the State', *Capital and Class* 43: 43–65.

Red–Green Study Group (1994) *What on Earth is to be Done?*, Manchester: RGSG.

Reflection Group (1995) *Progress report from the chairman of the Reflection Group on the 1996 Inter-Governmental Conference* Madrid, 1 September 1995, SN 509/1/95 (REFLEX 10) REV 1.

Saward, Michael (1994) 'Democratic Theory and Indices of Democratisation', in David Beetham (ed.), *Defining and Measuring Democracy*, London: Sage, pp. 6–24.

Sivanandan (1989) 'UK Commentary: Racism 1992', *Race & Class* 30(3): 85–90.

Turner, Bryan (1990) 'Outline of a Theory of Citizenship', in Chantal Mouffe (ed.), *Dimensions of Radical Democracy*, London: Verso, pp. 33–62.

Wainwright, Hilary (1993) *Arguments for a New Left: Answering the Free Market Right*, Oxford: Blackwell.

Weiler, J. H. H., Haltern, Ulrich R. and Mayer, Franz C. (1995) 'European Democracy and its Critique', *West European Politics* 18(3): 4–39.

Williams, Shirley (1990) 'Sovereignty and Accountability in the European Community', *Political Quarterly* 61(3): 299–317.

11 European Union citizenship as a model of citizenship beyond the nation state

Possibilities and limits

Theodora Kostakopoulou[1]

The 1992 Treaty on European Union (TEU) laid the foundations for a European civil society by introducing the institution of EU citizenship as a supplement to national citizenship. EU nationals have the rights of free movement and residence (Article 8a); the right to vote and to stand for election in the European Parliament and municipal elections in the member states of their residence (Article 8b); the right to protection by diplomatic and consular authorities of any member state in a third country where the citizen's own member state is not represented (Article 8c); the right to access non-judicial means of redress through the Ombudsperson and through petitions to the EP (Article 8d).

EU citizenship is expressly said to be a dynamic institution, progressively evolving in conjunction with the evolution of the EU (Article 8e). Despite this claim and several proposals to the 1996 Inter-Governmental Conference (IGC) for the strengthening of its scope through extension and deepening of the rights of European citizens and residents, the Treaty of Amsterdam has not added much to the legal substance of this institution. In symbolic recognition of national sensitivities, the treaty introduced the statement that EU citizenship shall complement and not replace national citizenship, and added a new third subparagraph to Article 8d stating that 'every citizen of the Union may write to any of the institutions or bodies referred to in this Article or in Article 4 in one of the languages mentioned in Article 248(1) and have an answer in the same language'. On the other hand, several other new provisions of the draft Amsterdam Treaty strengthen and improve human rights within the EU and have implications for citizens' rights.

EU citizenship as an institutional design offers both unique challenges and interesting possibilities. Among the latter is the prospect of a post-national political arrangement which facilitates multiple membership, by both natural and legal persons, in various overlapping and strategically interacting communities on supranational, national and regional/local levels. EU citizenship also entails the promise both of a heterogeneous community which values diversity and of a new form of citizenship which transcends the nationality model of citizenship.

Several of these possibilities, however, remain at present unexplored or frustrated owing to the inappropriate imposition of the logic and the language of the nation state onto the European level. A prime manifestation of this is the conditioning of the personal scope of EU citizenship upon tenure or acquisition of member state nationality. This has led to the exclusion of approximately 9.2 million third-country nationals (*Eurostat* 1996) who reside on a legal and permanent basis in the territories of the EU, and thus to their subsequent relegation to the periphery of the European civil society. The exclusionary nature of the personal scope of EU citizenship is coupled with its underdeveloped substantive content. As a result, theorists are led to dismiss EU citizenship as a symbolic plaything without serious content. Qualitative changes can only be made to this conception if the radical potential of EU citizenship is unearthed and a new agenda is articulated.

The purpose of this chapter is to highlight some of these alternative possibilities and to flesh out some ideas for further institutional reform. The particular relevance of such endeavour has been highlighted by the 'crisis of principled politics' in the EU and the modest reforms agreed at Amsterdam. Unearthing the radical potential of EU citizenship requires an abandonment of the category of the nation state as the lens through which to view developments in the EU (Wessels 1997). Modelling the emerging polity in the EU on the basis of ideas and patterns derived from the nineteenth-century process of national community formation, or imbuing it with functions and powers similar to those of the state, is not fruitful either methodologically or substantively. In methodological terms, such an approach appears to 'mobilize notions of the past in order to explain developments in the future, without any effort to justify why these notions might still be appropriate' (Koopmans 1992: 1049). In substantive terms, it undermines interesting possibilities for restructuring political life and for devising coordinate levels of government.

The radical potential of EU citizenship

The radical potential of EU citizenship may be identified in the possibilities for redefining community, rethinking membership, rearticulating citizenship, and enhancing democratic decision making that have sprung from the process of European political integration (see further Kostakopoulou 1996).

The institutionalisation of EU citizenship by the TEU precipitated the recognition that citizens may participate in and identify with multiple, overlapping and strategically interacting communities. The creation of an additional tier of rights and obligations from which citizens derive legal benefits (Closa 1992, 1994) shows that citizens' interests, concerns and identifications can no longer be confined exclusively to the national level, but extend both upwards to the supranational level and downwards to the subnational level. Regional, local, ethnic, linguistic and other identities can no longer be absorbed by the national state and overridden by a monolithic national identity (see Gilroy 1987, Karst 1989, Leca 1992, Silverman 1992). Citizens enjoy their plural identifications and have flexible commitments as a result of their shifting participation in various levels of government and their engagement with various projects. More importantly, within such a context, citizens are increasingly eager to use whatever opportunities are available on one level in order to induce constitutional developments on another and to halt centralising tendencies by national executives.

This process opens also the way for an alternative conception of community which is based neither on ascriptive membership, that is on thick communal attachments, nor on the liberal principle of consent (i.e. 'communities of shared values', 'communities of shared final ends'). The basic problem with 'communities of shared origin' is that they often lead to exclusion and domination. Liberal consensual communities of equal citizenship, on the other hand, have traditionally taken for granted the framework of a culturally homogeneous nation state (Anthias and Yuval-Davies 1992, Schuck and Smith 1985).

Europe's deep diversity and the profound disagreements over both the shape and the future of the European project prompt us to consider a novel conception of community; that is, one which is held together by the concern and willingness of its various constituent units to work together towards creating 'an ever closer union among the peoples of Europe' by designing appropriate institutions, whilst preserving and respecting the distinctive identities of its members (Clause F.1 of the TEU). What is distinctive about such a process is the absence of both consensus and certainty over the juridical–political shape of the outcome. What seems to sustain the sense of community in the EU is concern and a sense of commitment on behalf of the constituent units to participate in the collective shaping of this process and in institutional design.

Such a conception of community embodies a novel concept of politics and demos. It conceives the European demos as a genuinely heterogeneous European public – a European public which values difference, precisely because it is neither built on tangible homogeneity, nor requires cultural conformity. On this reading, European identity does not feature as a monolithic and overarching identity which seeks to level out differences or to absorb other allegiances, but, instead, as a civic and inclusive identity. Citizenship is thus the catalyst for the formation of identity and community at the European level rather than an institutionalised reflection of pre-existing, pre-political views about community membership and identity. As Preuss (1995: 108) has nicely put it, 'citizenship does not presuppose the community of which the citizen is a member, but creates this very community'. This line of reasoning stands in sharp contrast with the 'no demos' thesis of the German Constitutional Court (BVerfGE 1989, see also Gustavsson's chapter in this volume); that is to say, the claim that the EU is democratically deficient because there is not yet a European demos (Weiler 1995, 1996): it invites us to think of European demos as the product, and not the precondition, of Euro-democracy. What follows from this is a model of citizenship which, centred upon domicile, transcends the traditional nationality model of citizenship.

Domicile as a legal criterion for membership in the European demos encapsulates the idea of 'concern and engagement' as the elements required for community building. It is based on ascertaining certain factual conditions from which an intention to make that particular territory the hub of one's interests and life can be deduced. As such, it is considerably less exclusionary than the nationality principle, since it would include as full and respected members those who have made a particular territory their home, the centre of their economic life, pay taxes and are affected by state policies, send their children to school and participate in a whole web of social interactions which undoubtedly generate expectations. If EU citizenship were conditioned upon domicile, third-country nationals, who have been residing on a lawful and permanent basis in the territories of the EU, would not be deprived of the right to the benefits and the protection that EU law affords to Community nationals. Moreover, conditioning EU citizenship upon domicile appears to be consistent with the Community method, since the principle of domicile could easily be propounded as a Community law concept, thereby ensuring fair and uniform interpretation of the personal scope of EU citizenship across the territories of the EU.

Such a proposal is, in my opinion, considerably more attractive than subjecting the admission of third-country nationals to EU citizenship on the satisfaction of certain criteria, modelled upon those required by national laws, such as lawful entry and residence, age, employment, good character, loyalty to the aims of the EU, assimilation and so on (O'Keeffe 1994: 105). This proposal seems to entail sowing the seeds of a Euro-nationality. It grants third-country nationals only qualified respect thereby reaffirming their differential position in the emerging Euro-polity. And although others suggest either the relaxation of naturalisation laws in the member states (Evans 1994) or the introduction of legislative mechanisms to harmonise nationality laws for the purposes of free movement (O'Leary 1992: 384), EU citizenship needs to be disentangled from state nationality and affirm itself as a true supranational institution, if it is not to be robbed of democratic quality and substance.

Another potentially interesting development which is likely to have an impact on citizenship theory is the idea of multiple publics. Citizenship can no longer be confined to one privileged site, one unified public (e.g. as it was previously the level of the state), but it involves multiple, overlapping and strategically inter-acting publics formed on various levels. This allows for a complex and multi-faceted interrelationship of individuals, groups, 'interest groups and volun-tary associations, local and provincial authorities, regions and alliances of regions' with multiple, strategically interacting tiers of government (Meehan 1993: 185). This opens up new possibilities for more differentiated forms of citi-zenship and for more differentiated means to attack the structures of inequality and to combat social exclusion.

Differentiated citizenship could be articulated on the basis of four main areas of concern: race, gender, socio-economic inequality (class) and regional affairs. As regards the first two areas, Young's theorisation of justice as the project of empowerment of historically oppressed groups contains many fruitful insights and suggestions. Young (1989, 1990) argues that differentiated citizenship may be the best way to tackle the disadvantaged position of certain groups in society and, thus, to promote their participation in full citizenship. Differentiated citizenship entails the 'provision of institutionalised means for the explicit recognition and representation of oppressed groups'. It consists of guaranteed representation in political bodies, public funds for advocacy groups, veto rights over specific policies that affect groups directly (see also Abromeit's chapter in this volume), and group-differentiated policies such as language rights for Hispanics in the USA, reproductive rights for women, cultural rights for ethnic communities and so on. Young's fruitful insights could be applied to the EU and her basic idea could be further extended to cover socio-economic inequality and regional aspirations for increasing opportunities for self-governance.

The differentiated means to be employed in the EU, therefore, could include group rights that apply to certain categories of people by virtue of their specific circumstances. These are intended as a supplement to and not a replacement of the general tier of rights applicable to all. In this respect, the Committee of the Regions and the Migrants' Forum could be seen as the first step towards enabling the voicing of regions' or a group's analysis of how EU policies affect them. The Commission has also supported the setting up of a European liaison committee of non-governmental organisations involved in the fight against poverty. All these are initiatives designed not only to enable the voicing of the aspirations and viewpoints of groups and organisations, but also to generate development programmes and policy proposals by the groups themselves.

To be sure, current European sex equality law is not distinguished by its wholehearted acceptance of a group-oriented model. The Community's central objective has been to promote formal legal equality between the sexes, and not to tackle in a more direct way the structural causes of sex discrimination and thereby procuring substantive social change (see Case 184/85 *Hofmann* v *Bavmer Ersatzkasse* [1984] ECR 3047). However, Article 2(4) of Directive 76/207, which provides for equal treatment of men and women in the context of employment, leaves room for measures to promote equal opportunities for men and women, in particular, by removing existing inequalities which affect women's opportunities in the areas referred to in Article 1 (1). In addition, Article 6 of the Agreement on Social Policy allows for the adoption of affirmative action legislation. And although recent ECJ jurisprudence does not generate much optimism (Case 12/86 *Commission* v *France* [1988] ECR 6315; C-450/93 *Kalanke* v *Freie Hansestadt Bremen*, Decision of the Court of 17 October 1995), the incorporation of Article 6 in Article 119 by the Amsterdam Treaty is bound to trigger interesting developments in the future. Nevertheless, the ECJ has been instrumental in enhancing the rights of pregnant and birthing mothers (another example of group rights). In addition, the Commission, backed up by the EP, has introduced Positive Action Programmes, aiming, among other things, at eliminating sex discrimination beyond the workplace and promoting equal opportunity for women. A crucial feature of these programmes is the acknowledgement that women's educational and employment opportunities are closely linked to the sharing of family responsibilities.

In terms of regional rights for increasing opportunities for self-governance, the principle of subsidiarity could potentially be an important tool in the process of the distribution of competences among different layers of government. However, this genuinely decentralist meaning of subsidiarity has been compromised in the current formulation of the principle in Article 3b(c) of the TEU. The article is so designed as to appease fears that the uniting of Europe will encroach upon the member states' sovereign spheres of jurisdiction (Bermann 1994), rather than to coordinate levels of government. The current definition of the principle, both in the TEU and the Edinburgh Declaration (1992), postulates that competence belongs in principle to the member states, since the Community has only the powers attributed to it by the member states. Moreover, there is no mention of the allocation of competences between national and subnational levels, thus allowing each member state to determine how its powers are to be exercised domestically.

Despite such limitations, the promise of subsidiarity to empower has promoted interest in a 'Europe of the Regions'. In this context, it has increased calls by the German Länder, as well as the Spanish and Belgian regions, for a greater involvement by subnational government in EU policy making on the lines of 'co-operative regionalism' (Scott *et al.* 1994). Abromeit (this volume) goes a step further to suggest vesting regions with direct-democratic veto rights.

However, what may be called structural rights are also important. These would have as their central objective the tackling of the various facets of economic inequality. They may range from specific polices aimed at eliminating regional disparities in development and improving the structural adjustment of Europe's poor regions to measures designed to combat homelessness, child poverty and so on. Maintaining the inclusiveness of citizenship requires concern about the long-term effects of the replacement of adequately paid employment by unemployment, of poorly rewarded part-time work, of sporadic or low employment of various sorts. Unemployed people, women, old people, people with disabilities, informal carers, members of ethnic or religious communities, the homeless and travellers, all are at great risk of social exclusion.

The Commission's (1993) *Green Paper on Social Europe* addresses the issue of social exclusion and, accordingly, stresses the need for demarginalisation and reintegration of long-term unemployed, those without educational qualifications and single-parent families. The Commission's (1994) *White Paper on Growth, Competitiveness and Employment* acknowledges that the future of European integration depends on the effective combat of unemployment, but fails to specify the political initiatives needed to be taken at the EU level. In its *Resolution on the White Paper* (European Parliament 1995), the EP emphasises that economic prosperity, competitiveness, increased productivity and social progress must not be seen as conflicting ideals. The EP warns against attempts to dismantle the European social model under the pretext of promotion of employment, and confirms its commitment to fundamental rights to social protection. An important feature of structural rights is that they encapsulate a mixed (both individual and corporate) approach to welfare as they recognise that groups and regions could have legitimate claims for economic development and assistance.

The sadness of the potential? The EU and the citizen after Amsterdam

Despite these developments, EU institutions, perhaps burdened by the inherited failures of the member states, have failed to respond adequately to the promise entailed by EU citizenship. Despite rhetoric on citizenship and official pronouncements about building a 'Europe of law and democracy' which is respectful of 'difference' and rights, the reality of the EU's intentions reveals its adherence to an exclusivist mode of European identity and a restrictive conception of citizenship.

The TEU (Article 8 (1)) confined the benefits of EU citizenship to EU nationals only, thereby institutionalising the exclusionary personal scope of European citizenship. Member states can unilaterally define the term nationality and, thus, exclude third-country nationals from full membership in the European demos. Non-EU nationals do not enjoy free movement and residence, political rights, and, generally speaking, the protection against discrimination in the fields of employment, labour law, social security, vocational training, collective bargaining that EU law affords to EU nationals – unless, of course, they can derive rights from their relationship with an EU citizen or their employers' connection with the EU, or from the cooperation agreements signed by the Community and third countries. The Amsterdam Treaty did not alter the personal scope of EU citizenship. It has merely inserted in Article 8 the unnecessary statement that EU citizenship 'shall complement and not replace national citizenship', thereby giving symbolic recognition to national sensitivities.

Instead of capitalising on opportunities for designing a new form of citizenship, the Treaty has thus failed to promote a more inclusive identity than that provided by the Maastricht Treaty. This failure is not due to an absence of ideas and concrete proposals for institutional reform. Several institutional actors at both the European and national levels have campaigned long and hard and have put forward proposals for a new institutional dynamic in the domain of citizenship prior to and during the IGC. Community institutions, such as the EP, the Economic and Social Committee, and to some extent the Commission, have been aware of this problem of unjust exclusion and its implications for over a decade. Both the EP and the Commission have proposed, on occasion, reforms which, despite their vague formulation, have been designed to tackle the inequitable position of third-country nationals *vis-à-vis* Community nationals.

In 1985, the Commission drafted a background report calling for the granting of social and political rights to third-country nationals resident in the EU. The Council, however, ignored these proposals as national governments opposed such extension. The EP and the Economic and Social Committee, on several occasions, have recommended that freedom of movement should apply to all resident workers irrespective of nationality and that non-EC migrants should have the same rights of family unification as EC national workers (European Parliament 1990, 1991). It has also been proposed that non-EC migrants should enjoy protection from discrimination on the same footing as EC nationals and that they should be granted electoral rights. Non-governmental organisations too, such as the Starting Line Group, have highlighted the unfavourable position of third-country nationals in the EU, and have proposed either the liberalisation of naturalisation laws across the EU or the granting of EU citizenship to Europe's third-country nationals who have been lawfully residing in the territory of a member state for five years. Unfortunately, the Council has reacted negatively to these proposals.

The substantial work and intense lobbying done by a number of non-governmental organisations means that a new anti-discrimination clause has been inserted into the EC Treaty at Amsterdam. The new Article 6a enables the Council, acting unanimously on a proposal from the Commission and after consulting the EP, to 'take appropriate action to combat discrimination based on sex, racial or ethnic origin, religion or belief, disability, age or sexual orientation'. The new Article constitutes a major step forward in that it clearly places the issue of discrimination within Community competence. Also encouraging is the fact that the scope of this provision, in particular disability, age and sexual orientation, managed to survive the negotiations. But the new provision suffers from some important limitations too. First, its optional character (i.e. the Council . . . may) means that 6a is unlikely to give rise to individual rights which can be relied upon in national courts, and that the ECJ will not be able to adjudicate on actions against member states until directives have been produced. Second, the requirement of unanimity, instead of qualified majority voting, will undermine the effectiveness of this article, since any member state could block future proposals. Whilst the insertion of a directly effective anti-discrimination clause into EU citizenship which is supplemented by an equal opportunities policy still remains a future goal, in the short term, non-governmental organisations will need to keep the pressure on the Commission and the member states to introduce and adopt implementing legislation in this area.

True, sex equality fares better than other areas of equal treatment. It is expressly declared to be one of the goals of the Union (the new Article 2 EC) and is to be promoted in all its activities (amended Article 3 EC). More importantly, the full integration of the 1992 Social Agreement into Community law makes possible the effective realisation of equality through the adoption of group-specific measures. The new Article 119(4) affirms the principle of equal treatment, but also allows for member states to maintain or adopt specific measures in order to make it easier for the underrepresented sex to pursue a vocational activity or to prevent or compensate for disadvantages in their professional careers. This provision is supported by a declaration that priority must be given, in the first instance, to 'improving the situation of women in working life'.

The recent integration of social policy measures is a significant step forward in the direction of developing a genuine European social policy. Although the incorporation of the 'social chapter' annexes into Community law at Amsterdam manifests the EU's commitment to social rights, the new Common Social Policy is still limited. It needs to be strengthened in order to guarantee effective social rights: to incorporate employment rights such as the right to work as well as rights in employment such as minimum wage provisions, provisions on the right of association, the right to strike and night work for women. Such an extension would undoubtedly widen the EU's current focus on workers' rights by transforming them into citizens' rights. In addition, other important questions – like social security, redundancy or worker representation – still require the unanimous agreement of the member states.

With the possibility of consumer abuse across frontiers in the single market, EU citizenship should also be extended to the field of consumer protection. True, consumer protection is EU policy under Article 129, and the Treaty of Amsterdam reinforces the legal base. However, future incorporation of consumer protection in the material scope of EU citizenship may protect consumers by affirming the rights to health and safety and to protection of their economic interests. Similarly, future incorporation of a citizen's right to enjoy a healthy environment would facilitate civil liability for damage caused by pollution.

As far as political citizenship is concerned, Amsterdam added nothing on political rights. The TEU granted EU nationals the rights to vote and stand as a candidate for European elections and local elections in the member state of their residence. Given that residence is propounded as a sufficient condition for participation in local government elections, it seems unreasonable to deny EU citizens the right to participate in general elections, unless, of course, it can be unambiguously demonstrated that the differences between the two levels of government have a significant impact upon national interests. The most commonly held objection to this idea is that participation of EU citizens in national parliamentary elections is likely to dilute the national character of parliamentary elections or jeopardise national interests. But the argument that Community nationals should be ineligible for national elective offices because as MPs they would have access to secret information or would take part in deliberations of great importance to a state's security and defence, appears unconvincing for two reasons. First, defence and security issues appear to bear increasingly less weight in the load of normal parliamentary activities. Second, the plausibility of this argument has to be judged in light of the coordinated efforts to devise a common European security and defence policy. On this basis, it seems that objections to the idea of granting full political rights to domiciled EU citizens are underpinned by ideological and not political considerations. Nativism has been traditionally associated with loyalty and alien status with disloyalty. From the point of view of citizenship, however, political participation at the national level may be more important than participation at local level, since decisions of more direct relevance to the work of the Community are taken on the national level (Evans 1991: 210). One can only hope that member states will review the situation and revise their position in this respect. In any case, the local enfranchisement of Community nationals resident in a member state other than their own makes the disenfranchisement of domiciled third-country nationals difficult to justify.

Article 8b must be seen in connection with Article 138a, which provides for the right to political association – a necessary prerequisite for the exercise of voting rights. Article 138a acknowledges that political parties at the European level are an important contributing factor to European integration, as they constitute a means for the formation of a European awareness and the expression of the political will of the citizens of the EU. Whereas there is hardly any doubt that Article 138a must be applied and further developed, enhancement of citizen participation in the EU requires also the recognition of the rights of association and assembly within the context of EU citizenship provisions. In this respect, a future reform of the scope of EU citizenship may include the insertion of a new paragraph in Article 8b stating that 'every resident of the Union shall have the right to associate with other residents of the Union in order to represent their interests and defend their rights'.

Giving greater political substance to EU citizenship requires also the recognition of residents' rights to set up associations, foundations and organisations – provided, of course, that their purposes conform to European and national constitutional frameworks, coupled with a commitment on behalf of the EU to support those organisations which promote cooperation in various policy areas. In addition, political citizenship could be enriched by inserting provisions concerning regional rights, be it in the form of ensuring the administrative independence of regions and municipalities, or promoting interregional cooperation, or enabling legal persons to set up associations in order to promote their views and defend their interests. Finally, political participation can only be enhanced if citizens have the right to information together with appropriate means of redress. The Amsterdam Treaty contains an explicit reference to the principle of transparency. A new article (191a) provides for the right of any citizen of the EU, any natural or legal person residing or having its registered office in a member state to have a right of access to EP, Council and Commission documents. It allows each institution to draft its own code of conduct subject to the general principles to be drawn up by the Council and EP. Although the secret legislative process of the Council of Ministers is to continue (the Council has, nevertheless, agreed to make available all proposed third-pillar measures), this new provision commits the EU to greater openness in its institutions and their decision-making process.

Finally, the radical potential of EU citizenship has little chance to be realised unless the issue of immigration is seriously re-examined. This is not only because matters relating to the rights of third-country nationals resident in the EU have fallen within the ambit of justice and home affairs cooperation, but also because immigration shapes the boundaries and the content of citizenship. True, the IGC introduced some crucial reforms to the old framework of intergovernmental cooperation in Justice and Home Affairs (the so-called Third Pillar of the Maastricht Treaty) (on this, see O'Keeffe 1995a, 1995b). It 'Communitarized' the areas of immigration, asylum and the rights of third-country nationals resident in the EU alongside external border controls, visa policy, rules governing judicial cooperation in civil matters and administrative cooperation, thereby providing EU institutions with a greater role. In particular, the new chapter entitled 'Progressive establishment of an area of Freedom, Security and Justice' (a complex and often obscure piece of legislation which entails also three opt-out protocols for Ireland, Denmark and the UK) sets out a five-year transitional period from the entry into force of the Treaty during which the Council will continue to take decisions by unanimous vote, the Commission will share the right of initiative with the member states, but the EP will be consulted, and the ECJ will have jurisdiction to receive requests for preliminary rulings under Article 177 from national courts. Any move towards greater involvement of the EP or the introduction of Community decision-making procedures will require unanimous decision after this transitional period (Article G of the new Title). In addition, the Amsterdam Treaty incorporates the much criticised Schengen acquis (this includes the Schengen Agreement of 1985, the Schengen Implementing Convention of 1990, the Accession Protocols with related Final Acts and Declarations, decisions and declarations adopted by the Executive Committee and acts for implementation by the organs of the Executive Committee) into the framework of the EU, but leaves the Council to decide the legal basis for each of the provisions or decisions which constitute the Schengen acquis. Until such determination has been made, the Schengen measures will be regarded as acts adopted on the basis of the Third Pillar (Title VI TEU) (Article B of the Protocol on integrating the Schengen acquis).

No doubt, this positive, albeit initially limited, extension of accountability will please the critics of the Third Pillar. However, the new developments also involve risks and a new set of problems. First, the ECJ's jurisdiction is excluded from measures or decisions taken in the areas of external border controls, internal border controls and the rights of free travel of third-country nationals within the EU during a three-month period, which relate to the maintenance of law and order and the safeguarding of internal security (Article H(2)). This exclusion contradicts the concept of 'respect for the rule of law' which the amended Article F of the TEU (on fundamental rights) propounds as one of the foundations of the EU. Similarly, organisations set up in the context of the Third Pillar, such as Europol, are excluded from the scope of the new Article 213b EC on data protection and the EC Data Protection Directive which will apply to EU institutions processing personal data from 1 January 1999. Second, national executives decided to circumscribe the role of the ECJ and prune its integrative dynamic by restricting requests for preliminary reference rulings to courts of the last instance. National courts and tribunals can no longer refer cases relating to 'Freedom, Security and Justice' matters to the ECJ, and references by the courts of last instance are discretionary, not mandatory (unless the point is acte claire). Such inhibitions on the ECJ's jurisdiction come at the expense of legal certainty, the consistent interpretation of the European law across the EU, and are likely to yield undesirable implications for individuals who will now have to pursue their cases through the successive tiers of national jurisdiction. What is clear, however, is that the member states are determined to maintain as much control as possible over the shape of the new legal and institutional framework on asylum and immigration. But it would not be unreasonable to expect normative coherence, or at least a degree of sensitivity where the constitutive elements of EC law are at stake. Articles C(5) and H(e) of the new Title fail to display such a sensitivity; they contradict well-established principles of Community law. In opposition to the doctrine of pre-emption and the duty of solidarity imposed by Article 5 EC, Article C(5) seeks to preserve some measure of member states' competence in matters of immigration. According to the article, whatever the Community may do on immigration and on the conditions of residence of third-country nationals, the EU 'shall not prevent any member states from maintaining or introducing in the areas concerned national provisions which are compatible with this Treaty and with international agreements'. Similarly, Article H3 camouflages national disregard for EU law by resorting to the legal concept of *res judicata*. This provision states that rulings given by the ECJ in response to requests by the Council, the Commission or a member state shall not apply to judgments of courts and tribunals of the member states which have become *res judicata*. In Community law, issues falling within Community competence can only become *res judicata*, that is no longer open to further legal argument, if the ECJ has ruled on them.

Can one realistically hope that the new arrangements and the modest gains in democratic and judicial accountability will result in substantive changes in immigration and asylum policy? Will they lead to a questioning of the Schengen Convention as a model for the development of a European immigration policy (Kostakopoulou, forthcoming)? After all, it is the member states who designed the previous immigration regime, and have chosen to replicate the national restrictive immigration policies at the European level. Can national executives move away from the national path of exclusion and xenophobia and respond to the challenge of immigration by elaborating a principled, coherent and forward-looking European immigration policy which looks into the causes of the international refugee crisis with honesty? Naturally, the ideological redefinition of immigration as a 'law and order' problem affects third-country nationals negatively and reinforces their inequitable position in the emerging Euro-polity. A vivid proof of the way in which the Council views the position of the migrant population resident in the EU is the 'Resolution on the Status of Third-country Nationals Residing on a Long-term Basis in the Territory of the Member States (Council of the European Communities 1996). Instead of being welcomed as respectful and rightful participants with equal rights and opportunities in the workplace and society, third-country nationals are granted conditioned membership and second-class citizenship.

One cannot expect IGCs to alter completely the manner in which matters have been previously dealt with. However, growing levels of concern over the democratic deficit, the lack of transparency, and secretive negotiations which do not involve greater consultation with interested parties and public debate were something that member states' national executives could no longer afford to ignore. It is precisely this awareness that distinguishes the 1996 IGC, which resulted in concrete and positive, but still limited, attempts at redressing the balance. Perhaps, this awareness is enough to kindle hopes for the creation of a democratic and heterogeneous European public, and to sustain institutional actors' work and pressures to finish the unfinished rights' agenda of EU citizenship and realise its radical potential.

Note

1   The discussion in this paper states the law as at August 1997.

References

Anthias, F. and Yuval-Davis, N. (1992) *Racialized Boundaries: Race, Nation, Gender, Colour and Class and the Anti-racist Struggle*, London: Routledge.

Bergmann, A. 'Taking subsidiarity seriously: federalism in the European Community and United States,' *Columbia Law Review* 94(2): 332–455.

BVerfGR (1993) *Bundesverfassungsgericht, Entsheidungen* Vol. 89, Judgment of 12 October 1993.

Closa, C. (1992) 'The Concept of Citizenship in the Treaty on European Union', *Common Market Law Review* 29(6): 1137–69.

Closa, C. (1994) 'Citizenship of the Union and Nationality of Member States', in D. O'Keeffe and P. Twomey (eds), *Legal Issues of the Maastricht Treaty*, Chichester: John Wiley, pp. 109–19.

Commission of the European Communities (1993) *European Social Policy – Options for the Union*, Green Paper, COM (93) final.

Commission of the European Communities (1994) *European Social Policy – A Way Forward for the Union*, White Paper, COM (94) 333 final.

Committee of the Regions (1995) 'Opinion on the Revision of the Treaty on European Union', *Bulletin* EU 4/1995, point 1.9.2.

Council of the European Communities (1996) 'Resolution on the Status of Third-country Nationals Residing on a Long-term Basis in the Territory of the Member States', *Official Journal* 96/c 80/02, March.

European Parliament (1990) *Resolution on Free Movement of Persons*, A3 0199/91, 91/C 159/05, OJ C 159/12–15.

European Parliament (1991) *Resolution on Union Citizenship*, OJ C183, 15/7/91.

European Parliament (1995) *Resolution on the White Paper on European Social Policy – A Way Forward for the Union*, A4–0122/94, OJ C43/63, 19 January 1995.

Eurostat N. 31/96, 22 May 1996.

Evans, A. (1991) 'Nationality Law and European Integration', *European Law Review* 16(3): 190–215.

Evans, A. (1994) 'Third Country Nationals and the Treaty on European Union', *European Journal of International Law* 5: 199–219.

Gilroy, P. (1987) *There Ain't No Black in the Union Jack: The Cultural Politics of Race and Nation*, London: Hutchinson.

Karst, K. L. (1989) *Belonging to America: Equal Citizenship and the Constitution*, New Haven, CT: Yale University Press.

Koopmans, T. (1992) 'Federalism: The Wrong Debate', Guest Editorial, *Common Market Law Review* 29(6): 1047–52.

Kostakopoulou, T. (1996) 'Towards a Theory of Constructive Citizenship in Europe', *The Journal of Political Philosophy* 4(4): 337–58.

Kostakopoulou, T. (forthcoming) 'Is There an Alternative to Schengenland?', *Political Studies*.

Leca, J. (1992) 'Questions on Citizenship', in C. Mouffe (ed.), *Dimensions of Radical Democracy: Pluralism, Citizenship and Community*, London: Verso, pp. 17–32.

Meehan, E. (1993) *Citizenship and the European Community*, London: Sage.

O'Keeffe, D. (1994) 'Union Citizenship', in D. O'Keeffe and P. H. Twomey (eds), *Legal Issues of the Maastricht Treaty*, Chichester: John Wiley, pp. 87–107.

O'Keeffe, D. (1995a) 'The Emergence of a European Immigration Policy', *European Law Review* 20(1): 20–36.

O'Keeffe, D. (1995b) 'Recasting the Third Pillar', *Common Market Law Review* 32(4): 893–920.

O'Leary, S. (1992) 'Nationality Law and Community Citizenship: A Tale of Two Uneasy Bedfellows', *Yearbook of European Law* 12: 353–84.

Preuss, U. (1995) 'Citizenship and Identity: Aspects of a Political Theory of Citizenship', in R. Bellamy, V. Bufacchil and D. Castaglione (eds), *Democracy and Constitutional Culture in the Union of Europe*, London: Lothian Foundation Press, pp. 107–20.

Schuck, P. and Smith, S. (1985) *Citizenship without Consent. Illegal Aliens in the American Polity*, New Haven, CT: Yale University Press.

Scott, A., Peterson, J. and Millar, D. (1994) 'Subsidiarity: "Europe of the Regions," v. the British Constitution?' *Journal of Common Market Studies* 32(1).

Silverman, M. (1992) *Deconstructing the Nation: Immigration, Racism and Citizenship in Modern France*, London: Routledge.

Weiler, J. (1995) 'Does Europe Need a Constitution? Reflections on Demos, Telos and the German Maastricht Decision', *European Law Journal* 1(3): 219–58.

Weiler, J. (1996) 'European Neo-constitutionalism: In Search of Foundations for the European Constitutional Order', *Political Studies* XLIV: 513–33.

Wessels, W. (1997) 'An Ever Closer Fusion? A Dynamic Macropolitical View on Integration Processes', *Journal of Common Market Studies* 35(2): 267–99.

Young, I. (1989) 'Polity and Group Difference: A Critique of the Ideal of Universal Citizenship', *Ethics* 99(2): 250–74.

Young, I. (1990) *Justice and the Politics of Difference*, Princeton, NJ: Princeton University Press.

12 European Union citizenship and supranational democracy

Carlos Closa

Introduction

The aim of this chapter is to discuss the connection between supranational democracy and European Union (EU) citizenship. There are two ways in which this linkage might be established. The first is normative, concerned with such questions as whether there should be a supranational democracy. Within this normative domain this chapter is concerned with the fundamental problem of identifying a model of democracy in which the 'people' are constituted as a self-defining entity. The second aspect is an empirical or sociological one, concerned with the characterisation of functioning contemporary European democracies.

In seeking to relate these aspects, the normative and the empirical, the first section draws attention to the implicit understandings of political agency within a democracy contained in each approach and argues that normative ideals cannot and should not be deduced in a mechanistic fashion from a pre-existent sociological reality. Instead, discussion of democratic procedures should follow from an analysis of political agency within a democracy. The second section sets out the sociological limits for EU democracy. Taking into account these limits, the third section explores the possibilities for stimulating the development of an EU public sphere (the sociological prerequisite of democracy) as a possible way of connecting sociological reality with normative models. Some institutional developments of EU citizenship that are nevertheless consistent with nationally bounded normative discourses on democracy and citizenship will be suggested. Then in the fourth section the changes introduced by the new Amsterdam Treaty in respect of citizenship are briefly reviewed. The conclusion suggests that empirical difficulties by themselves are not sufficient to support a normative model that precludes the possibility of supranational democracy.

The political subject of democracy in normative and empirical dimensions

The fundamental theoretical assumption of this chapter is that democracy can be conceived both as a normative ideal and as an analytical concept with descriptive content (Sartori 1987, Dahl 1986). The meaning of democracy cannot be reduced exclusively to only one of these understandings, since normative models provide self-correcting criteria for empirical forms of democracy.

The *analytical* separation of these two aspects of democracy, the empirical and the normative, is necessary because the current set of 'peoples' is often treated both as 'natural' and as the paradigms for demoi – as happens in historicist and organicist accounts. Yet, such organic conceptions of the demos, for example those based on a supposedly homogeneous objective characteristic such as race or language, suffer one of two problems. Either they are simply inconsistent with democracy or they allow for the justification of any political regime whatsoever (Sartori 1987: 23). Even when this organic conception is reduced to the softer version of a need for shared values and beliefs, it states at most a facilitating condition rather than a prerequisite for democracy, since democratic forms are in fact superimposed on either heterogeneous or homogeneous communities (Sartori 1987: 90).

Such conceptual problems stem from the identification of empirical models with normative forms, as usually happens when the democratic nation state is made a benchmark or reference point. As is well known, the traditional theory of the state presupposes not a demos but a population, a pre-democratic aggregation of individuals, on which the demos is constructed. Political unity is achieved through political representation which need not exclusively be associated with democratic procedures. Such representation transforms pre-democratic political institutions into instruments of democracy (and, in this sense, democratises aggregations of individuals with no other democratic basis). The confusion of empirical and normative concepts of democracy is a mistake that should be avoided, however. Conflating national representation with democracy has the effect of elevating to a normative category what is contingent. There has been a historical coincidence between national representation and democracy, but the former is merely an historical manifestation of the latter's transformation (Dahl 1994, Duverger 1994).

A link between representation and democracy must therefore be explicitly secured through the procedure used to generate representation, namely universal free elections. The governing people, the demos in the act or the role of governing, manifest themselves at elections (Sartori 1987: 86). From this perspective, the majority principle implies shifting majorities, with the various parts of the body politic able to alternate in wielding power (Sartori 1987: 33). An electoral majority is thus largely an artefact of the electoral process and thereby largely an artefact of the party system functioning as a system of canalisation (Sartori 1987: 136).

The essential consensus for a democracy is a procedural one, involving a consensus on rules for the solution of conflicts. Unless and until the majority principle is generally accepted, a democracy has no rule for processing internal conflicts (Sartori 1987: 91). Similarly, Habermas argues that the consensus achieved in the course of discussion in an association of free and equal citizens stems in the final instance from an identically applied procedure recognised by all (Habermas 1994a: 24). Thus, the idea of a social contract, that is the idea of an agreement among everyone on some fundamental rules of convenience, even if this is the only rule of majority, is indissolubly linked to the ideal of democracy (Bobbio 1981).

The idea of democracy as a procedural mechanism linking individuals is only possible if real individuals are thought of in terms of the idea of citizenship. In this way, the people acquire political agency as a set of citizens. A citizen is an individual enlightened by reason, who is free from class prejudice, not tied by economic circumstances and who is also able to offer an opinion on public affairs abstracting from his/her personal preferences (Burdeau 1959: 30). Corresponding to this rationalist notion of the citizen there is, in the opinion of Burdeau, an empirical counterpart: the 'situated' person, who in daily life is characterised by his/her profession, lifestyle, tastes, necessities and available opportunities. Empirical forms of democracy thus act on certain sociological preconditions, most notably that of identity.

It is against this background that the question of the validity of the defining criteria of the political subject of a democracy needs to be reconsidered. Obviously a democratic polity requires some kind of criteria to delimit its boundaries and the participating individuals. In legal terms, defining membership of the demos involves, first, the constitutional rules defining personal qualifications for exercising voting rights and, second, in most constitutional orders, conditions of nationality. In most cases, nationality laws crystallise (although not necessarily in an exclusive form) ethno-cultural criteria. Thus, the intrinsic problem of such defining criteria is that they inscribe, at the very core of democratic forms, an organic definition of the people in which the legitimacy of majority rule does not derive from a political procedure but from the pre-democratic elements that brought a people together.

Descriptively, of course, it is true that sovereignty is based on national citizenship which implies bonds of mutuality and social obligation that are more exacting than the moral obligations which every person owes a fellow human being (Preuss 1995: 275). But can this constitute a legitimate claim to be the normative understanding of democracy, especially as it elevates one historical form of democracy into a paradigm of universal validity? The question is particularly important, since the approach simply accepts the dependence on a constituted political subject prior to the demos whose identity is not, certainly, derived from the democratic process. Finally, it does not allow a normative reorientation of the outcomes of the democratic process towards a redefinition of the original pre-existing entity in a democratic direction.

Theoretically, it is possible to detach the subject of democracy, the demos, from nationality. Dahl (1986) identifies five relevant criteria: voting equality, effective participation, enlightened understanding, control of the agenda and inclusiveness. The last in particular requires that the demos must include all adult members of an association except transients (Dahl 1986: 221). Whilst the association might be any human grouping, the essential (defining) characteristic of membership is being subject to the rules. This bears a strong similarity to Habermas's argument:

> the united will of citizens is bounded, through the mediation of universal and abstract laws, to a democratic legislative procedure which . . . only admits regulations that guarantee equal liberties for all and everybody: the procedurally correct exercise of popular sovereignty simultaneously secures the liberal principle of legal equality (which grants everybody equal liberties according to general laws).
>
> (Habermas 1994b: 11)

Although the empirical counterpart to this normative conception reflects an impoverished reality, the processes by which there is a generalisation of citizenship rights to all individuals within the boundaries of nation states point towards this ideal.

If a normative concept of democracy is applied to functioning democracies, there is then an implicit obligation to revise and reformulate the pre-democratic elements of those polities, otherwise the sociological analysis of democracy may have the effect of transferring to the normative level those pre-democratic components on which empirical forms of democracy rely.

European Union democracy

The normative case for EU democracy rests upon an evaluation of the operation of national democracies within Europe, in particular the limits they face to their autonomous capability for self-determination. We are witnessing a decline of the paradigmatic institutional framework for democracy, the nation state, as an arena for the reconciliation of private autonomy and public self-determination. Given that EC law is constructing a supranational sphere for economic activity, the EU is increasingly becoming the arena within which individuals exercise their autonomy, whilst the public regulation of this private sphere is removed from the traditional framework of the state. The existing practice of citizenship grounded in the plurality of EU nationalities has not been sufficient to secure a democratic decision-making process and, therefore, it seems that (at least in formal terms) the reconciliation of private autonomy and public self-determination which is at the very basis of the idea of democratic citizenship has been substantially weakened by the process of European integration.

In this situation, nation states are facing a democratic dilemma: the ability of citizens to exercise democratic control over the decisions of the polity versus the capacity of the system to respond satisfactorily to the collective preferences of its citizens (Dahl 1994: 28). Habermas too identifies the gap between the nation state's increasingly limited manoeuvrability and the imperatives of modes of production interwoven world-wide which create the illusion of real sovereignty. In his words, 'the greater danger is posed by the autonomisation of globalised networks and markets which simultaneously contribute to the fragmentation of public consciousness' (Habermas 1995a). The effects will be post-industrial misery because of the 'surplus' population and moral erosion of the community. In this context, national self-determination is more a chimera than a reality whilst supranational processes have a logic of their own which relegates to the sidelines not only democracy but also politics itself.

Political sociology has emphasised the extent to which democracy presupposes a form of mediation between the scope for the realisation of individuals' autonomy (the market) and public power, in the form of political culture, civil society or a public sphere. In Habermas's account, the public sphere presupposes a triadic model which explicitly recognises the normative zone between public power and the market (Somers 1995: 124).

It is, however, scarcely even possible to disagree with the diagnosis that the prerequisites for EU democracy are largely lacking: there is no 'Europeanised' party system, no European associations or citizens' movements, no European media. The biggest obstacle, however, seems to be the absence of a common language, so that political discourse remains bounded by national frontiers (Grimm 1995: 294–6). As the German Constitutional Court noted, a common language is important because of the requirement that the decision-making processes of the organs exercising sovereign powers and the various political objectives pursued should be capable of being generally perceived and understood by citizens. In this way, citizens entitled to vote can communicate in their own language with the sovereign authority to which they are subject (German Constitutional Court).

The definition of the demos contained in this judgment is, however, basically organicist, although, as Weiler (1995) notes, there are two distinct substrands: the 'soft' Not Yet version (a European organic demos may come into existence sometime) and the more radical No Demos (a European demos is impossible and undesirable). The central question, however, turns on the discussion of the sociological conditions of democracy or, in other words, the character of the public sphere. The German Court's Maastricht ruling explicitly grounds democracy in 'pre-legal' elements: democracy is dependent on the presence of certain pre-legal conditions, if it is not to remain a merely formal principle of accountability. Political processes of will-formation take place giving expression to what binds the people together (to a greater or lesser degree of homogeneity) spiritually, socially and politically.

In this line of thought, spiritual, social and political bonds, as well as a certain degree of homogeneity, precede democracy. Identity is not an explicit outcome of democracy but a constitutive element of a nation on which democracy is superimposed. This opinion is also shared by some scholars of nationalism. Thus, Smith (who considers national identity the essential element for the kind of political communities on which democracies operate) argues that the idea of cultural identity embodies a sense of shared continuities on the part of successive generations of a given unit of population, shared memories and the collective belief in a common destiny of that unit and its culture (Smith 1992). More cautious authors merely claim that what is required is a collective identity with sufficient awareness of belonging together on the part of its members that could support majority decisions, social solidarity and the capacity discursively to communicate about its problems and goals (Grimm 1995: 297).

For this line of thought, then, identity (national or cultural) is a foundation for democracy and the lack of a European identity appears as the primary obstacle to EU democracy. For Smith, Europe is deficient both as an idea and as a process: it lacks a pre-modern past, a prehistory which provides it with emotional substance and historical depth. At best, European countries have partially shared traditions and heritages which constitute a 'family of cultures'. The new Europe's true dilemma is presented as a choice between unacceptable historical myths or memories on the one hand, and on the other a patchwork, memoryless scientific 'culture' held together solely by political will and economic interests that are often subject to change (Smith 1992: 74). The obstacles to EU democracy are thus the weakly developed collective identity and the low capacity for transnational discourse (Grimm 1995: 297).

However, the methodology underlying these conclusions rests upon partial assumptions (Habermas 1995a, Weiler 1995), since within this approach the concept of democracy is constructed according to the concrete sociological features operating in a given national context. These features are reproduced as a model of the public sphere and then elevated to a normative status, thus neutralising alternative proposals which are not explicitly grounded on the empirical model of the national democratic state. From this perspective, conceiving democracy above the nation state becomes not only empirically difficult but also normatively questionable. It is empirically difficult because there is an obvious problem of identification of a model of a national public sphere in a supranational setting. It is normatively questionable because in this view a supranational public sphere would be incompatible with national ones.

On the empirical side, the argument has provoked replies, though sometimes of an implausible sort. The need to make identity a fundamental prerequisite of democracy has stimulated optimistic interpretations of a 'European' identity. This empiricist approach links in logical succession two different strategies of European construction: traditionalism (the foundation of European unity in a spiritual fact, e.g. religion – see Marquand 1995) and modernism and constructivism (involving the creation of a homogeneous cultural space through communication technologies; Ferry 1992: 42–3). Some argue that Europe (not the EU) constitutes the widest possible frame for citizens in terms of their social identity. The problem of European identity derives from its lack of distinctiveness due to its universalisation and the extension of European values and forms of life world-wide (Giner 1993) as well as the lack of coincidence between the EU and the geographical framework of a European identity. There is also a problem of establishing coincidence between the political and institutional framework and the geographical entity which that framework allegedly reflects. For some, common experience and traditions of thought that may form the substrate of a European political community transcend the mere affirmation of political will by some states. On the contrary, those reside equally in all the peoples of Europe (Tassin 1992: 171). Despite this, there is a strong convergence among EU countries in the sense of the development of parallel or similar structures which allows one to conclude that the incipient advent of a European society is clearly in sight (Giner 1993).

The discussion on the role of language for democratic forms is similarly informed by the national model and its specific combination of empirical and normative dimensions. Language has a different normative value if it is conceived either as a cultural expression of uniqueness (national or otherwise) or, merely, as a means of communication. Some argue that democracy within national/linguistic units is more genuinely participatory, precisely because of the pre-democratic elements. Political communication has a large ritualistic component, and these ritualistic forms of communication are typically language specific (Kymlicka 1996). Probably, it would be very difficult to disentangle these two aspects, and, in fact, they seem to be conflated when it is argued, for instance that language-based political units are in fact the most consistent with freedom and equality, since language helps to construct a society of free and equal citizens (Kymlicka 1996). However, it is worth pointing out that languages had a rather different function in totalitarian regimes where they were instruments and justifications for eroding freedom and equality. No doubt, an emphasis on the communicative side makes the problem of a shared European language a practical rather than a normative one (Bakke 1995: 10). If the process of creation of national languages was intrinsically linked to the process of nation building, the tendency within the EU is towards the consolidation of a diglossia with English as the dominant language for reasons of communication. And communication necessities (and not the fostering of any form of alternative identity) is the source of threats to national languages. Thus, although the disappearance of national languages is unlikely, their robustness, in the long term, is dependent on continuing state support and protection (Swaan 1993: 252).

However, the empiricist line does not seem the most solid methodological avenue because the survival of an exclusively nation state model of the public sphere as epistemologically valid can be questioned. The (explicit or implicit) reaffirmation of territorially bounded public spheres and nationally integrated political communities for the realisation of civic or communitarian solidarity has been theoretically challenged (Soysal 1996). The traditional account of public spheres becomes spurious if the postwar reconfigurations of sovereignty, citizenship and national communities are taken into account. In particular, Soysal contends that public spheres are realised internationally or transnationally, and the referent is no longer national citizenship but an abstract individual entitled to claim the collective and bring it back to the public sphere as his/her 'natural' right.

If this is a possible assessment of empirical traditions, a normative design for EU democracy grounded on the traditional empirical perception would be wrong. An alternative is to evade 'substantive' definitions of identity and to pursue, instead, a procedural one: *une identité dont la définition n'est jamais considerée comme simplement donnée, ni liée à un contenu fix semantiquement, mais constantement refor-*

mulée dans le cadre d'une discussion démocratique[1] (Berten 1992: 82). Habermas's criticism of Grimm's thesis takes this view. He argues that the burden of majority and solidarity formation

> must not be shifted from the levels of political will formation to pre-political, presupposed substrates because the constitutional state guarantees that it will foster necessary social integration in the legally abstract form of political participation and that it will substantially secure the status of citizenship in democratic ways.
>
> (Habermas 1995a)

There is no automatic or self-evident normative relation between national identity and democracy.

Thus, one possible scenario for an eventual EU democracy is one where the cultural or identity context of a more or less homogeneous nation would have to be substituted by something different. In this line, Étienne Tassin argues that a common space of European peoples should be protected both from the chimera of an original common identity to be reconstituted for the planned union, and from the phantasm of a unitary will to be forced out of nothing so that common politics should become possible (Tassin 1992: 188). If anything, there is a basic agreement on the critical character of European identity, either as a moral identity (Camps 1992) or as a reflexive identity in which the relevant socialisation processes, as well as economic, political and juridical processes, are the object of a permanent critical evaluation. The result is *une instabilitée potentielle de l'ensemble des institutions, mais également une possibilité ininterrompue de rationalisation, de correction et de réorientation en fonction d'objectifs qui surgissent du sein même de la réflexion*[2] (Berten 1992: 93). Critical reflexivity thus allows a reference to universal elements embedded in national political constitutions as well as international judicial space. Culturally distinct national identities can enter into a political community through their compatibility with the axiological referent framework without this implying a culturally homogeneous society (Ferry 1992: 50–1).

EU citizenship as the institutional foundation of a European public sphere: possible developments

Democratic citizenship in place of national identity is an outgrowth of the liberal political culture implicit in the status of EU citizenship. This, of course, has to be a very rich status:

> a liberal political culture can hold together a multicultural society only if democratic citizenship . . . can be recognised and appreciated as the very mechanisms by which the legal and infrastructure of actually preferred forms of life is secured. Forms of life comprise not only liberal and political rights, but social and cultural rights as well.
>
> (Habermas 1995a: 33–4)

EU citizenship defines a status for individuals with a fundamentally liberal profile (Closa 1996). It is liberal in the dual but interlinked senses that (1) the market is the model of public space on which EU citizenship is grounded, and (2) almost all socio-psychological traits normally associated with nationality and the communitarian understanding of citizenship are absent. This model of citizenship thus resembles a libertarian ideal of democracy the essential characteristic of which is the assumption of private law as a fundamental constitutional principle along with a lack of provision for political self-determination. Yet, in its current form, the status of EU citizenship is insufficient to become the institutional foundation of an EU democracy.

The emergence and survival of this political culture depend on EU citizenship becoming recognised and valued as the very mechanism which secures preferred forms of life. Rather than a comprehensive ensemble of rights, which is more coherent within national contexts, EU citizenship requires the development of rights in careful balance with those available under national citizenship. The development of EU citizenship will need to pay attention to the interplay between market, social and political rights. Under EC law, individuals have seen those rights greatly enhanced with respect to the realisation of their private autonomy in the market place. The consequence has been a selective, market-led logic in the creation of EU social rights. The further development of social rights with a redistributive profile seems to require a previous process of will-formation (Closa 1996). The decisive point is to recognise the effect of political institutions in inducing political will-formation as a result of the process of constitutionalisation (Habermas 1995a; compare Tassin 1992: 189).

To be sure, citizenship is not only a question of conferring a political and social status; it is also a question of creating the sphere for citizens' action. Although the causal relationship between citizenship status and the creation of a public sphere does not seem to be empirically supported (Soysal 1996), the absence of a coherent legal status of citizenship is not irrelevant in normative terms. So, an interpretation of EU citizenship along these lines would lead towards the identification of practical requirements which may assist in gearing a legally defined status of individuals towards praxis, that is the creation of arenas for public deliberation. EU citizenship has the advantage of a sort of quasi-neutrality because of its disentanglement from nationality (Closa 1995, Weiler 1995) and the lack of pre-democratic elements which prejudice national political subjects. On the other hand, it would be a status with high reflexive psychological demands for individuals: it requires permanent rationalisation and objectivisation processes that substitute for myths and routinised narratives. This citizenry would need to develop a sense of critical awareness towards 'performative contradictions' in EU policies and it would need to devote explicit attention to the reconsideration of recent and historical narratives as well as the construction of a community of feelings (Pérez Diaz 1994).

Although democratisation may seem an unavoidable future necessity of the Euro-polity (Schmitter 1996), such a project is neither normatively neutral nor unchallengeable. Given a lack of normative consensus, practical endeavours to constitute an EU political sphere out of EU citizenship can only be legitimately accepted if they satisfy the paradoxical condition of being compatible with processes of public deliberation about the normative self-understanding of national democracies. Although this may seem to imply a process of 'denational-isation' of states, in which the idea of a European fatherland may be replaced by that of a public space of disparate communities (Tassin 1992: 190), it is more plausible to place this normative strategy within the context of 'post-national' citizenship. Thus, the development of EU citizenship is part of a more general tendency. The revalorisation of legal personality as a meaningful and alternative status to national citizenship developed by legal theorists (Ferrajoli 1993) finds its empirically grounded counterpart in 'actorhood' rather than membership as the essential element in defining participation (Soysal 1996). In other words, this normative strategy grounds EU citizenship (understood as a status) and the concomitant public sphere on the universalistic elements embedded in particu-laristic settings. For some, this is congruent with the 'essence' of the modern liberal community: the abundance of altruistic norms that effectively manifest a belief in the intrinsic value of all members of the community (Howe 1995: 39).

One profitable approach in this context is to identify specific problems for the emergence of a European public sphere along with the possible developments of EU citizenship which can be grounded in particularistic settings of principles but, nevertheless, can assist in resolving these obstacles. These are not discussed in depth here. It is enough to remember three of them pointed out by Pérez Diaz: first, the absolute priority of domestic matters combined with the expecta-tion that they should be resolved by national governments; second, the 'performative contradiction' of EU politics where everyday behaviour tends to follow the logic of self-interested nationalism and contradicts thus the rhetoric ideal of a common interest; and, finally, the difficulty of creating common feel-ings from diverse histories (Pérez Diaz 1994: 17).

There are, however, some developments possible in the current status of EU citizenship which would extend its practical scope. It is important to note that institutionalisation requires reformulating national citizenship and, for this reason, it may stimulate discursive interchanges among individuals and the kind of reflexive and rational 'identity' on which EU citizenship may be based. Of course, no automatic process can be assumed when considering practical proposals like the following.

First, inclusion of the principle of equality within EU citizenship (with proce-dural guarantees in order to avoid discriminatory effects on non-EU member states' nationals) is important. Existing derogations from this principle of non-discrimination offer a shelter to certain communitarian understandings of the relations between individuals and the state premised on nationality. Anxieties about national identities are well protected by current EU provisions.

Second, there should be full constitutional provision made for the political status of individuals on which this public sphere might be constructed. This implies completing the procedural conditions for political interchange within the nation state. Whilst it may be disputed whether a high degree of participation implies a similarly high degree of legitimacy, it is undeniable that the absence of formal mechanisms for participation is a source of lack of legitimacy for any regime. A fuller definition of the political rights of EU citizenship is a likely result of spillover from existing rights. It has been convincingly argued that the rights to vote and stand as a candidate already included under EU citizenship cannot be effectively exercised without guarantees of full political freedoms, including expression, assembly and association (Lundberg 1995). Whilst freedom of expression falls into the category of human rights (and is consequently widely accepted in all member states), rights of assembly and association have a more discretionary interpretation by EU members' national legislations. Germany's Aliens Act, for example, expressly provides for the possibility of restricting or forbidding non-nationals political activity, and the Portuguese Constitution establishes the right of a government to withhold permission to engage in polit-ical activities. However, these examples are not necessarily problems in practical terms. As Lundberg argues, it is likely that if difficulties (deriving from these restrictive interpretations) appear in the exercise of the political rights estab-lished by Article 8 of the TEU, the ECJ will probably remove them by recourse to the doctrine of *effect utile* and the principle of equality (Lundberg 1995: 129).

Third, some spillovers are to be expected from current provisions for EU citizenship, specifically on nationality laws. Although determining nationality is still an exclusive member states' competence, the ECJ has established in the Micheletti ruling an obligation to observe EU objectives and principles. Nationals from third countries at present can expect different conditions to attach to access to the exercise of EU citizenship rights, depending on the country where they are seeking naturalisation. A coherent interpretation of the equality principle might suggest the harmonisation of naturalisation rules. At present EU citizens have unequal opportunities for the exercise of political rights entitled by naturalisation rules in each member state. Moreover, there are cases where there is no reciprocal treatment of citizens between two member states regarding those rights. In a coherent construction, harmonisation should precede a form of plural nationality. The advantage of this kind of develop-ment is that these measures still keep competence within member states' hands and outside EC law. Furthermore, they force national processes of deliberation to take place on the acceptability of EU citizens as participants in national political life.

Fourth, it seems fully consistent with the development of the discursive capa-bility of a European demos to promote increased forms of direct participation. Even diverging or opposed arguments about the public good have the functional effect of identifying focal points of interest. In this sense, proposals for holding EU-wide referendums on carefully chosen topics (Schmitter 1996) seem to make sense, since the possibilities of transcending national aggregation seem to be greater around an either/or issue. The obstacles to this development are obvious: referendums are incompatible with certain conceptions of representa-tive democracy. On the other hand, they are one of the institutions most closely identified with the actualisation of national sovereignty.

Fifth, direct participation cannot be considered only in a static framework. In such a static framework, participation refers to decision making within the current institutional and legal framework. In a dynamic framework, participation refers to the process of transformation to which the EU is committed either as reform or enlargement. Citizens' rights have to be considered both in respect of structure and process. Democratisation of the Euro-polity thus starts with this constitutional aspect. After the Maastricht debates, referendums have become a pressing demand from national citizenries, and this is supported by normative considerations. In the words of Dahl, 'the people of a democratic nation are not only fully entitled to explore the trade-offs between system effectiveness and citizen effectiveness, but I believe that commitment to democratic values obliges them to do so' (Dahl 1994: 34). The current requirement of unanimous reform, however, shields national processes of will-formation from the burden of generating a common interest. Institutional devices allow strategic behaviour by national citizenries which leads towards complex package deals rather than agreement on principles. Thus, requirement of unanimity prevents the emergence of a form of social contract among individuals. Granted, in a 'contractarian' context such as the EU, any minority is free to aim at self-determination. But democratisation would require that constitutional decisions were not subordinated to the wish of a minority.

Citizenship in the Amsterdam Treaty

Modifications of EU citizenship in the new Amsterdam Treaty are mainly concentrated under two headings: freedom, security and justice on the one hand, and the EU and the citizen on the other. These headings reveal the new centrality of citizens in EU politics even if only in a rhetorical form. In terms of the themes pursued in this chapter, these changes have several implications.

First, the new provisions continue the trend of inculcating the common values of the European civil society into the European polity. Thus, respect for fundamental rights as principles of Community law (Article F.2) improves slightly the former wording. Two Declarations to the final Act follow suit: the Declaration on the abolition of the death penalty and that on the respect for the status of churches and religions in each member state. Whilst in the case of fundamental rights this is an enforceable provision and a full constitutionalisation may follow from ECJ activity, the importance of the Declarations lies in their potential to make explicit principles for the European polity that are coherent with national practices.

Second, provisions on non-discrimination have been strengthened in a more universalistic way (Article 6.a TEC), particularly in respect of gender equality (Articles 2 and 3 TEC). These two Articles are coupled with a Declaration in the final Act regarding persons with a disability. The first provision – allowing action against discrimination based on sex, racial or ethnic origin, religion or belief, disability, age or sexual orientation – was originally proposed by the Irish Presidency. It is a positive clause since it establishes the base for action and complements the former exclusively negative prohibition. Two objections might be raised. The first is its itemised form (i.e. the singling out of possible causes of discrimination) rather than a general approach (i.e. prohibiting in general any kind of discrimination) (Shaw 1997: 7). The second is that implementation is left to the Council's judgement, since the Council may take action to combat discrimination.

Third, the guarantees for national citizenships have been reinforced by the new wording of Article 8.a: citizenship of the EU shall complement and not replace national citizenship. This wording borrows from the Danish declarations on citizenship and its meaning is subject to interpretation.

Fourth, the inclusion of employment provisions involves the creation of a policy issue often mentioned as one of the main preoccupations of European citizens. It provides opportunities, slim as they may be, for the contestation and argument essential to democratic politics over important matters. As the example of EMU shows, the European debate will proceed on a common topic but within segmented (i.e. national) constituencies. Yet common sentiments may still be enhanced. The new provision in Article 8.d enshrining the right of every citizen to write to EU institutions and have an answer in the same language has the same value for enhancing a sense of Europe closer to its citizens.

Finally, a new Protocol regulates the conditions for the application of asylum rights in EU member states. The initially ambitious Spanish proposal was based on an implicit model of federal citizenship. But it was introduced at a time when member states where not prepared to substitute commitments under international law *vis-à-vis* other member states' citizens with a constitutional system of guarantees. Nevertheless, the consolidation of asylum rights for EU citizens and the provisions allowing for the suspension of certain EU membership rights (Article K1 TEU and new Article 236 TEC) have emphasised the EU as guarantor of member states' democracy.

Concluding remarks

Rejection of the possibility of supranational democracy is based exclusively on a mechanistic identification of national identity, national representation and the nation state, on the one hand, with democracy, on the other. If this conceptual view is not avoided, supranational democracy is not only empirically unlikely but also normatively undesirable. The normative setting for an EU democracy is grounded in the erosion of national democracies and, specifically, in the increasing divergence between the levels where there is scope for individuals' autonomy and where there is scope for political self-determination. The active subject of a supranational democracy can only emerge from the development of the universalistic elements embedded in particularistic settings. The model of political culture of this demos is a highly rationalised and reflexive one, where identity cannot have a founding role but results only from the practice of citizenship.

Notes

1 'an identity of which the definition is never considered as simply given, nor bound to a fixed semantic content, but continually reformulated in the context of a democratic discussion'.
2 'a potential instability of the collection of institutions, but equally a permanent possibility of rationalisation, of correction and of reorientation in connection with objectives, which rise up from the heart itself of reflection'.

References

Bakke, Elisabeth (1995) 'Towards a European Identity?', ARENA Working Paper 10/95 Oslo.

Berten, André (1992) 'Identité européenne, une ou multiple? Réflexion sur les processus de formation de l'identité', in J. Lenoble and N. Dewandre (eds.), *L'Europe au soir du siècle. Identité et démocratie*, Paris: Éditions Sprit, pp. 81–97.

Bobbio, Norberto (1981) 'La regola di maggioranza: limiti e aporie', in N. Bobbio, C. Offe and S. Lombardini (eds.), *Democrazia, maggioranza e minoranze*, Bologna: Il Mulino, pp. 33–72.

Burdeau, Georges (1959) *La democracia*, Barcelona: Ariel.

Camps, Victoria (1992) 'L'identité européenne, une identité morale', in J. Lenoble and N. Dewandre (eds.), *L'Europe au soir du siècle. Identité et démocratie*, Paris: Éditions Sprit, pp. 99–105.

Closa, Carlos (1995) 'Citizenship of the Union and Nationality of Member States', *Common Market Law Review* 32(2): 487–518.

Closa, Carlos (1996) 'EU Citizenship as the Institutional Foundation of a New Social Contract: Some Sceptical Remarks', RSC Working Paper EUI.

Dahl, Robert A. (1986) 'Procedural Democracy', in *Democracy, liberty and equality*, Oslo: Norwegian University Press, pp. 191–225.

Dahl, Robert A. (1994) 'A Democratic Dilemma: System Effectiveness Versus Citizen Participation', *Political Science Quarterly* 109(1): 23–34.

Duverger, Maurice (1994) *Una metamorfosis inacabada. La Europa de los hombres*, Madrid: Alianza (trans. from original French version).

Ferrajoli, Luigi (1993) 'Cittadinanza e diritti fondamentali', *Teoria Politica* 9(3): 63–76.

Ferry, Jean-Marc (1992) 'Identité, et citoyenneté, européennes', in J. Lenoble and N. Dewandre (eds.), *L'Europe au soir du siècle. Identité et démocratie*, Paris: Éditions Sprit, pp. 99–105.

Giner, Salvador (1993) 'The Rise of a European Society', *Revue Européenne des Sciences Sociales* 31(95): 151–65.

Grimm, Dieter (1995) 'Does Europe Need a Constitution?', *European Law Journal* 1(3): 282–302.

Habermas, J. (1994a) 'Citizenship and National Identity', in B. van Steenbergen (ed.), *The condition of citizenship*, London: Sage, pp. 20–35.

Habermas, J. (1994b) 'Human Rights and Popular Sovereignty: The Liberal and Republican Versions', *Ratio Juris* 7(1): 1–13.

Habermas, J. (1995a) 'Remarks on Dieter Grimm's "Does Europe Need a Constitution?"', *European Law Journal* 1(3): 303–7.

Habermas, J. (1995b) 'The European Nation-State. Its Achievements and its Limits. On the Past and Future of Sovereignty and Citizenship', *Rivista Europea di Diritto, Filosofia e Informatica* 2: 27–36.

Howe, Paul (1995) 'A Community of Europeans: The Requisite Underpinnings', *Journal of Common Market Studies* 33(1): 27–45.

Kymlicka, Will (1996) 'Identity, Language and Democracy. Commentary on Veit Bader', Paper prepared for the Conference on 'Social and Political Citizenship in an Age of Migration', EUI, Florence, February.

Lundberg, Erik (1995) 'Political Freedoms in the European Union', in A. Rosas and E. Antola (eds.), *A citizens' Europe?*, London: Sage.

Marquand, David (1995) 'Reinventing Federalism: Europe and the Left', in D. Miliband (ed.), *Reinventing the left*, London: Polity.

Sciences, Institute Juan March, Working Paper 1993/42 41pp.

Pérez Diaz, Victor (1994) 'The Challenge of the European Public Sphere', ASP Research Paper 4/1994, Madrid, 18pp.

Preuss, Ulrich K. (1995) 'Problems of a Concept of European Citizenship', *European Law Journal* 1(3): 267–81.

Sartori, Giovanni (1987) *The theory of democracy revisited*, New Jersey: Chatham House.

Schmitter, Philippe (1996) 'Is it Really Possible to Democratize the Euro-polity? And if so, What Role Might Euro-citizens Play in it?', Manuscript, IUE, Florence.

Shaw, Jo (1997) 'European Citizenship: The IGC and Beyond', *European Integration online Papers* (EIoP) Vol. 1, No. 3; http://eiop.or.at/eiop/texte/1997-003a.htm.

Smith, Anthony (1992) 'National Identity and the Idea of European Unity', *International Affairs* 68(1): 55–76.

Somers, Margaret R. (1993) 'Citizenship and the Place of the Public Sphere: Law, Community, and Political Culture in the Transition to Democracy', *American Sociological Review* 58(5): 587–620.

Somers, Margaret (1995) 'What's Political or Cultural about Political Culture and the Public Sphere? Toward a Historical Sociology of Concept Formation', *Sociological Theory* 13(2): 113–44.

Soysal, Yasemin (1996) 'Changing Boundaries of Civic Participation: Organized Islam in European Public Spheres', Manuscript, EUI, Florence.

Swaan, Abram de (1993) 'The Evolving European Language System: A Theory of Communication Potential and Language Competition', *International Political Science Review* 14(3): 241–55.

Tassin, Étienne (1992) 'Europe: A Political Community?', in Ch. Mouffe (ed.), *Dimensions of radical democracy*, London: Verso, pp. 169–92.

Weiler, Joseph (1995) 'Problems of Legitimacy in post 1992 Europe', *Aussenwirtschaft* 46(3–4): 411–37.

13 Environmental protection in a liberal democratic Europe

Constitutional aspects

Marcel Wissenburg

Preliminaries

The European Union (EU) has reached the point where constitutional choices on fundamental issues have to be made. The informed citizen's educated guess would be that these issues include the distribution of authority between the EU and member states, the division and relative weight of the administrative, legislative and judicial powers within the EU, as well as the extent of the EU's rule. Whatever the issues are, constitutional decision making (CDM) on them will have to be accomplished under higher-level conditions. It is these conditions in which I am interested here, or at least two of them: care for the environment and the preservation of the European liberal democratic heritage.

I shall assume that Europe needs two things: a constitution to delineate its powers relative to its members (states, regions or citizens) and a social contract to secure its legitimacy. More precisely, it needs a constitution that is, at the same time, a social contract (cf. Abromeit, Beetham and Lord, Føllesdal, and Kuper in this volume).

What would be the content of such a constitution? We can broadly distinguish between two major issues. One is the existence and capacities of institutions designed to protect and uphold the substance of the constitution, the other is the substance itself: the policy areas with which the EU is concerned and the values which it is to protect or advance. Note that none of these functions requires the EU actually to be a union of states, or a federation, a superstate or a state in its own right; it could perform all of them equally well if it were merely a shared administrative service of independent nations. Now, at first sight, it appears that care for the environment can, but need not, be included among these policy areas, whereas there is good reason to believe, even a priori, that the liberal democratic heritage will be included among the values the EU should endorse.

As to the latter, the nations of Europe are products and guardians of a set of post-1789 values collectively labelled as 'liberal democratic'. These values are appreciated widely, even by the powers that matter. In the process of CDM, the new and higher authority of the EU cannot avoid decisions that will determine whether, where and how this heritage is protected. One might argue that the values of liberal democracy are more than merely normative conditions, more than things certain people just happen to appreciate. On this account, they are (also) actual cornerstones of our European societies, even defining characteristics. Had our societies not incorporated traits like freedom of conscience and expression, freedom of movement and contract, social and legal equality, they would not have been what they are today or would not even have existed at all. Hence, the room the EU offers to liberal democratic values will be of more than average importance both for the viability of the EU and for the moral stature of its constitution.

Given the prominent role liberal democracy must have in the EU, environmental issues will also be more important than on average. For one thing, there are few problems, perhaps only nationalism, that may constitute a greater challenge to liberal democracy than this one. According to the doomsday scenario that ecologists have advanced over the last decades, we are in the middle of a global environmental crisis, on the edge of total depletion of nearly all natural resources, of desertification, floods, skin cancer, extinction of species, genetic damage, and so forth – and all at the same time. Even if the risks are smaller, more remote and less interrelated, environmental problems do point to the possibility that there are limits to growth – hence limits to the wealth and welfare societies can deliver, and hence limits to the possibility of consensus building and social peace.

So far, we have only established that environmental protection is a political problem and that the EU could be a good instrument in dealing with the issue. But should it also be mentioned in an EU constitution? First, note that it *can* be included (assuming environmental care and liberal democratic values to be compatible). Constitutions like the Dutch or the German ones mention the areas in which governments are expected to be active, the positive and negative rights of individual citizens and, in general terms, the policy aims of governments. There is no reason to assume that an EU constitution could not do the same with an environmental protection clause in one form or another. As a matter of fact, clauses to that effect *are* already included in the Single European Act of 1987 and in the 1992 Treaty on European Union and were acknowledged in the (draft) 1997 Amsterdam Treaty. Second, there are reasons to assume that an environmental clause should be included. The reasons why policy areas, policy aims and positive rights concerning welfare, housing, education or health are delineated in some constitutions seem to apply with equal force to the environment: because they are all understood to be vital for the survival of citizens as citizens – in the broader sense of citizenship as full membership of society. Whether any of these rights should be part of an EU constitution is of course open to debate, but if one is included, the rest should logically follow. (Compare on both points Blackstone (1991) and Kostakopoulou and Kuper in this volume.)

It seems fair to say then that these two reasonable assumptions – that an EU constitution can include an environmental protection clause and that it will incorporate liberal democratic values – define an interesting new conflict area, since it is not obvious that concern for the environment and concern for liberal democratic values harmonise all that well. In the next three sections I shall develop a rough characterisation of the main areas of conflict between liberal democracy and ecology. In the first of these sections I discuss the substance of the liberal democratic heritage and formulate a series of criteria that are relevant to our topic. The second section performs a similar task with respect to environmental questions. In the third section I confront these two sets of criteria with one another. I end in the concluding section with a summary of the rather conservative (as it turns out) results of this exploration and with a short discussion of the consequences these results have for the shape of a European environmental protection clause and, in general, for an EU constitution and EU democracy.

Liberal democracy, European and universal

The trouble with liberal democracy is that it is a kind of 'hurrah' word – a vague multifunctional term with pleasingly positive connotations. Political scientists and theorists normally do not bother to analyse it beyond the point of remarking that it has something to do with democratic control over rulers, with civic liberty, and with equality in some form or other. The theorist usually moves on to a formal or normative analysis of what any one of these three concepts can and should mean; the empirical scientist investigates their permutations in concrete cases. Even if it was not designed to fit the specifics of the European context and the case of environmental care, the characterisation of liberal democracy that I am about to offer would, therefore, still be destined to be idiosyncratic. Yet I do not believe that it is also implausible; it seems compatible with classic statements of the liberal democratic ideology by Tocqueville (1951), Paine (1989), Publius (1962), Dahl (1956) and Rawls (1972), as well as with Closa, Føllesdal and Weale in this volume.

The three basic ingredients (democracy, liberty and equality) are, to use another 'hurrah' word, essentially contested concepts; that is to say, no one doubts that these elements are essential to liberal democracy but what they mean, exactly, is open to debate. Democracy, for starters, may be short for 'the rule of the people', 'of' meaning both by and over, and it may necessarily be representative, but this is as far as agreement goes. A first cause of controversy is the degree of representation: for one school of democratic thinkers, anything other than direct democracy cannot be democracy. For others, notably the representatives of liberal democracy, the essence of democracy lies in adequately representing the will rather than the bodies of the people. But here we find a second source of conflict: what exactly is meant by the will of the people?

Proponents of liberal democracy have a hard time determining their views on this matter. On the one hand, they believe that the wo/man on the Clapham omnibus should be free to make her/his own mistakes when voting in elections; in this respect, every interpretation of 'the will of the people' is acceptable. Yet on the other hand, the people's representatives are expected to be different and to represent not so much the will of the people, undiluted, unpurified, as rather their *interests*, their cleansed will. And yet, paradoxically, those same representatives are chosen by and expected to represent imperfect citizens and their imperfect ideas. It is here that advocates of liberal democracy point to the checks and balances provided by control mechanisms like the division of powers, majority rule, constitutional protection for minorities and so forth. At the very least, if even representatives cannot be trusted to behave like ideal citizens, it is hoped that the procedures and the deliberative process in representative bodies will somehow produce a collective expression of the ideal citizens' will: sincere, sufficiently informed, aware of consequences, prudent, responsive to needs rather than desires and directed at a common good (see the elegant analysis of 'will' in Day 1970).

I mention a third source of controversy in democratic theory only in passing: the question of whose wills are to be represented, of who is to be recognised as a citizen: adults only, natives only, and so forth. Questions of this sort deal with the concrete form given to the idea that all those who are governed should have a say in how they are governed, which makes them questions of equality rather than questions about the legitimacy of democracy as such.

Equality, liberal democracy's second pillar, is in our context perhaps less contentious than might be expected on the basis of the amount of controversy it motivated in moral philosophy. The truly necessary traits of liberal democratic equality can be formulated in far more general terms as the numerical equality of citizens and proportional equality of recipients. The usual argument for numerical political equality is made partly in terms of liberty: in the absence of an authoritative standard by which to judge the worth of persons, no moral standard, and hence no individual plan of life, and hence no individual, should be privileged over any other. If there is no relevant difference between persons or their views, it follows that citizens should be equal before the law and that they should have an equal opportunity for political participation: one man, one vote; universal freedom of organisation; universal freedom of speech; and so forth.

The second criterion, proportional equality for recipients, relates to the originally Aristotelian understanding of distributive justice as treating equal cases equally and unequal cases in proportion to their inequality. In its distributive capacities, the liberal democratic state is expected to treat the recipients of its benefits and burdens according to a moral standard that meets this criterion. The exact measure of (in)equality is, as said before, open to debate, but there are limits. One does demand that it be a *reasonable* measure; that is, that it is supported by good reasons and open to amendment should better reasons emerge.

As indicated above, liberal democracies know (at least) one area of conflict on equality other than that of the exact standard of equality: who is, or whose interests are, to be considered by the rulers? It seems to me that there are two minimum requirements, one of which is consideration of all human beings legitimately living within the borders of a state. Any limitation of this set seems incompatible with the egalitarian nature of liberal democracy and its perpetual quest for maximum legitimacy. Any extension of the set, on the other hand, say to include animals, might be seen to overstretch the idea of equal concern. Although extension is by no means impossible, the mark of a liberal democracy is not so much that it is a perfect state where the ideal of equality has been fully realised, but rather – and this is the second minimum requirement – its openness to reasonable arguments for the inclusion of outsiders in the in-group. Hence, consideration of the interests of out-groups like (members of) foreign societies, for whom a state may carry a legal or moral responsibility, is *not* a necessary trait of liberal democratic equality, unfortunate as that may be.

Over the past forty years, the analysis of the concept of liberty has led to the existence of roughly three vested schools of thought plus a large collection of dissenters. For all, liberty is a special type of freedom: political freedom, both as rights recognised by the polity and as the freedom required to be truly part of the polity. In the first tradition, true liberty (true freedom) is negative: freedom from interference or hindrance by others. The second school identifies freedom with positive freedom: that is, having the ability, the means, the opportunity etc. to do x.[1] A third school refuses to see a fundamental difference between positive and negative freedom, for two reasons. First, at a hypothetical level of so-called basic acts, both always come down to the same thing: being able to do x with means y to purpose z – where y can stand for both corporeal and extra-corporeal means (Wissenburg 1994; cf. Parent 1974). On this account, negative and positive (un)freedom are special cases of (sets of) such basic freedoms. Second, at the everyday level where liberty and freedom refer to complex sets of these basic freedoms, negative and positive freedom seem to presuppose one another. A (positive) freedom to the means of survival cannot exist without a (negative) right to life, obviously, but neither can a negative right to vote be taken seriously if there never are elections, if the ballot boxes are inaccessible or hidden, if there are no pencils, paper or computers to vote with, no one to count the votes, take notice of the results or implement them.

The great advantage of this third approach is that it allows us to describe liberty in terms that seem to be acceptable for proponents of both positive and negative liberty. The specific version of liberty that characterises liberal democracy, in particular, would then be described as a combination of three ideas: the recognition of a series of purely formal rights to do x, minimum interference with the formulation of purposes z, and a strong commitment to empowerment, that is to securing and enhancing the availability of means y.

Obviously, one can say of any government that it recognises certain rights, avoids some forms of interference and promotes the availability of some means. What makes it a typically liberal democratic government is the precise content of the recognised (etc.) list of rights. To make a long story short, typically liberal democratic rights seem to fall into two main categories: one defining political rights for members of the polity and the other defining a private sphere free of collective or government interference (cf. Rawls' (1972) famous two principles). In both categories, liberal democrats recognise value pluralism, that is the existence in practice of a non-reducible pluriformity of equally worthy views on the good life. In the context of this chapter, the following rights or freedoms appear to be most important: the right to vote; freedom of expression and free access to information; freedom of trade; freedom to design and pursue any reasonable plan of life (I shall refer to this from now on as 'the liberty of life'); and, within these limits, freedom of lifestyle.

These then are some of the demands liberal democracy poses on CDM in general. The European context adds one important aspect: the fact that the EU is a multilingual and multicultural entity. In principle, the more the process of unification proceeds, the greater the number of lifestyles and plans of life will be that become possible for individuals. In practice, this same process of unification might actually result in a cultural struggle for life and a reduction of individual choice if more dominant cultures or customs eliminate the weaker ones. And even though culture, like nationality, is morally undeserved (cf. several contributions to Barry and Goodin 1992), consistency would oblige a liberal democratic EU to protect value pluralism both at the individual level *and* at that of member cultures.

Environmental ethics and policies

In designing environmental policies, decision makers have a long series of questions to answer and choices to account for, all of which can be relevant to CDM. Some of these are (nearly) metaphysical: are environmental problems interconnected to such a degree that no single issue can be handled without addressing (all) others? Are they flaws in the machine Earth or is 'the' environment a self-sustaining, self-repairing organism? Others are of a political nature: how important are environmental considerations in comparison with other human concerns? Is a greener society still possible if it is based on or offers room for socialist, liberal or feminist principles? Finally, there are ethical questions and questions of strategy: what is valuable in this world, and why?; how does one go about protecting it? It is on these last two groups of questions that I shall focus here, and not merely for reasons of lack of time and space. For one, the answer to many political and even metaphysical questions will be implicit in the answer to our initial question: we want to know if an EU environmental policy can be compatible with the demands of liberal democracy. Second, the ethical questions logically precede both the political and the policy questions, in the way the formulation of ends precedes the search for means.

In the field of environmental ethics, the most prominent topic of debate concerns the *object* to which value is assigned. A policy to save the malaria virus from extinction is, for instance, not likely to be justifiable if only the object 'humankind' or 'human interest' counts. Although I only distinguish three positions here, there are far more subtle distinctions possible – see for instance Barry (1995: 20), Vincent (1993: 254) or Wissenburg (1997). In our context, it suffices to distinguish between *anthropocentrism*, attributing value to humans only, *pathocentrism*, attributing it to all sentient creatures (the official view of the EU in the draft Amsterdam Treaty), and *ecocentrism*, attributing value to all of nature.

Second, value can be attributed in either of two ways: *equally* or *hierarchically*. In the first case, assuming for example that we are dealing with an anthropocentric theory, all humans are of equal worth; in the latter, assuming a pathocentric theory, we can put a higher price on humans than on animals.

I ignore here the distinction between theories that attribute intrinsic value and those that give only instrumental value to objects or situations. Including it adds little to our analysis and in fact only complicates matters since belief in intrinsic value by definition interferes with the policy logic of means and ends.

As regards policy strategies, decision makers have less issues to deal with than environmental activists. For them, questions like whether political action in the field of environmental care is possible at all or at which level action should be taken (world-wide, regional, etc.) are matters of expediency rather than principle.

A question that does matter concerns the level of action. One possibility for green policies is that they are collective: that is, deliberate attempts by the institutions of a society to transform or preserve a status quo. Most environmental policies are of this type, and most political action is directed at promoting or inducing such collective policies at the national, international or subnational level. A second option is that of group action, in which one or more segments of society neglect the collective route and start operating on their own. Famous examples of this approach are Greenpeace, the RSPCA in its early days and Earth First! If neither of the above applies, green policy will be a purely individual act. The latter is especially an option for those who believe in invisible hands, the self-regulating capacities of the free market or the ineffectiveness of political coercion.

Second, 'green' policies can be basically of only two types: radical or reformist. The distinction is based on one made by Karl Popper (Popper 1960: 64) between utopian and piecemeal engineering. The reformist approach presupposes that problems should *in principle* be solved separately, one by one, one after the other, in their smallest possible shape, with the lowest possible amount of energy at the lowest possible speed. The idea is to offer a maximum opportunity for testing and adapting policy hypotheses while avoiding as much as possible any undesirable and unpredictable side-effects. The radical approach, on the other hand, assumes that problems should be solved as radically, speedily, completely, directly and fundamentally as possible, precisely because there is always a chance that something (pressure groups, new issues and problems, second thoughts) comes in between the first steps towards X and the realisation of X.

With these two dimensions, we can characterise six important policy ideal types (see Table 13.1). Probably the best-known approach to green policy is ecological modernisation (collective, reformist), the background of which has been described in detail by, amongst others, Weale (1992). Note that, unlike the way in which I am using the term here, ecological modernisation is far more than just a policy style. It is a complete theory of environmental politics, based on, amongst others, the proposition that environmental protection can be a source of economic growth (Weale 1992: 76). The reason why I use the term here to designate a policy style is simply that it seems to be the archetype of a reformist collective approach. One can contrast it with what might be called ecological utopianism (collective, radical), the preferred approach of radical ecologism. From this viewpoint, the industrial and post-industrial modes of production are responsible for an imminent ecological disaster, and the only solution is a kind of ecorevolution, a complete transformation of the way we live, cooperate and produce and of the desires we try to satisfy.

Clearly distinct from these two are the radical policies of groups like Earth First! and the Animal Liberation Front or lone rangers like the UNA-bomber, policies that have been described as ecoterrorism (group/individual, radical). Both believe in the necessity to eradicate fundamental problems with radical means; neither one believes in the virtue or need of collective action to start their revolution. Green consumerism (individual, reformist), buying green and selling green with green intentions, needs no introduction. Examples of green civic action (group, reformist) are boycotts, cartel agreements and covenants between an economic branch and environmental groups.

The compatibility of liberty and nature

At this point, we have collected a long list of criteria that European CDM should somehow meet if Europe is to be liberal democratic, of possible strategies for an EU environmental policy and of types of environmental ethics that it may or may not adopt. The number of (im)possibility theorems that could be formulated on the basis of any combination of these propositions is enormous and certainly too high to discuss in any text of this size. What I want to do instead is develop some general hypotheses of a more practical nature about the fields where one would expect liberal democratic and environmental concerns to harmonise best or conflict most deeply.

Liberal democracy and environmental policies

It is clear that a liberal democratic EU cannot use or accept terrorist methods for any purpose, ecological purposes included. Nor can it be reconciled with ecological utopianism, since this radical approach demands that all debate on criteria of equality and concern should be terminated *as a matter of principle*, and that civil

Table 13.1 Types of environmental policy

Level of action	Type of action	a.k.a.
Collective	Radical	Ecological utopianism
Collective	Reformist	Ecological modernisation
Group	Radical	Ecoterrorism (group)
Group	Reformist	Green civic action
Individual	Radical	Ecoterrorism (individual)
Individual	Reformist	Green consumerism

liberties should give way to the overwhelming importance of the citizens' best interest, again as a matter of principle.

Indeed, it would seem that the only policy strategy that is fully compatible with liberal democratic principles is ecological modernisation. The two non-interventionist strategies, green consumerism and green civic action, are essentially control mechanisms of a civil society, a free market. Hence, they give us the usual problems involved in combining economic liberalism with political liberalism. For one, the free market, even if it operates in a pro-environment way, dispenses with all democratic debate on the criteria for (in)equality since it recognises only one such criterion: financial power. It may also violate individuals' and cultures' freedoms of lifestyle and life-plan, and in the case of green civic action particularly consumer freedom, simply by making some goods unavailable. The only way to fit non-interventionism into a liberal democratic Europe would be by making it operate within possibly very broad but certainly strictly defined borders set out by a policy that can deliberately accommodate liberal democratic demands, that is ecological modernisation.

Green policies and environmental ethics

Although no environmental ethic necessarily commits one to any specific type of green policy, nor vice versa, some combinations are more compatible than others. Perhaps the anthropocentric hierarchical ethic is the least interesting version of environmental ethics; at any rate, it is the least discriminatory. On this view, nature is worth what it is worth to humans, while at the same time not all humans are necessarily equally worthy – as might be the case in a neo-Thomistic green ethic. This view seems to be one of the few that are compatible with ecoterrorism, as it allows some interests to be sacrificed for the benefit of others. Although both the strategies and the effects are far less radical, the same argument applies to the equally compatible strategies of green consumerism and green civic action. One might, however, suspect that even on an elitist view of life, collective action for a common good (ecological modernisation and ecological utopianism) will be more appreciated than these possibly divisive strategies. Among the collective strategies, ecological modernisation will then rank higher for the same reason. The pathocentric variant of this view will recognise more subjects (i.e. animals) but yield the same results.

An ecocentric hierarchical ethic will take full account of the interconnectedness of all life and all environmental problems, and hence of the need to act carefully and securely. Even if it requires a radical change in the human mindset, its proponents will if rational want to avoid both large-scale radical strategies (ecological utopianism) and all non-coordinated action of individuals or groups. This leaves only one alternative: ecological modernisation.

Virtually the same observations apply to the unqualified ethic of deep ecologists, ecocentric egalitarianism. In principle and in politics, the need for effective control will overrule all other considerations; it is only in cultural affairs – possibly – radical. The interconnectedness of all nature and hence of all environmental problems, a central tenet of deep ecology, suggests carefully controlled protective policies on the one hand and a radically new approach to life, customs, desires and nature on the other. However, the constraints on radical activities of groups and individuals will be less. The urgency of an action to save, say, the last ten unicorns and with them their species may well outweigh the importance of a well-balanced, carefully implemented general environmental policy – it may even outweigh the lives of unicorn hunters.

Since the arguments regarding pathocentric egalitarianism are essentially identical to those regarding anthropocentric egalitarianism, albeit with more subjects to be considered, they can be treated as one. On either view and at least in principle, ecoterrorism will be the worst possible policy, concentrating the authority of equals in the hands of what is in practice an elite. Non-coordinated reformist strategies will do only marginally better, since they are, like ecoterrorism, obviously hard to control. As collective strategies, only ecological modernisation and utopianism may be indisputably free of any suspicion of violating equality, and of these two, only ecological modernisation is genuinely open to control. Yet pathocentrism, like ecocentrism, may allow a deviation from this ranking in the interest of a threatened species.

Liberal democracy and environmental ethics

Since we have already assumed that the EU, to be viable, needs legitimacy and that to be considered legitimate it must accommodate liberal democratic values, we can ignore the question of whether and how liberal democracy fits any environmental ethic and concentrate on the other side of the equation: whether and how environmental ethics fit liberal democracy.

For starters, liberal democracy and an anthropocentric hierarchical ethic are clearly incompatible. The latter violates all principles of equality as well as the criteria for concern: it would make some individuals outsiders relative to more worthy others. With one exception, the same is true for pathocentric and ecocentric hierarchical ethics. Only if humans are considered as mutually equal in worth and if humankind stands at the top of the ladder of concern can these types of environmental ethics be successfully blended with liberal democracy.

Second, eco- and pathocentric egalitarianism escape these objections: there is no reason to believe that either one must necessarily reject proportional equality, deny political equality to humans or go for the absurd option of enlarging the electorate with rabbits and cabbages. In fact, both are pleas for the inclusion of other interests in political deliberation, for 'extending the circle of compassion', as it is called.

Third and obviously, anthropocentric egalitarianism and liberal democracy are perfectly compatible: the former has always been the dominant morality within liberal democratic thought.

There is, however, one area in which it is doubtful if any environmental ethic other than anthropocentric egalitarianism can be reconciled with liberal democratic ideas: that of civil liberties, in particular those liberties that concern the liberty of life. First and most conspicuously, any material or mental sacrifice made by x or any possible benefit denied to x on behalf of y can be, and can be understood as, a restriction of x's liberty. Yet even if the 'can' in this proposition were (incorrectly) replaced by 'will necessarily', the y in it could still be equally well a fellow citizen, a cuddly species or a foreign landscape; the difference is only gradual. The interests of any newcomer, indeed of any other citizen, can limit an individual's choices and opportunities. The fact that interests, desires, plans of life may conflict is practically the *raison d'être* of political institutions, liberal democratic or not. The addition of more subjects and interests to a polity is therefore nothing new, nor is it a reason why liberal democracy would have any specific problem with an extension of the circle of compassion. It may have bigger problems but it is not an essentially new challenge.

A more consequential reason to suspect that liberal democracy and non-anthropocentrism might conflict is that the sacrifices made or benefits foregone 'on behalf of y', y being something non-human, do not advance or protect y's plan of life. The best if not only justification liberal democracy has for limiting one individual's liberty of life is that this will in some reasonable way serve to protect the same liberty of others. With the possible exception of some animals, it seems, however, that no non-human entity has anything remotely similar to a plan of life, nor a capacity to use the liberties of life, nor therefore anything that can serve to justify limits to human liberty. At this point, we should avoid getting entangled in the famous and incessant debate among green philosophers on criteria for the moral relevancy of subjects. In this chapter, I have opted for the idea that what matters about people relates to their having or executing plans of life, but there are of course alternatives. However, I would argue that these alternatives either do not make a difference or, if they do, would disfigure our idea of liberal democracy beyond recognition.

First, consider alternatives in which, say, reason, reasonability, freedom of will or autonomy (cf. e.g. Nozick 1974, Ackerman 1980) are seen as the defining marks of moral relevance. To determine whether non-humans possess any of these characteristics, we need to communicate with them, and any claim to having discovered any of the traits mentioned is bound to be contentious in a far more fundamental way than claims to being able to communicate with foreigners or simply any other human. Second, the utilitarian alternative of pleasure and pain might seem to escape this objection (albeit merely with regard to some animals) because it requires emotional rather than intellectual communication. But it puts pleasure and pain in the eye of the beholder, and thus appeals to gut feelings – feelings we do not necessarily share, and above all feelings that do not even need to lead to an extension of the circle of compassion since they remain anthropogenetic. Third and finally, we could appeal, in the style of Levinas, to 'otherness' rather than 'likeness' as the defining mark of moral relevancy (Cooper 1995). Yet even if this would only lead to the replacement of anthropocentrism by pathocentrism, it appears that the result will again be either an in-the-eye-of-the-beholder recognition of other subjects of concern – or an understanding of politics, society and membership of society that is so totally different from anything we know that any political system, including liberal democracy, would have to be redefined.

Our question was whether and which environmental ethics fitted liberal democracy, not the other way around; our conclusion must be that only anthropocentric egalitarianism does.

Conclusion: European CDM on environmental issues

Given this last conclusion, the results of our analysis can be shortly and simply summarised as follows. Provided that the EU is liberal democratic, its attention for environmental issues will have to be inspired by an anthropocentric and egalitarian appraisal of the value of the environment. Its concrete policies may offer room for the non-radical private initiative, but only within limits set by an overall strategy of ecological modernisation. Being liberal democratic, the EU would offer room for dissenting opinions on environmental ethics. Yet it cannot implement these except on the basis of an anthropocentric consideration, that is when the means and ends of dissenting views on environmental politics happen to coincide with the interests of its citizens.

In the course of the political debate on European CDM, the issue of the constitutional status of the environment and of environmental policy is likely to pop up, since similar issues are already on the political agenda in many of the EU member states: animal rights in the UK for instance, the intrinsic value of nature in Germany and the Netherlands. In view of our analysis, one should observe that a constitutional recognition by the EU of the intrinsic value of nature, at any rate, will be nearly meaningless except as a political move. It may serve to gain support from environmentalists, but it cannot serve to inspire a liberal democratic green policy; the latter will necessarily be inspired by anthropocentric considerations. The same is essentially true for animal rights. Unless the basic tenet of liberal democracy, the sanctity of plans of life, is amended, there can be no constitutional protection for the welfare or interests of any creatures other than humans. For deep ecologists, this may be a diabolical conclusion; for others, it may reek of *Realpolitik* – but even idealism cannot prosper without an informed judgement of reality.

As regards the possible inclusion of an environmental protection clause in a European constitution, we can draw three conclusions, all of which appear to keep their validity (*mutatis mutandis*) regardless of whether the EU becomes a superstate, a collective administrative service or something in between. First, since liberal democratic values and care for the environment can be compatible, we can safely assume the *possibility* of inclusion of such a clause. Second, we note that it can be included both as an 'area of concern' type of clause and as an individual positive right: both options are compatible with anthropocentric egalitarianism and ecological modernisation. Third, concerning the precise wording of an environmental protection clause, all we can say is that it would have to be rather open-ended or non-committal. It cannot mention either the exact means or the definite ends of environmental policy; it can refer to environmental ends only as aims, not as sacrosanct duties or side-constraints. The prior commitment to non-radical, deliberative, democratic solutions and to the individual liberty of life excludes too substantive a commitment to any one particular ideal of a sustainable Europe. Finally, one conclusion that we cannot draw is whether an environmental protection clause should actually be included in an EU constitution. That still depends on our answer to the normative question of how important we judge the environment to be for empowering individuals to shape the life of their own choice, relative to other positive rights or needs.

This brings us to a final observation on the EU and CDM. As we have seen, a European environmental policy will encounter several problems of a more or less contingent nature. It may, but need not, contradict the principles of equality and justice. It may, but need not, conflict with principles of liberty, especially the liberty of life, either directly by limiting choices and opportunities or indirectly by controlling production. It may, incidentally, also endanger the cultural diversity of the EU. But the most serious problem for European policy makers is one that has little to do with environmental ethics and everything with the ambiguous nature of democracy, based as it is on a distinction between the will of the people and the interest of the people. What applies to the questions of extending the circle of compassion and amending the plan-of-life ethics applies equally to all radical changes in established doctrines: they cannot be legitimated by an appeal to reason or morality alone, nor by an appeal to the previously established legitimacy of procedures, nor finally by an appeal to the representatives' better insight in the interests of those they represent. Even more than the recognition of rulers and representatives as being in the best interest of those concerned, they require the support of the governed subjects themselves. The implication is that, in matters of constitutional choice, we have to demand more than full consensus or widespread agreement among constitutional decision makers, more even than a sincere etc. consensus. What is most urgently needed is a population that for once expresses its considered interest *itself*, and its considered interest rather than its uncleansed will. One might see a rather paradoxical trait of democracy in this: people who cannot as a rule be trusted with their own interest must now suddenly be trusted when it comes to constitutional decisions. On the other hand, one might consider it a sign of courage, confidence and respect if an elite trusts its subjects with their fate.

Note

1 Note, though, that there is a second interpretation of positive freedom as being free of internal obstructions to freedom: that is, freedom as being one's true self (cf. Berlin 1969, Day 1983).

References

Ackerman, Bruce (1980) *Social Justice in the Liberal State*, New Haven, CT: Yale University Press.

Barry, Brian (1995) *Justice as Impartiality. A Treatise on Social Justice*, Vol. II, Oxford: Clarendon Press.

Barry, Brian and Goodin, Robert E. (eds) (1992) *Free Movement. Ethical Issues in the Transnational Migration of People and of Money*, New York: Harvester Wheatsheaf.

Berlin, Isaiah (1969) *Four Essays on Liberty*, Oxford: Oxford University Press.

Blackstone, William (1991) 'Ecology and Rights', in Kristin S. Shrader-Frechette (ed.), *Environmental Ethics*, Pacific Grove, CA: The Boxwood Press, pp. 131–7.

Cooper, David E. (1995) 'Other Species and Moral Reason', in D. E. Cooper and Joy A. Palmer (eds), *Just Environments. Intergenerational, International and Interspecies Issues*, London: Routledge, pp. 137–48.

Dahl, Robert A. (1956) *A Preface to Democratic Theory*, Chicago: Chicago University Press.

Day, J. P. (1970) 'On Liberty and the Real Will', *Philosophy* XLV: 177–92.

Day, J. P. (1983) 'Individual Liberty', in A. Phillips Griffiths (ed.), *Of Liberty*, Cambridge: Cambridge University Press, pp. 17–29.

Nozick, Robert (1974) *Anarchy, State and Utopia*, New York: Basic Books.

Paine, Thomas (1989) *Political Writings*, Cambridge: Cambridge University Press.

Parent, William A. (1974) 'Some Recent Work on the Concept of Liberty', *American Philosophical Quarterly* 11: 149–67.

Popper, Karl R. (1960) *The Poverty of Historicism*, London: Routledge.

Publius (Alexander Hamilton, James Madison, John Jay) (1962) *The Federalist Papers*, New York: The New American Library.

Rawls, John (1972) *A Theory of Justice*, Oxford: Oxford University Press.

Tocqueville, Alexis de (1951) *De la Démocratie en Amerique*, Paris: Gallimard.

Vincent, Andrew (1993) 'The Character of Ecology', *Environmental Politics* 2(2): 248–76.

Weale, Albert (1992) *The New Politics of Pollution*, Manchester: Manchester University Press.

Wissenburg, Marcel L. J. (1994) 'Justice From a Distance. An Outline of a Liberal Theory of Social Justice', PhD Thesis, University of Nijmegen.

Wissenburg, Marcel L. J. (1997) 'A Taxonomy of Green Ideas', *Journal of Political Ideologies* 2: 29–50.

Index